High Adventure in the Great Outdoors

Art to Choke Hearts

Pissing in the Gene Pool

One from None

Bang!

Black Coffee Blues

See a Grown Man Cry

Now Watch Him Die

Get in the Van

Eye Scream

Do I Come Here Often?

Solipsist

THE PORTABLE

HENRY ROLLINS

March 4, 1989. Vienna, Austria. 7:59 a.m.: It rarely gets better than this. I'm in the breakfast room of this old hotel. The gray light of the Austrian morning puts a soft cast on the empty tables tha[...] Across from where I'm sitting is a long table of food: eggs, cheese, bread rolls, butter, jam, milk, orange juice, m[...] a large pot of coff[...] halfway through the [...] it is awesome. There [...] of sweat developing on [...]

I have stayed in [...] before, in 1987. The [...] playing acr[...] Eur[...] ten-week tour. The table sa[...] is to my left. What a great, mighty morning it was. We ate so much food that I think they were going to throw us out if we so much as even looked at the food table again. It was fantastic, an exercise in overeating, "sport eating" we used to call it in Black Flag. After we had eaten much too much food, we made sandwiches for the road, put them in our pockets, and exited.

I have finished the first cup. I ask the friendly young woman if I can have some more coffee. Her reply endears her to me until checkout time. "Yes, of course," she says. She understands. The second cup has arrived.

This hotel is across the road from the train station. In 1987 I walked the streets here [...]t into the station and watched an amputee try to sleep on a bench. He wa[...]usted [...] expelled. I [...] the whores work the [...] in their thigh-high [...]stic boots. Last night [...] getting back from the [...] ought about taking a [...] to where I saw this [...] blond whore hold up the side of a building. She was a hot icy set-me[...]ant machine. Last night I thought about her as I stared into the darkness of my room. I wondered where she was—maybe still out on the boulevard, maybe dead. Was she still as pretty as I remembered? Is anyone? How memories lie to us. How time coats the ordinary with gold. How it breaks the heart to go back and attempt to relive them. How crushed we are when we discover that the gold was merely gold plating thinly coated over lead, chalk, and peeling paint.

She comes forward, a pot in each hand. "Would you like

THE PORTABLE

HENRY ROLLINS

HENRY ROLLINS

VILLARD
New York

Published in the United States by Villard Books, an imprint of The Random House Publishing Group, a division of Random House, Inc., New York, and simultaneously in Canada by Random House of Canada Limited, Toronto.

VILLARD BOOKS is a registered trademark of Random House, Inc.

Library of Congress Cataloging-in-Publication Data
Rollins, Henry.
    The portable Henry Rollins / Henry Rollins.
        p.   cm.
    ISBN 978-0-375-75000-7
    1. Title.
    PS3568.05397P67   1997
    818'.5409—dc21   97-2931

www.villard.com

Printed in the United States of America on acid-free paper
20 19 18 17 16 15 14 13 12 11

BOOK DESIGN BY DEBORAH KERNER

Acknowledgments

Thank you: Villard, Gail Perry, Richard Bishop, Peggy Truxis, Vega, Selby, Bajema, Shields, Carol Bua, Ian Mac-Kaye, Mitch Bury of Adams Mass.

JOE COLE
4.10.61–12.19.91

Contents

Contents

Introduction

I started writing on the road when I was in a band called Black Flag. I was young and the road held much to open the eye. So many things were happening day-to-day, I thought it would be a good idea to start writing about it. The more I wrote, the more I liked writing. After a while, it occurred to me to make a book. I saved money that I was supposed to use to eat with.

After several months I had enough to make a fold-and-staple photocopied chapbook. I sold five hundred of them and used the money to make another run. I made a paperback later that year. A friend told me that I had to have a name for my company. Company? I was just making some books at a cheap printer in downtown LA and selling them out of my backpack. I took his advice and came up with 2.13.61 Publications. Those numbers stand for my birthday. I figured I will be the only one on the label, so why not?

Time went on and more paperbacks came out. I got an office and some staff to deal with the mail order and store accounts. We started putting other people's work out. More time passed and we kept moving the company to larger places and needed bigger storage space for all the titles.

As it is now, we are a small book company that puts out everything from photo books to short-story and poetry books. We do okay.

I was at Villard one day in 1996 for a meeting with Craig Nelson. He asked me if I would consider doing an anthology of my work. I thought that was an interesting idea. The excerpts from my books included in this volume were chosen in hopes of presenting a fully rounded view of what I do writing-wise, and I hope you enjoy it . . . or something.

—HENRY ROLLINS

HIGH ADVENTURE IN THE GREAT OUTDOORS

This book contains some of my earliest writing. Upon rereading it I was surprised that I still liked some of it. The material in the book was released in three separate, smaller books and was put together years later.

Numbers are perfect, infallible and everlasting. You aren't. Numbers are always right in the end. You may see an incorrect figure, but that's not the fault of the number, the fault lies in the person doing the calculating. How many times will your heart beat during your lifetime? Of course you don't know! But there's a number that will provide you with this small bit of information. Numbers are dependable! The sun may explode, you may lose your job, you may never be able to get it up again, but at the end of the day five is five. Get it? Good! Numbers do not cut in line at lunchtime. Numbers do not write bad checks. Numbers sound cool, like when a fucking pig gets a call on his pig radio to go answer a 2-11. You can go to buy coffee at 7-Eleven. Numbers make good names. Like at a party or soirée. I always wear a sticker that has a martini glass and the words HI MY NAME IS: printed on it; underneath the printing I write in "2-13-61." So I can say, "Hi, my name is 2-13-61, what's yours?" Then you can say to girls or guys, "Hey you're really the bees' knees! What's your number?"

▼

I see walking bombs on the street
Hearts not beating, but ticking
I am talking about detonation!
You're in McDonald's
And some guy's head explodes
Brains everywhere

I think there's some faulty circuitry here
You see some guy in a business suit
Walking home from work
Look at him closely
He's slumped over
There's smoke coming out of one ear
There's a buzzing, crackling sound coming from his head
Blown fuses
Poor machine!
But it's ok
The parts are interchangeable
We'll install a new one

▼

In a state of delirium I dreamt that I came upon a female cockroach the size of a girl. She smiled at me and told me to come closer. She kissed me. The feeling of her belly scales against my flesh made me convulse and sweat. We made love. She wrapped her six legs around my back and pulled me close. Her antennas lashed my back. No girl ever made me feel like that before, ever. By morning I was covered with sweat, blood, and a noisome yellow-green mucus. She had my children (twenty of them). They were semihuman in form, could reproduce in weeks not years, and could lift up to six times their own weight. We are breeding. In the alleys in the sewers in the back rooms and brothels. Not a day goes by where my children don't grow in size and strength. We are everywhere. You try to kill us with motels and poison. This is snack food for us. You will never rid the world of us. We will rid the world of you.

▼

I woke up this morning in the truck. I like sleeping in the truck. It's quiet and dark. Rain was falling on the roof. Sounded nice. Outside I heard tires screeching followed by a loud crash. I looked out the window. Head-on collision. The song "Dead Joe" by the Birthday Party immediately came to mind. There was a child lying sprawled on the sidewalk in the rain. The mother was in hysterics. The child kept screaming, "Mommy! Mommy!" I tried to imagine what the mother saw when she looked down at her child. Was the child's head bashed in? Were any bones exposed? Was the child's blood mixing with the falling rain and making rivulets of bloody water into the grass? Did their eyes meet? When the child would scream, the mother would jerk as if hit by lightning. Do the jerk mom, c'mon mom, do it in the rain. C'mon ma, jerk it. Use your hips mom. Jerk it.

▼

She lit my soul and inhaled deeply
Flicking my ashes occasionally
Finally, she ground me out
After a time, she reached for another
Cracked
Crumbling
Ruptured soul
Shattered
I wrote out a road map to get back home
I threw it away
Here I am
In uncertain time
And a shaky place
And this is all right
Not somehow
But all right
This isn't the way it is
It's the way it is around these parts

▼

I was in a men's room at one of those big gas-rest-food stops. At the urinal I saw six men pull down their zippers and pull out their cocks almost simultaneously. It was fantastic, like a firing squad, or like some kind of secret Masonic pud-grab ritual. Men act differently in the men's room. They don't talk much, and if they do, it's real loud as if to say, "Hey, I'm not afraid to talk in the men's room!" They act very manly in the men's room lest someone think they are gay. There are no weaklings in the men's room! We are in the men's room. We have our cocks in our hands. We are urinating our way. Right. A man who is henpecked and owned by his wife or girlfriend transforms into a virtual bedrock of masculinity upon entering the men's room. It's a temporary club, where men, united by a need to urinate, are men.

▼

I poured salt on a large slug. The slug writhed and squirmed. The slug tried to escape me and my burning salt. The slug made no sound. I'm sure if I was turned inside out and dipped in salt, I would scream. I remember how the slug glistened and respirated until I put the salt on it. I remember how it tried to get away, secreting yellow-green mucus in great quantities that bubbled slightly. My fascination turned into revulsion as the slug writhed and tossed from side to side, secreting even more yellow-green mucus to try and beat the salt. It was a losing battle for the slug, because when the slug had succeeded in rubbing off some of the salt, I would simply turn the salt shaker over on the slug and the game would start again. Eventually I got bored and left the slug, still writhing, trying in vain to get free of the salt bath that would eventually suck the slug dry. Later I imagined that my whole body was a tongue, and I was dipped in salt.

▼

Home. The streets lie, the sidewalks lie. You can try to read it but you're gonna get it wrong. The summer evenings burn and melt and the nights glitter, but they lie. Underneath the streets there's a river that moves like a snake. It moves with smooth, undulating, crippling muscle power. It chokes and drowns and trips and strangles and lures and says, "Come here, stay with me," and it lies.

▼

I saw a man slither down four blocks of gutter with his face pressed against the ground. He called himself the snake man, said he could do just about anything. He didn't say a word about right or wrong or once or twice. He just talked about doing it. He bled dirt, he was down in the gutter, crawling low, he was invincible. I saw a man jam a needle into his arm. He looked my way and told me he was free. I saw a man who had cried so much that he had trenches bored into his face from the river of tears. He had his head in a vise, and every once in a while he would give it a little twist. I saw a man who was so run-down that he was pissing blue. He was pissing the blues, now that's what I call blue.

▼

I was playing at this club in Birmingham, Alabama, called the Nick. I was sitting at the bar staring at the picture of Amanda Strickland. I had found the flyer at a restaurant a bit earlier that evening. The guy next to me said, "Yeah, they found her."

"In how many pieces?" I asked.

He said, "One. She was shot twice in the back of the head." The two abductors had her about six to eight hours, drove her to Atlanta, killed her, and tossed the body. The body was found about two weeks later. The guy next to me added, "She was bisexual. You know, kind of strange. A real nice girl."

▼

On the day of October 1, 1984, Katherine Arnold bought a shotgun at a K mart in Lincoln, Nebraska. Katherine, twenty-eight, mother of a son, took the shotgun into the parking lot of the K mart, sat down against a retaining wall, and blew her brains out. On October 2, I came to Lincoln to play at the Drumstick. The Drumstick is one hundred yards away from the K mart. I sat most of the day in the Drumstick writing. Now and again I would hear snatches of conversation about how "this lady blew her brains out." Later on that evening some people were telling me about it. This kid came up with a McDonald's cheeseburger wrapper all wrapped up. He opened it. Inside was some of Katherine Arnold's brains. After the show I took a flashlight and went out to the K mart parking lot. I walked down the lot, parallel with the retaining wall. I saw chalk markings on the pavement. I made a right and hopped over the wall; I shined the light against the wall. I found the spot. The wall was tinted brown from blood and gunpowder. The grassy area around the stain had been clipped. There was a sliver of brain still stuck on the wall. I peeled it off. There was a very strange smell in the air. I have never smelled anything like it before. I felt around in the surrounding area. I found some portions of brain tissue. I sat there alone with the remains of K. Arnold and that smell. It seemed to be in my pores, in my brain. I remember getting the feeling that this was a very special place, some kind of hallowed ground. I wanted to stay longer, I wanted to sit down exactly where she had. At this point I was overcome by a feeling of being watched, watched from the trees or from someplace outside the distance of the flashlight's reach. It was time to leave. I picked up the pieces of brain tissue from the grass and went back to the club. Waiting outside to leave, I sat down and thought about the whole thing. After a while, the blood would wash off the wall, the grass would grow back, and it wouldn't look like anything out of the ordinary. Maybe some kids would come there in a car, park, and drink some beers, legs dangling, feet hitting against the spot where Katherine Arnold's head rested. I wondered if the partyers would become aware of an odor. I wondered if they would just get up without a word and get the hell out of there. I found the article on Katherine Arnold in the local newspaper. I cut it out, and drove all night to Minneapolis.

Katherine, who would ever think that your trail would end at K mart? Did anyone tell you? If you were alive right now, I mean if your brains hadn't been blown out of your skull with that shotgun you put to it, would you have believed that you would have done such a thing? Katherine, you didn't see what I saw. Oh girl, some kid had a hunk of your brains in a cheeseburger wrapper and was showing it to people. I went to the place where you shot yourself, you know the place I'm talking about, you were there about twenty-six hours before me. Katherine, I searched through the grass with my hands, I found pieces of your brain covered with dead grass and dirt. I peeled a piece of your head off the wall. You might be interested to know that your husband found you. Imagine what he saw, you with your brains all over the place. Katherine, I hope you aren't angry with me. I kept part of your blasted-up brain. I wrapped it up in a piece of tinfoil and put it in my backpack. I think about you from time to time. Hey, you made the local papers and everything. Who would have thought your trail would end at K mart?

▼

I just got off work. I work at an ice cream store. I scoop ice cream into cups, cones, pint containers, quart containers, coffins, and body bags. I work behind a counter. I'm kind of like a bartender. I watch the pretty girls pass the window that looks out onto the sidewalk. I'm the guy in the ice cream store. I have been here eleven hours. My legs ache. I just got off work, it's 2:30 a.m. I'm hungry so I go to the only place that's open. 7-Eleven. I get the same thing every night. I sit alone on the curb and eat. I have to walk to my apartment. My apartment is home. I don't want to go home. Home is dark, home is lonely. Home is cold storage. I'd rather go almost anywhere except home. I just got off work. I signed on for extra hours at the ice cream store so I could have somewhere to go. I go back into the 7-Eleven to get a Coke for the walk to the apartment. It's a long walk. I don't want to go to the apartment. The apartment knows I'm coming. The apartment knows I have nowhere else to go. The apartment is smiling. It shuts off the heat and waits for me to fall in. I leave the 7-Eleven and walk down Wisconsin Avenue. I walk past the ice cream store and check the door to make sure it's locked. I just got off work. I hate my life. I hate myself. I feel ugly, unwanted, mad, mean, cold, and condemned. I make the walk to the apartment. I pull out my folding shovel and dig down six feet to my front door.

▼

Fuck you Alan: I have been here all day. It's 6 p.m. I look forward to getting off work. It's cool not to work at night for once. I got nowhere to go, but still . . . I'm waiting on Alan to come in and take over. It's 6:15, he's fifteen minutes late, fuck you Alan. Forty-five minutes later, Alan comes in, he's bleeding from his eye, his forehead is smashed up. Alan also works at this fancy shoe store up the street. At 6 o'clock the shoe store got robbed and the robber beat Alan's head in with the butt of a gun. Alan wants to know if I can pull his shift for him so he can go to the hospital. I ask him if he is sure he can't work. Alan stares at me in disbelief. Alan goes off to the hospital in a cab. The night shift is here. I might as well be here. I don't need the extra money and the store beats the apartment, but still . . . fuck you Alan.

▼

I played this club in San Francisco. The night before, another band played. All night long the guitar player sat in a small room with the lights out. He spoke to no one. He played two sets, he stood in the shadows and played his guitar. Between sets he went back to the small room and sat in the dark. The next day they cleaned up the room, they found the ashtray full of Camel nonfilter butts. The ends were caked with heroin. What a life.

▼

I've got a place
I've got a desert
I've got a good thing going
Don't climb down here
You put me on the outskirts of town
Now you want in?

You think you do
I'll turn your lights out
I'll take your virginity away again
I live in a hanging garden
Suspended from your world
In alienation: No Sears, Roebuck dreams
No credit is good
In alienation I am whole
Complete
The full circle realized
In alienation
In the alienation
In the peace of 21361 minds
It's only cold in your world
When I'm with you I'm cold
Alien
Your world is such a lonely place
When I am there
I am cold
You are a bad trip
That's why I quit you
That's why I spat you out
That's why I went upriver
Into the desert
Into the jungle
Into the sun
I exist in alienation
I am not alone
I am joined by those who know that paradise
Lies

▼

I'm looking through the window at these guys sitting at a bar.
They stare into the darkness, they smoke, they drink, they try not to

exist. They drink and curse and burn and weep and drink and hate it, and drink and grind their teeth, and drink and wring their hands and drink and live a slow lifelike death and drink and sink into their stools.

▼

When I was nineteen, I worked for a while at a lab facility in Rockville, Maryland. The place had mice, rats, and rabbits. I was a drone. Monday I mopped the facility. Tuesday I loaded dirty cages into a huge washer. Wednesday, Thursday, and Friday would pass in similar fashion. One day while I was transferring the three hundredth batch of mice into a clean cage, Mike, the head man, came into the room. He told me that there was an outbreak of a rodent disease called ectromelia throughout the entire facility. All the animals in the facility were to be killed and incinerated.

Mike: Henry, do you want to do it? I mean would it make you squeamish?

Me: Hell no.

Mike: So you'll do it?

Me: Sure.

Fine. By order of the National Institute of Health, fifteen to seventeen thousand little beasts were to be destroyed. Fine, clean their cages, mop their floors, sterilize their rooms. Now I kill them. Most of the staff were relocated to another facility. It was pretty much just me and the animals. I had a room all empty and waiting. I was to gas them. The procedure was simple enough. I would put twenty to thirty animals in a plastic bag, squeeze the air out, stick in the gas tube, turn on the gas. Fine. I would go into the rooms and pull out the carts that held cages. I would wheel the cages into the death room. I had the bags and the gas tank of CO_2. I would kill, cage by cage. When the boxes would fill up with dead rats and mice I would take the boxes over to the big N.I.H. facility where I would incinerate them. From 7:30 in the morning until 4:30 in the evening, I killed them. Each time I would gas, I watched the animals die. When the mice would be put into the bag, they would crawl around, sniff, and try to figure out what they were doing there. Then when I stuck the tube in and turned the gas on, they would leap up the sides of the plastic bag as it ballooned full of the gas. They looked like they were jumping for joy or something. They would fall back down to the bottom, gasping, soaking in their own urine. They always died with their eyes open. I would look through the bag and look at their eyes, their bodies stacked in a heap. The bottom of the bag was always warm from their piss and shit. I would tie the bag off and throw it in a specially marked box. That sound, I'll never forget that sound, the gas hissing, and the scratch of the little claws scurrying up the inside of the bag. They always died the same, wide-eyed and with no idea why. I was Adolf Eichmann. I was ordered to terminate. I was not a murderer. I was just trying to get the job done with maximum efficiency. I would terminate and incinerate. I like the way that sounds. Yes, I brought them to the camp in carts that held up to two thousand at once, efficient. I gassed them in enclosures that contained the bodies, their wastes, and their disease. Efficient! The corpses were taken to the ovens and incinerated, leaving behind disease-free ashes, efficient. They called me a murderer. A saint maybe, a murderer, no. After all, it was I who cured the illness. It was I who stopped its spread. I destroyed the ill and the weak, those who were not fit for survival. Can't you see? I did a job that had to be done. I tried to give rise to a strong, perfect, disease-free race, and you call me a criminal? I am a humanitarian in the strongest sense of the word.

Inside of a week and a half the facility was silent. All were incinerated, except for one load that I dumped in Burger King and 7-Eleven dumpsters. I quit the month after and started working in an ice cream store. A while ago, I was thinking that it would have been a lot more fun to distribute the boxes in more interesting locales. How about taking boxes of dead mice and rats to a nice residential neighborhood and putting a box on each doorstep? How about UPS-ing a whole bunch to your old high school or girlfriend's house? You could open up the boxes and bomb people on the sidewalk. How about taking a bag, putting it on someone's doorstep, lighting the bag on fire, and ringing the doorbell? The guy comes out and stomps the fire out and . . . gross, rodent flambé underfoot! You could freeze 'em and throw 'em at people in Westwood—fun!!! With an open mind, the possibilities are endless.

▼

Life's abandonment is painless
Life's abandonment is silent
The abandonment grows inside
Like a freezing, killing, crawling cancer
Born, and left in the dust
The sun comes up
You're walking down the street
You realize that you've been left in the house all alone
It's cold inside
The doors are locked
You're never coming out
Who left you?
No one left you
You're looking at yourself
And there's nothing wrong
You're looking at yourself
And there's no one home inside
You say: Hey where have I gone?
You went nowhere
That's the abandonment
I open my eyes and I see it
I feel it
It consumes me
That's the abandonment
Turn me off

Or cut me
Take my mind off my mind

Come home
Close the door
Lock the door
Make sure you lock the door
Pull back the curtains
Look outside
The streets are full of killers
Snakes at your feet
Feel the dirt touch the disease
Cure the illness
Stop the hurt
Cure the illness
Stop the vision
Still the turbulence
Sit down on the couch
Take a load off
Take out the gun
Put the barrel in your mouth
Close your eyes
Think of the filth
Think of the alienation
Become the isolation
Embody the alone
Use it as a weapon
Alienate others
From yourself
From themselves
Use the weapon
Pull the trigger
Show them what you're made of

Stop flailing around
Pull the trigger
End the joke
Make it real
End it

▼

They're at a bar, sitting at a table. The waitress comes over to take their order. She orders a dry martini, he orders a cup of coffee. Shortly after, the waitress comes back with the drinks. She says:

"I'm confused, who is who?"

The lady says, "I'm the martini."

The gentleman says, "I'm the coffee."

The waitress puts the drinks down and leaves.

She is the gin. Cold, intoxicating. Gives you a rush, makes you warm inside, makes you lose your head. Take too much, it makes you sick and shuts you down.

He is the coffee, hot, steaming, filtered. You have to add stuff to it to make it taste good. Grinds your stomach, makes you jittery, wired, and tense. Bad trip, keeps you up, burns you out.

Coffee and gin don't mix, never do, everybody keeps trying and trying to make it taste good.

▼

Madonna. She makes me want to drink beer. She makes me want to drive fast and go bowling. She makes me want to shop at Sears. She makes me want to kick vegetarians. When I hear her sing, I know she's singing to me. She wants to get nasty with me. When I see her face, her eyes, her lips, talking to me, telling me to come on. I get to feeling mean. I get to feeling like I wanna do a whole lot of push-ups, or go to a hardware store. Then I have to cool down. I gotta cool down, man. It's either gonna be a cold shower or a Bruce Springsteen record.

▼

Man and woman
Forever ruptured
Forever severed
Clutching
Clawing each other's flesh
Fucking in shallow graves
Rolling in blood-soaked dirt
He looks into her eyes
He reaches inside her
Deep inside her
He rips her uterus out
And shakes it in her face
He screams:
Whose idea was this?

▼

Cockroaches are your gods. You are weak. You should pray to them. They are a more perfect life-form than you. You are fucked up, with your idiotic idiosyncrasies. You have analysts, tranquilizers, you need vacations, you start wars, you commit suicide, you steal, you lie, you cheat. You are weak. You cannot survive, you are too busy hauling around that big brain of yours. You have to build jails to keep your own kind from killing you. You kill everything. You live in fear. You could never live with the simplicity and beauty of the roach. You have abortions. You engage in meaningless activity. You are weak, cockroaches are your gods. You're not even fit to kiss the smooth belly scales of the mother roach. You are repulsed by them, you fear them. There are more of them than there are of you. You get squeamish at just the sight, they make you sick. You are weak. Cockroaches are your gods. Give up your plate of food to them. Whether you do or not, they will survive you and your stupidity. You try to kill them with gas and poison just like you do to your own kind. The roach comes back, stronger, faster, immune. You watch television, you lock your doors to protect yourself from your species. You put needles in your arms, you sell your bodies, you find new and inventive ways to mutilate yourselves and others. You are weak. Cockroaches are your gods.

▼

She touches me
The jungle lights up with incinerating fire
Looks like a flaming serpent
I look into her eyes
I see a movie flickering
Car crashes
People kicking corpses
Men ripping their tracheas out and shaking them at the
    sky
I think to myself:
I don't want to survive this one
I want to burn up in the wreckage
Cooking flesh in the jungle

▼

My father died this winter. He just died. I am glad that he died in the winter. Just the idea of it, his body, sealed off in the season of cold. Doesn't it seem more clean to you? Like less decay? I like that. I can almost imagine his face in death. The eyes, staring, tilted slightly upward. The mouth gaping open. Looking like almost every picture I have ever seen of a victim of the Nazi death camps. Yes, he died in the wintertime. Sealed off in cold. That is my memory of his death. Cold, frozen, stagnant. Totally unaffected by the heat and damp of the summer. A heat that makes my thoughts fester and boil in decay and rot. No, memories of him live in the freezer of my soul. The warmth of compassion and tender feeling will never reach there. These feelings do not exist anyway. I did not attend the funeral or any of the gatherings that preceded the funeral. I missed the two events that I would have liked to be present at. I missed his last breath. I would have wanted to have had my eyes so close to his that his last breath would have blown right upon me. I would have breathed in every single solitary particle of his last breath as I stared into his eyes. I would have savored this breath of air for as long as I could before expelling it into a jar for later use. I also missed the autopsy. I would have loved to have seen his guts, his brains, his body. Mutilated in cold, precise surgical fashion.

. . . In my dream I hover above and study his gutted, sliced features. He looks pathetic. His cock, shriveled up gray-blue. He looks like dog meat. He looks helpless and stupid. I hate stupidity. I descend from my perch above and kick his brittle ribs with my steel-cap jack boots. The coroner waves me off and asks me to hold off until he has conducted his investigation. Respecting a job that has to be done, I sit in a folding chair and read a magazine. I cannot concentrate on the magazine because the cutting up and squeezing of my father's corpse is captivating. I ask to help. I am refused, of course, as it is normal policy for the next-of-kin to have no part in the autopsy. . . .

I would have asked the coroner for my father's cold, dead heart. Having received the heart, I would have taken it home and cooked it in a hearty bouillon. I would have invited very special guests over. We could chat about small, unimportant matters, sip mineral water or white wine, and sup upon my father's heart. To me that would be a very spiritual and intimate send-off. This would take a lot of intestinal fortitude on my part because I am a vegetarian. However, the opportunity to dine on my father's heart is one that is irresistible to me.

▼

When she comes:
She pulls you close
She breathes in short bursts
Her eyes close

Her head tilts back
Her mouth opens slightly
Her thighs turn to steel and then melt
She is perfect
And you feel like you are everything

PISSING IN THE GENE POOL

All this writing in *Pissing in the Gene Pool* and *Art to Choke Hearts* came from one frame of mind. The two books were eventually put together and released as a single volume. A great deal of the material was written in Venice, California, in 1986. I was living across the street from a very active crack house. Business was conducted day and night. At one point, there was a drive-by shooting and apparently some girls died. The crack house folded soon after.

saw it on TV. An L-1011. Full-color footage. It looked like a ruptured toy. The men were out with their garbage bags, picking up limbs. There was luggage, clothes, bodies, and big hunks of metal all over the place. I'll never forget the sight of that enormous plane ripped apart and gutted like a big foot had kicked it around. I wonder what that must have been like. Picking up heads, arms, fingers, and assorted guts and loading them into plastic bags. I wonder if those guys go through the pockets of the dead, maybe get a little beer money. Why not? What the fuck is a stiff going to do with money? There must have been flies all over the place, being summer and all. Ask any fly and he'll tell you, there's nothing better than fresh guts on a summer day! The telecast turned to the chief coroner. He said that identification of the corpses would take a long time. He said that most of the bodies were covered with jet fuel, a lot were burned beyond recognition. He asked that the relatives bring any photographs, dental records, and doctor's info (operation scars) that they had to help speed up the process. In a few days *Time* and *Newsweek* will have good color pictures of the twisted metal and destroyed bodies. I dig those pictures; a few months ago they had some great color shots of dead bodies stacked high at the Belsen concentration camp. But anyway, when those mags come out with those airplane pictures, I'm gonna buy 'em, yes sir. And I'm gonna say: "Boy! Am I glad I wasn't on that plane! Look at all those people. They're dead, naked, and burned up!"

▼

To me, she's not even human, she's some kind of a germ. A concoction. She is neurotic, nasty, and abusive. *Pathetic* is a word that springs to mind. When she is loud and drunk, it's torture being around her. She treats marijuana like some life-preserving drug. She is most lively when she has a chance to get "fucked up." Whenever she's spazzing out and drooling over pot, I think to myself, "coke whore," but I change the word *coke* to *pot.* She doesn't bathe much, and sometimes the stench can be quite noxious. I don't like being associated with her because I see how nasty she is with people that I work with. When she comes into a room, I either leave or try to get out of earshot of her. I hope she goes on her painful little way and leaves my sight. Not a bone in me hates that girl. She has managed to turn off everyone around her. She sure did it to me. I never set out to feel like that, no way. Now it's at the point where it's totally irreversible. I avoid her whenever possible.

▼

I overheard some people talking. This girl was complaining about having to shell out money every time her period came around. She said that Midol and tampons should be given away in welfare boxes. I had never thought of that before. She had a point there. What if a guy had to put out a dime every time he took a piss. It would be nothing at first, but after a while those dimes would start to pile up and you might try and hold out to make that dime go a bit farther. Imagine saying, "Fuck, I spent a buck on urine today!" What if you were into beer? What if you are out of $$$? What if you had to write a check? A credit card? What if you had to say, "Brother, can you spare a dime? I gotta piss." You would be in bladder hell pal. Think about that!

▼

It's cold here, cold and raining. It's August but it feels like October. Even the air smells like autumn. Autumn time makes me think of working at the ice cream store in Washington, DC. I lived in this really dingy apartment in the fall of 1980, and I used to avoid it as much as possible. I would do this by hanging out on the street and working extra shifts at the ice cream store. I would spend a lot of time alone. While my car still worked, I would go for drives at night with all the windows open, just to have the cold air wash over me. I would drive through different neighborhoods in NW just to clear my head. I later stopped driving as much because I started to enjoy walking more.

I would go for long walks by myself. That made me feel old, getting enjoyment from going for walks by myself. I'll never forget how the autumn air smelled that year. I spent a lot of time out and around because I only used the apartment as a last resort. At the time it seemed that everything frustrated me. I would work behind the counter at the ice cream store, and the customers would just wear me down. I would take orders all day long. I felt like an old shirt going through the laundry over and over. By the end of the shift I was burned out on people, their talk and their bullshit. The walks did me good. It was so great to be outside when the air was clear and cool. Everything looked good.

Sometimes I would get invited to a party or to go out to dinner by one of them and I would decline. Part of me wanted to go, but those kind of outings always made me feel even more alienated than usual. Hearing them talk made me feel lonely and hateful at the same time. Lonely because I didn't fit in, never did. When I was reminded, it hurt. And hateful because it reaffirmed what I already knew, that I was alone and on the outside.

I spent a lot of time feeling alienated and lonely. But with all of that also came a real solid feeling of independence. I came to enjoy eating alone and spending my off time for the most part alone. I was walking down the streets here today, cloudy sky, on-and-off drizzle, and it all came back to me in waves, perfectly structured memories. That was the autumn I remember most clearly. I was no longer in school, and it was a strange feeling for it to be autumn and for me not to be sitting behind a desk. I was more aware of each day and each night and all the time in between. Sometimes I miss that way of life. I enjoyed the nights at the ice cream store. A place to be doing something that wasn't the apartment. I would walk home slowly, enjoying the street lamps, smelling the cold air. The apartment was like a prison cell. I felt like kicking myself every time I slept late. It was a long walk to Georgetown, but I knew the sooner I got out of that apartment, the better. Damn, I was lonely that autumn. I wished for a girl I could hang out with. I never really did anything to meet girls, too shy, too fucked up. Autumn makes me think of women.

At the ice cream store I would get one or two days off a week. But as I took on more responsibility at the store, the days off decreased to almost none. That autumn I almost always got Friday nights off. Friday is my favorite day of the week. Friday night was either spent walking around until I got tired or spent at Mike's or Chris's house. We would sit around, drink Cokes, and play a lot of records. That became one of my favorite memories.

I'll never forget how the depression and loneliness felt good and bad at the same time. Still does. The sidewalks, the trees, the storefronts, they became my friends. Every time I would pass a house that had a wood-burning fire, I would try to imagine what the people inside were doing. Sometimes I felt so outside of everything that I wanted to die. I felt terrible, but then out of nowhere would come an overwhelming wave of relief and calm. It was my life! My depression! Good for me! The air and the leaves and the streetlights would smile at me and I would feel okay. I realized that autumn that yes, I was alone in this world, totally alone. Alone and on the outside, but at the same time I wasn't alone, I had myself. I was always alone as a child growing up, but this was the first time that I ever clicked on what it meant to be alone. I felt invincible. I felt as if I could withstand the longest winter ever.

I feel uneasy when my mind gets crowded with memories that I can't shake. I write them out of my system and hope it works. I run breathlessly from one word to the next. Sometimes I think I'm dissecting my brain into little pieces. When I'm forced into a frame of mind and time by outside elements such as season or geographical location, it drives me nuts. I feel I have to write a telephone directory–size book to get it out of me.

Nothing gets me like autumn, though, nothing. I can see myself walking down P Street right now, I can feel it. I can smell the fireplaces on O Street right now. I can see the street lamps glow on R Street. But at the same time, I can feel the consuming emptiness that paralyzed me and made me sullen and cold. I can remember sitting in that dark apartment that reeked of paint and insecticide wanting out so bad but not having the slightest fucking idea where to go. Every time the air turns cold, I am transported back to all those places. I have visions of the fluorescent glow of the ice cream store when it's observed from the People's Drug Store across the street. The place looks busy and cheerful. A lit glass cube in a dark, cold wall. It makes me feel like I'm watching the world from the outside. Walking the streets on the outskirts of earth. Alone and on the outside.

▼

How are you today? Are you climbing that ladder? They told you all about that ladder. Climb that ladder and find that salvation. Sure is a hard climb I bet. Arms getting tired? Sure is a long ladder. Faith, is that the word they used? Hope? I've been watching you from a long ways off. You're not climbing on any ladder. You're running on a treadmill.

▼

This summer has left me on an island all by myself. My mind goes its own way, usually to the streets of my hometown. Walking alone on MacArthur Boulevard at night. Muggy, unmoving air. Watching the moths play around the street lamps. I walk through the night, ill at ease and alone. The sun will never rise on this street. MacArthur Boulevard is always dark and quiet. The street lamps are small yellow planets that keep me from falling into the distance. I feel the isolation. I sink inside myself so deep that I turn into the most pathetic, lonely, ugly animal there ever was. Summer becomes a jail, a ship run aground, a ladder to nowhere. Summer brings back the thoughts of the girl and her house. I would feel so small that I would sink into the cracks in the brick sidewalk. The summer animal, I can never outrun or hide from it. The journey in my mind continues along, and I find myself standing in front of a house with a roofed front porch on Beecher Street. I see myself and others I recognize sitting on the porch, they are unmoving. They are statues. Suddenly I grow heavy, as if filled with water or sand. I grow tired, lazy, and thoughtless. Stagnant and breathless. I know what I am, but I don't know what I'm supposed to do. When in doubt, I move. So I leave and walk somewhere else, trying to walk out of the mouth or asshole of the summer beast that has consumed me. The sunsets are the worst. They sink slowly and mournfully, burning and waving good-bye. I want to reach out and grab the sun and throw it back up high in the sky so I can have more time to figure out this dilemma. I know that it's too late to turn to other shores. I wouldn't even if I could. The summer bores me out, turns me into a hollow carcass. Fueled by insomnia and a thirst for everything. I turn into boneless limbo man caught in the middle. My skin turns to leather, I turn inside in. I seal off. Every pore, every orifice. Underneath this leather exterior I scream, twist, convulse, and burn silently. I wonder to myself wouldn't I be better off far from everything that bears the least resemblance to this? You can change the scenery that surrounds you. You can run from the fists that pound you, but you cannot escape your feelings. I've crawled every sewer from here to there and I've never done it. And I burn silently.

▽

I had a dream the other night. I lay on the floor and closed my eyes and the creatures came to life: A snake is crawling along a desert trail that parallels a straight, black paved road. The sun is going down but it's still quite bright outside. Over the horizon walking down the road in the opposite direction is a woman. The two get closer and almost pass each other, but each stops just in time. They both step into the area that runs between the trail and the road. The wind gusts suddenly, and the snake is instantly transformed into a man. He has dark hair. He is marked with scars and symbols, patterns of his tribe. The two walk toward each other and embrace. Another gust of wind comes and blows all vestiges of clothing off them both. The sun holds still for a moment and starts to slowly rise, and as it rises it turns a deep crimson and gives off a low, metallic whine. The couple are fully embraced and perfectly still. Their bodies fit together like two parts of a jigsaw puzzle. Another gust of wind comes and blows the flesh and organs off the man and woman so all that's left are two skeletons locked in embrace. Their jaws open and they start to grind into each other, bone on bone, tooth on tooth. The sun is emitting a pitch that is making the ground rumble. The skeletal bodies grind together as if trying to destroy each other. Another gust of wind comes and forces the two to totally intertwine with each other until only one is visible; this lasts for the blink of an eye before the image implodes and turns to a pile of sand. The pile of sand conflagrates with white-blue flame, and nothing is left. The sun has now changed shape, transformed itself into a double helix, bright red and twisting. It sinks into the distance, and the rumbling quiets as the light fades.

▼

I like my headaches, they're pure. The ones I've been getting lately are the ones I like best. The pain jumps all over my head. Sometimes they come out of nowhere. The pain rushes through my head like splinters of lightning. The pain is sharp and pure. I see cold blue shards in my brain. They make my head expand, contract, and distort into vile shapes. The pain sometimes makes me squint. Like a bullet entering my brain and then altering its normal path and wriggling about like a snake plugged into a light socket. Sometimes I think that something wants in, and sometimes I think that something is trying to rip its way out of my head. Like a rising sun. Ulcerating. Burning. Destroying my brain cells. Spinning and aborting constantly. Maybe I harbor a colony of fugitive rats in my head, turning my brain into a ghetto and a rancid nest for dreams and hallucinations. They eat away at the center of my brain consuming white and gray matter. Fortifying themselves, strengthening themselves so they can employ and embody plague and infestation. The pain strengthens and educates me. Forces me to understand, acknowledge, assimilate, and enjoy pain and pain's by-products: vision and brutal, absolute forward movement. I like my headaches.

▼

I'm a multicolored man scar tissue. I'm a self-inflicted kind of guy, and I'm self-inflicting down the road. DRAW THE LINE! I'll fall short. I guess I forgot to mention the overflowing cowardice, stupidity, and sheer unadulterated pettiness. But I'm a stranger in your face and my mood swings like a guillotine and my hands aren't connected to my head bone and I got crazy muscles and wavy eyes and I got an urge with no name I don't know what to do with it muscles, cock, brain, knife—whatever. I just want to do it.

▼

Me and Ian went for a drive in his car. We went over Key Bridge where I used to walk home from work. We drove down M Street. We drove down R Street, past the place where that black dude slammed my head against the wall of the alley and took my tape player, past the place where that dog looked me in the eye a split second before he got hit by a car, covering my shoes with blood. Past the block where a hippie girl put flowers in my hair while her male companions turned over cars. Past Montrose Park. Past Jackson School, where I went for first, second, and third grade and got beat and harassed because I was white in 1969. Got held responsible for the death of Martin Luther King. I could still remember hearing them chant: "Fight, fight nigger and a white, beat him nigger, beat him 'cuz the white can't fight." I could still remember how my stomach would twist and my head would grow light. Down Thirtieth Street, over to Q Street, past my old bus stop, past that apartment where that young white boy was raped and made to play games with that black dude. Back on Wisconsin Avenue, past 7-Eleven, past the library, past the Safeway.

We keep driving, we stop at Ian's parents' house. We park the car, we walk to Wisconsin Avenue. Ian goes into the bank; I take a short walk over to the building that once held the pet shop I worked at for years. The building is a restaurant now. I walk behind the building to see the back steps, the steps that I walked up and down for years hauling out garbage. The steps that I sat on and ate my lunch. The steps that I stood on and destroyed litters of sick animals. Cats, rabbits, you name it. People would come in with their sick animals to have them put to sleep. Of course, we had no facilities for such things. Didn't matter to my boss. He took the money and I took the animals on the back stairs and killed them. Some, I broke their necks with a sharp twist. Others I took and bashed their heads against the wooden rail. The move was smooth and swift. I used to go home with my shoes covered with blood. The back steps. One time I went out to dump the trash, and I saw a guy getting head from a stripper from the bar next door. I walk back up the alley and reemerge on the street. I look around me, almost every building in the area has been torn down. I walk past the restaurant and look inside. A family of well-dressed people sit at a table, they look up and see me, their eyes swell up. I pull away from the glass and walk back to Wisconsin Avenue toward the bank. I'm thinking about that family eating their food, their feet tapping on the floor. The floor that acted as a roof for more rats than you will ever know. We had rats all over that place, ratshit everywhere. Piles of it stacked high and rotting into every two-by-four in the joint. A miniature ghetto of sorts. Upstairs from where the family eats is a room where my boss used to fuck his boyfriends. One day he told me how hard it was to get the Vaseline out of the sheets.

Keep eating, lady, the rats squirm, crawl, and shit below you. Neurotic fags fuck and moan above you. You're surrounded, entrenched in shit, sweat, and Vaseline, eat up, sleep tight. It gets so twisted, so distorted, that I lock myself out of my own house. I look at myself looking at myself, inverse to inverse, turning inside out and the other way around.

I'm going to wait until the ghosts come out again. I'll see my boss walk through the rear wall, naked, heaving, smelling of shit, complaining of the sheets and how bad he hates "the niggers in this city." That was one of his obsessions. He had a huge dog that he trained to hate blacks too. He would say, "Tannis, don't you want to eat a nigger?"

There's ozone in the air now. I'm sitting in a room with an open window. The ozone air comes flowing in gently. So gently, I might just drift off with it. I get lonely when the ozone comes out. The smell of it makes me remember lonely times, always. Gray, cool, and empty, leading to a cave-in. I've been to that window ledge before. I never jump, I never have the guts. I just sit in a chair and contemplate my body falling through the ozone. Thinking of girls, thinking of how it never works. Never. And then you die or just go to sleep . . .

▼

I go out on the street. I hear the cars and the people, but that's not what I want. I want to hear jungle music. It's all lies out there. I think I understand the difference between dirt and filth. The dirt is clean and the filth is filthy and it's everywhere. It rips at my eyes. I can keep a better grip than a lot of people I know. And when I make an effort, I can maintain out there. But sometimes I get pushed and my brain goes into automatic pilot and I feel like kicking and walking a straight line right into their diamond minds. But you know you can't do that. You will never touch their minds. That would be like punching at thin air. If you're going to get all the way into it, you might as well take that straight line right into their flesh. You know what I'm talking about. With a smile on your face speak the international language: dirt and filth.

The noise comes in, crowds me out of my brain. At first, the sound of children laughing mixes with the sound of rain. The sound of the children fades out and is replaced by the sound of gunfire. The gunfire remains at a steady pitch as the rain fades. Now I hear the sound of people talking, laughing, screaming, crying. Reminds me of when I was in the hospital. All night long they would scream for their medicine, they wanted to get better. The old woman in the room next to mine sounded like she was being cooked alive in her bed. The whole place was screaming. Made me think that I might lose my mind in there. In there, out there, I don't know the difference anymore. The sound, I can't shut off the sounds of their voices. When I'm all alone in my room I can still hear their voices screaming in my ears. I know that I am to blame for letting them in. I want to get better myself. I'm not running from anything, I'm just trying to free myself from their sounds. If I don't, I'll become accustomed to them and that will be the end of me. The sound of rain, pelting down on boxes holding the dead. The rain mixing with dead children. What I see, what I hear. The whole place is an insane asylum. A screaming shit house. Gunfire off in the distance. The bodies are falling, crying, trying to get better, doing anything to get well. And you know how bad the emptiness feels when you're full of it. They fill you with emptiness, and then they come to get their pay. They want their pay, but they don't want what's coming to them.

It never fails. My weaknesses are always strong enough to knock me to the ground. My weaknesses are the greatest weapons I have when I turn on myself. It won't always be like this. I'm getting better every day. Maybe someday I won't want, I won't be such a sucker. It's all one big insane asylum, a screaming shit house.

The sound of children splattering, sounding like gunfire. For every voice, a bullet. For every scream, every prayer, every day, annihilation inside my room.

▼

S&D Vacation Package Pt. 1: Organize leisure air tours during wartime. Vacationers who could afford it would be flown over battle sites and would have the opportunity to drop napalm and bombs on the villagers below. I can see them now. Wagner's *The Valkyrie* blasting through the quad system. Fat white tourists dressed in polyester pantsuits and those silly Hawaiian shirts sit in their seats, each with his own personal trigger. "Can we do it now?" they ask.

A smiling stewardess gives them a knowing wink and says, "Soon, very soon."

"But I want to drop fire now! I want to kill now! I want to incinerate now! Now!" says a fat balding man.

"Calm down honey," his wife says. "You heard the stewardess. We'll be in bombing range soon. See honey, the music's starting and everything." Soon they are dropping fire on the cities below. The conversation in the plane resembles one that can be heard in a boxing arena on a good night. The vacationers come home with pictures and souvenirs. Some pose with charred dismembered bodies. They smile and give the thumbs-up to the camera. Some are wearing strings of ears around their necks. The women all want their pictures taken with the captain. People will come back with their own stories about the number of gooks they killed, each will exaggerate like crazy. Each will have a story about the one that got away. "One of those little bastards was hiding in a rice paddy. I was so plastered on those goddamn huge drinks they were serving that I missed him. Madge blew the little son of a bitch right out of the water. What a woman."

▼

I used to think that red, blue, green, and yellow were my friends. For a while there I thought that lines could go in circles if I wanted them to. I know better now. Black and white and the straight line are my friends. Inside my room I am free. Colors burst forth anytime they want to. The lines go wherever they please. Outside of my room I am not free, and that's where the black and white are by my side, and that straight line is my chosen direction. I know what it does to you. I know how it makes you feel. There is another side to this blade and I know that one too, and I am tired of playing games with you. Thank you for all the gifts. I'll return them one of these days.

▼

It hurts to let go. Sometimes it seems the harder you try to hold on to something or someone the more it wants to get away. You feel like some kind of criminal for having felt, for having wanted. For having wanted to be wanted. It confuses you, because you think that your feelings were wrong and it makes you feel so small because it's so hard to keep it inside when you let it out and it doesn't come back. You're left so alone that you can't explain. Damn, there's nothing like that, is there? I've been there and you have too. You're nodding your head.

▼

Cold outside, cold inside, the smell of grease and disinfectant. The guys behind the counter look like they hate everybody who comes in. It's one of those jobs that you get, and all the while you're telling yourself that it's just temporary until the right thing comes along. It's one of those jobs that when you look up, you would swear that the clock hasn't moved a second since you looked at it an hour ago. The kind of job that you realize you've been at for over a year now. Sure, you hate it, but it doesn't feel as bad as it used to. The brain numbs itself to everything except hate and the ability to take orders. But then again, who the fuck am I to say anything at all? For all I know, these guys might think that waiting on a bunch of meth dealers and whores is quite a great thing to be doing. Nobody understands anybody's anything.

▼

Labels on records. Why not labels on booze? For example, a label that ran like so: Warning: Use of this product can cause vomiting, blurred vision, loss of control, loss of memory, severe headaches, dry mouth. Prolonged use of this product can lead to a dependency on this product. Prolonged use of this product can lead to the destruction of self-confidence. Prolonged use of this product can lead to the total destruction of self-respect. Prolonged use of this product can lead to the destruction of the soul.

▼

I found out what there is for me. Nothing. Nothing I can see. There are only things to learn from and forces to make myself aware of. My brain is on a different wavelength now. Names, faces, I don't remember them. They don't matter. More and more, day by day, I break from them. There are no answers, just a lot of questions. No, scratch that. I don't have any questions anymore. No questions, nothing to explain. I can't talk to them. They have proven that to me over and over. I used to think that I could talk to her, but sometimes I don't know. Sometimes when I talk to her I think that I'm being quietly laughed at. That's how I felt today. I held the phone in my hand and stared at it. Finally I just hung it up and walked away. Those phone booths are almost like coffins. I wonder if anyone ever gets buried in them.

▼

Sometimes I think of myself as this guy holding on to a propeller that is going full speed. My body twists and turns as I hold on for dear life. Pulled along. In motion but not really in control.

If I close my eyes, I can see myself and this propeller go ripping by, the propeller cutting a path through dense underbrush and tree limbs. The propeller does fine. My body gets mangled as it slams into tree trunks, branches, and bushes.

I need to make friends with the machine. I need to understand the power, to harness it and direct it, not be dragged along by it. I need to become one with the machine. I've got to stop holding on to the monkey's tail. I must get on the monkey's back.

▼

I can see it in your eyes. They're wet like a dog's. You're looking for a leg to climb to keep you from drowning. Your hands reach out, clutching for something solid to hold on to. You're weak and in need. You want something to hold so you can have something to blame. Don't reach out to me. I'm drowning too.

▼

Take my no man's body and point it toward the sun. Going home. You got me feeling like a hole dug in the ground. I got to fill up the hole. I fill it up with dirt. You got me feeling like a hole dug in the ground. I open up my window and I take a look around. I see killers looking back at me. Killers walking in the sunshine. Dirt hole man. Dig it. Dirt hole man. Pass me by. I got nothing to give you. Pass me by. I'm digging myself. I dig myself. I dig my hole alone. Don't want nobody in my hole with me.

ART TO CHOKE HEARTS

Originally I was going to call this "I Will Incinerate the Pepsi Generation." Like I said in the intro to *Pissing in the Gene Pool,* this book was the second half of one big, turgid block of mid-eighties stress-related expression. Read on, please.

Walking to the store. The first thing that hits me as I go out into the light is the smell. Dog-shit all over the grass. I walk down my street and watch the homeboys watch me. I have to look right at them, I can't help it. They piss me off when they stare. I feel like shooting their little heads off. I turn onto the main street and walk past the family-planning center. A worn-out street dude looks at me and waves and nods his head like he knows me, that random recognition always leads to the hit-up for some change. I keep walking. There's bums and garbage all over the place, it looks like some low-grade war was being fought. Bum soldiers. They look battle-torn, bloodshot eyes, slow stumbling walk. They pick through garbage like they're picking over corpses. I keep walking. The store signs are mostly in Spanish. Little Mexican children run by me screaming and chasing each other. I see a bum in a doorway; his stench is so strong that I can smell him from almost ten feet away. His fingers are yellow from cigarettes. I breathe in, it's like trying to breathe in a rock. My breath just seems to stop like it doesn't want to go any further. I turn the corner and go into the store and get what I need. The lady at the checkout asks me how I'm doing, and I know she doesn't really want to know so I don't say anything. These people always make me want to destroy. All I can think of is the flamethrower and the destruction. I leave the store. The side of the shopping center is the place where several buses pick up and let off. Run-down people of all types. They look like they're on their way to work, they all have that bottomed-out hopeless look. The more beaten-down they look

41

the longer the shift is I bet. I pass the bum again, and again I get that smell. I turn my head to the street, and I see a beautiful girl on her bike. She has long blond hair and a blue tank top; her hair is streaming behind her. As she goes, I look back at the bum and then back at the girl—what a view, what a trip. I go to the bakery to get a loaf of bread. There's a line out the door. I squeeze in and pick out some bread. The line is made up of two distinct groups, old Mexicans and old Jews. The Mexicans look like they have worked the night shift of every shit job there ever was. They are silent and they wait patiently. The Jewish folks are very talkative, they make a bunch of comments about how long the line is and how strange that is for this time of the week. They look like they have just gotten off a Miami golf course. The men have their pants pulled way up past their waist. I finally get out of there and make my way back to the apartment . . .

Have you ever thought that the night could be hungry? Like it wants to eat you up? That's the feeling I get sometimes. I don't want to move because if I do that, I won't want to stop and I'll get all wrapped up in some crazy shit that I won't be able to deal with. But the night, it seems, is always there, waiting around, looming over me. It's the feeling I get when I'm in this room at night. I want for something, but I don't know what and I feel so isolated but at the same time I think I could run right through the wall if I really wanted to. No matter what I do I think I'm wasting time when I should be getting on to the real thing, but I don't know what the hell that is. I tell myself that something's coming. I don't know what, but it's coming . . . but it never does and I knew that it wouldn't in the first place. But to think that something's coming makes me feel like living a little more. Sometimes I don't feel like that at all, living I mean. Sometimes I crave something so big that it will be big enough to really knock me out, or do something. I sit here and I can hear all this noise and shit outside and I wonder if any of it's for me, if any of those noises are supposed to be telling me something. I listen intently. I don't want to miss the right one. What a drag, but I don't know what's dragging. The night is the only constant. But that doesn't help much right now.

▼

I wanted this to be the real thing. I wanted it to finally be the real discipline. The discipline that I had been so well preparing myself for. I needed something to be real. I saw all things around me falling apart, all people caving in. I asked myself how long I was going to live this lie, how long I was going to let myself down and blame someone else. Finally I kicked through the wall. It was like a junkie who busts through the scar tissue that keeps him from hitting. It was like slashing through the womb with your teeth. It's the lies that are killing me. The lack of discipline. I was killing myself and I didn't even see it. I couldn't feel it. The painless days are over.

▼

I went to a show last night. I went to help the soundman set up his system. What shitty bands. What a poor excuse for music. I looked at the crowd all night. There was nowhere else to go. All I could do was sit there and listen to this shit. I cannot count all the times that I wanted to take a flamethrower and fire it into the crowd. I wanted to incinerate the whole mess. That's what it was, a fucking mess. The only thing I liked the whole night besides all the people leaving was the pig's guns. I liked their clubs too. It would have been great to have rammed one of them down their throats. The show was at a university. Those kind of shows are always a joke. There's something about colleges that really sets me off. I guess it's all that idiotic knowledge going on. Like sheep getting trained for the slaughter. When I walk down the halls, I always get the strangest looks from the students. Makes me wonder if they would survive a war on these shores, or even an afternoon in a bad neighborhood. If some bad shit ever did go down, I bet they would make good prisoners of war, patient, obedient. When I walk the halls of these schools I feel that these guys are really getting taken for a ride, on their parent's money; I guess that's the way it should be.

43

The music, what a mess. All of it was so hollow. The opening band was called Guns n' Roses, and they blew the headliners off so hard it was pathetic. Even the applause after a number was hollow, well, that makes sense. The audience and the performers go hand in hand. Seemed really depressing that this is the stuff that these people are playing in their rooms at night. What a shitty world to go home to. I was so glad when all the people finally left. It was a joy to load the equipment out and get out of there.

Some music might be alternative for a while, but if it is any good, it gets sucked into the big scene, and then that's when they get their pants pulled down in front of everybody. There's nothing like a little success to dissolve anything good about a band that had little to start with. Most bands have so little to start with these days. There's this thing where alternative bands get to be real shitty and not get pinned to the wall for it. That's the funny and stinking thing about the music business, it's all bullshit, on every level. You just have to find the pile that smells the best.

I choose to do what I want and not get in the light with a bunch of faces who are in competition with each other for the trophy. Gone are the bands that want to destroy and fuck the place up. This place needs fucking up. . . .

▼

Goddamn I want a gun. The heat is making my brain stick to my skull. I'm thirsty. I want it so bad that I could crawl up the wall, grind my nails into the plaster. I wish I could kick my own head in. I wouldn't think. I wouldn't know shit. A bare bulb in the ceiling, that's my brain. Hot and hollow. I wish I could scream the walls down. I can't scream. I can hardly move. Hot prison man. If I wrap my arms around myself tight enough maybe I could collapse my rib cage. No I'm not getting out of here. I'm not getting out of this night. I'm not getting out of this brain. The brain I'm in. Prison, bastard, fucker, self-mutilator. I'm all those criminals. If I could somehow turn it all around. If I could some-how breathe life instead of death all the time. Then I could get out of here less painlessly than all the rest. I don't have the guts to go out like you.

▼

We have a little war going on here. I just heard an ambulance go around the corner. What will it be tonight? The son who kicked his mother down the stairs? The father who beat his wife to death with the telephone? The baby who got forgotten by his mother because the drugs were real good today? You never know. You never know and you never get to know unless it's you, and if it's you, well, you don't want to know. Maybe tomorrow it'll be me. I'll fuck up and walk on the wrong side of the street, and then someone will teach me a lesson and the ambulance will come for me and I can be the star for a while. Oh, there goes another siren. Holy shit, they're dropping like flies out there. Tomorrow is just another day. You pack your lunch in a brown bag, make sure your gun is loaded, and get your ass to work. You don't want to be late.

▼

A man sits in a jail cell serving a life sentence. He doesn't want to live anymore. To live the way he must live now means no women, no safety, no life, no nothing. Just the rest of his life sitting behind bars waiting to die. He wants no part of it. He wants to die, better death than God knows how many years in the hole. Every day he looks for ways to kill himself. The guards took everything they could think of so he couldn't do it after he tried to hang himself with his shoelaces. The guards love when they get a guy who wants to die. They know they cause the man great amounts of pain by keeping him alive. They have no concern for his life, they enjoy the amounts of suffering they can cause a man. They pride themselves on the duration of the man's suffering. They know full well that at some point the man will find a way to kill himself. Imagine seeking death as fully as you would seek to regain your freedom. You would do anything! Imagine wanting death so bad. Imagine death as freedom. Wouldn't you hate the men who

45

kept you from your death, your freedom. All night, you would lie in your bed all alone, thinking about your death like you were thinking of your lover far away. You would miss what you never had. You would find a way to kill yourself. You would, you would die somehow. Some die inside, the guards can smell that a mile away, they can tell when a man's dead from the inside. They give up. They leave the man alone, they let him get fed to the sharks.

That's how I feel sometimes, dead from the inside. I look into the mirror, I look dead, my eyes look tired and gone. Sometimes when I walk down the street I think that no one can see me; that's when I wonder if I'm dead. I feel like a bottomless pit. Like a big garbage hole. You can put stuff in, but it never gets full. In fact you never see any of what you put in again. Kind of like in one ear and out the other, but down and out of sight. That's where I'm at right now. I'm nothing and I'm passing time without the guts to make a move in out up down or otherwise. That's the name of my tune. That's the ring on my hangman's noose. That's my death row hallway walk. I'm fake, artificial. I think at one point I had it. I had it down but now I'm a swinging man. A cold breeze from way down the hallway blows my dangling body back and forth from day to day. Life has nothing in it worth living for, not in my mind. I tried all the things that were supposed to make me feel more alive, and they damn near killed me. I was lucky once.

▼

I'm always right when it comes to me
I used to think that people got in my way
Until I realized how little they have to do with what I'm
  doing
I live in one man's land

▼

I'm riding on the bus. I hear these youths sitting in the seats behind me. They're talking all this shit about how they were at this party, and the one is going on about how hot this girl was when he had her in the hot tub and how soft she was and how her boyfriend in the other room was getting all jealous and shit. The other guy says that yeah, he knows that the girl is fine since he was with her last week. Then they start talking about all these fights they had gotten into last week, tripped me out. They were talking about how one dude got it with a chain in his head and how another got all messed up and had to lie to his folks saying how he had taken a fall down a flight of stairs. All this shit is going down right behind me. I was too scared to look around at these guys. I thought they might kick my ass too. The thing that was funny about it was the Californian accents they had. They're telling all these way-out tales of sex and violence, and it sounds like a bunch of rich surfers. So I'm hoping to fuck that these heavy mothers get off the bus soon before they get any ideas about knocking me around. About two stops later they get up to leave. They filed past me and didn't give me even a second glance. You bet your ass I checked them out. I couldn't believe it. They were fat kooks, and they were wearing these New Wave clothes that you could tell cost a lot of money. The last one to get off the bus is the one I can't forget. Thick glasses, big butt, with a denim jacket that said THE CURE written in marker on the back. What the fuck is wrong with these people? The Cure? I'll bet those kids raid their parents' liquor cabinet and get out the Lite beer. Whatever happened to juvenile delinquents? It's too late, I think. There should be a law: Anyone under the age of twenty-five will not be sold any weak alcohol products. It's going to be malt liquor, whiskey, or nothing. Anybody who wants to purchase Lite beer will have to be over forty and have the identification to prove it.

▼

The palm trees make it all look like such a lie
They make the streets look like they're part of a movie set
Bums and palm trees
Garbage and palm trees
Urine-soaked hallways, puke-stained stairways
And palm trees

47

Like a postcard
There should be a postcard
That shows a dead street-gang member
Lying in a pool of blood
His dead body resting at the foot of a palm tree
The desert ghetto
Dogs lifting their legs and pissing on palm trees
Palm trees lining the front of a star's home
Anyone can have them
Limbs of Barbra Streisand's severed corpse
Thrown all over her front yard
Her fat head resting on a palm frond
Her crossed confused eyes looking up
At the warm California sun

▼

The bums in Venice should get together and form a gang. They should get some patches to put on the backs of their filthy jackets. The initiation would be to shit and piss in your pants, without changing them, for a year and a half. They could rumble with other gangs of derelicts in parking lots by the pier. They would square off and bum change off the tourists. The gang who had more dough at the end of the night would be the winner. Not to mention the most fucked up by the dawn's early light.

▼

Have you ever got the feeling that there's no time left? Or maybe that it's running out faster than you think, faster than you could possibly imagine? Do you ever get to feeling like that when you're lying in your lover's arms talking a bunch of shit that seems to make sense at the time but not really because you know that tomorrow you're not going to feel that way? And you know it all the while and still you go along with it for some reason and you don't know what that reason is but you never stop to question it because you're too wrapped up in some shit that's making you blind?

Do you ever get to feeling like that when someone is stringing you along to your death by wasting your time with bullshit and lies that feel good? Do you ever get that feeling? Do you? Ever at all? Do you think that you'll be here forever? Do you ever think that wasting time is losing time? Do you ever think that losing time is gaining on your death? Not death that doesn't touch you, like in a movie or in a magazine or some fucking cause that you give your filthy money to, but your death. The real death, the one that takes your life. Do you ever feel like there's no air to breathe? Like things are getting tight and heavy in your chest? Do you ever get that feeling in your guts like it's going to be over sooner than later and sooner as every hour passes, as every minute, as every second goes by? Do you ever feel like the air is being sucked out of you? Do you ever feel like running until you burst into flames and explode?

I do.

I've got a stopwatch strapped to my brain. Got a death-trip man screaming in my ear. I got a part animal part machine vision digging its spurs into my side screaming, "Faster, you idiot, the sun is coming up!"

▼

Do you ever get the feeling that there's no way out? Everything around you closes in. The walls that have all of your favorite pictures become your enemies. It's suffocation. Every thing, every thought, every movement, everything becomes a knife slashing at your face. You start to think that existence is a dirty trick. A sucker punch. You're a punched-out sucker waiting for the air to not be so hard to breathe. You have to look out because you're walking into coffin walls all the time. You turn around and something says: Don't breathe, don't think, don't move. Don't do anything to remind yourself that you're alive. Maybe then you'll be okay. Okay for now or as long as it takes

49

your heart to beat once. Don't close your eyes, don't do it. Don't even blink. You don't want to miss a second of it.

▼

In the evenings the noise outside escalates to the point where everyone is yelling at each other. I keep waiting to hear that gunshot, that scream, that siren, something to tell me that someone has blown their top. It never comes. I wish there was a schedule I could look at. I would stay home so I didn't miss the men taking the body out of the apartment across the street or the two men squaring off in the middle of the street to kick the shit out of each other. That would make having to put up with all this noise a lot more worth it. I think it would relieve a lot of tension in these parts. I can see it in myself, all night long I have to listen to these assholes outside yelling like they're getting burned alive. Three in the morning and they're out there blasting that shitty music and yelling a bunch of shit. Tension, yes, the tension needs to be released. All I feel like doing is getting a gun and picking them off from the upstairs bedroom. That's what I call tense.

That's the problem though. All windup, no release. No fire. No pow pow pow. Why can't these guys get into some heavy thing with the cops? All the time those choppers are hovering right over the block, they never do shit. What the fuck. Why can't there be one of those SWAT guys on the roof, someone like that guy Hondo from the TV show. I can see him now, his cap on backward so he can see better, a cigarette dangling out of his mouth as he picks off those shitty little kids on their way home from school. Nothing like that ever happens here. All we get are these overweight social workers who come and hang out, score their drugs, and leave. I'm not advocating death and destruction, well I guess I am but what the fuck? All bullshit and no death and mutilated assholes make Jack a dull boy, dull and tense.

▼

Push them around. Don't you ever feel the need to kill them over and over? I do all the time. They make my teeth grind, they make the bile rise in my throat. They force my eyes to hate. When I see them die, I feel good, I feel like I'm alive again. I feel like I've been reborn. I am part animal part machine. Do you feel what I'm saying? Do you feel it? Yes you do, I know how you think. I know the whole thing inside out. I tell you, I think I'm going to explode. Have you ever felt like you wanted to rip your fucking face off? Burn it and feel the pain that comes when you live in this place. I want you to see this place in the middle of a firestorm because you know it would feel so good to know that they're burning like a fucking torch.

▼

I was walking up the avenue. I saw a gold Mercedes parked with its hazard lights blinking. There was a man and a woman in the front. Two black guys come walking up the avenue toward the Mercedes. When they get to the car, one of them starts shouting and bouncing the car up and down with his foot on the bumper. The other one just stands there watching. The guy gets off the bumper and grabs the hood ornament and makes like he's going to pull it off, then he takes his hand off. He goes around to the passenger side and sticks his arm inside; he comes out with some kind of necklace. He goes around to the front of the car again and bounces it some more. Then he grabs the hood ornament again and pulls it off. He throws it across the street; it lands on a roof. He goes around to the passenger side again and yells into the car window. He turns away, and he and his friend go walking on up the street.

▼

I'm exhausted but I can't sleep. Every time I close my eyes, these bright white dots go shooting through the space between my pupils and my eyelids. My body stiffens and jerks backward to dodge the dots. My spine is an animal occupying my body. My jaws are clenched tight. When I notice I relax my jaw. A short time later my teeth are grinding again. My stomach is a hard knot. I'm sweating, my armpits and crotch itch. I feel like screaming but I'm afraid of scaring myself to death. My heart aches, I wait on each beat to be the one who jams my heart into my windpipe. My head aches, it feels twice its normal weight, it feels like it's going to explode. I can almost see it ripping out of my skull, flying across the room, and smashing against the wall.

▼

He took off his clothes and his watch and left them in a pile in the living room. He went to the bathroom and ran the water for the bath. He paced the hall waiting for the tub to fill. He didn't want to go into the bathroom until the tub was full. The last time he tried this, his face staring at him in the mirror made him chicken out. The tub filled with water. He walked in, avoiding the mirror. He picked up the razor and put it to his wrist. He took a deep breath and pressed down. The pressure on his skin made him stop. He wasn't afraid to die— that's what he wanted. He was afraid of the pain and the blood he knew he would see. He put the razor back to his wrist and closed his eyes. He pressed down firmly and evenly. He pulled the blade from his wrist to the crook of his arm. The pain wasn't sharp as he expected it would be. It was a deep and dull throbbing ache that he could feel in his chest and head. The razor dropped from his hand. His knees went a bit weak. He caught himself on the shower curtain, which amazingly did not come down. He got in the tub and lay down. His breathing was heavy, the air felt tightly packed as he drew it in. He looked at the faucet and the soap holder. The air was getting heavier. The phone rang in the kitchen. He laughed and let out a long sigh, his eyes closed, his head tilted forward stopping when his chin hit his breastbone.

▼

I don't understand you. I don't think I ever did. For years I tried. I'm no closer now than I was then. It doesn't make me hurt, but it makes me wonder. Back then I had ripped wounds and a head full of nothing. Thinking of you now makes me think that perhaps I haven't changed much at all.

▼

I have dirt under my nails from digging this hole I'm in. When they talk to me, they get my imitation. I treat the flesh on my hands like it's Playtex. They shake my hand but they never touch me. When I extend myself to them, it's as if I have put a sign on my neck saying: DESTROY ME. When I extend myself I always become the victim of some kind of cruel joke. Now, I'm all for destruction, I think it's all right, but I would rather do it to myself.

▼

Downward spiraling man. Forehead pushed in, walleyed. I rip his throat out. I push him. He falls away leaving a trail of exhaust fumes.

▼

She points her finger. His porcelain mask falls to the ground and breaks into many jagged pieces. She looks at the face that she had never seen before. She walks away, leaving him alone with his undoing all around his feet.

▼

Florida Highway, 1986. Lonely slum. I passed through on low wheels. It was hot outside. Shacks, gas stations that didn't work, dead corn in fields, children on the road, retarded and dulled by the heat. Two girls waved as I passed.

▼

The sun is setting on my street. I live on Sunset Avenue. The drug dealers are having a meeting in the parking lot of the apartment across the street. They pull up in Cadillacs and BMWs. The little kids watch in silent reverence. To tell you the truth, it blows me away too. Seeing these guys with their gold and the nice cars, they look real smooth. Their hands wrap loosely around the steering wheels. Steering wheel one day, LA County prison bars the next.

▼

Clear blue sky, palm trees, offshore breeze, nice sunset. Well-dressed black boys on my street selling drugs. Last night I was getting out of the car and one of them came up to me and asked, "Lookin'?"

I pointed to the apartment where I lived and said, "No, living."

He smiled and said, "I heard that."

▼

A fly was crawling across my window. I crushed him with one of the blinds. I watched him crawl with his guts trailing behind him in a snotty little trail. No I didn't stick my face in and clean it up with my tongue. You don't know me as well as you think you do. I watched it crawl until it was too weak to haul its own guts. What a way to go. No complaining, no pleas for mercy. No cries for mamma. A while later I was looking out the window at the drug pushers across the street. I saw the fly again. It was still stuck to the glass by its guts. Another fly was eating him. I wish I could be like that. My girlfriend blows her brains out in the bathroom and I take her body downstairs and live on it for weeks. I couldn't do that you know. I wouldn't have the guts. I thought of that fly again with its buddy standing on top chowing down. That fly has more guts than I do.

▼

Hello Mom, do you read me? Over. Yes son go ahead. Over. Mom the sky is real red now and all you can smell is gasoline. You could look around at all the dead bodies and say that we're in some kind of hell. The choppers are so loud I can't even hear myself think, which is okay in a way because it keeps out all the bad thoughts. Nothing to think about except death. It's not here yet but I know it's only a matter of time. Over. That's a big 10-4. Over and out.

▼

The Mexicans on their bikes
I see them around sundown
Riding slowly down the street
I'm still asleep when they go to work
They always ride fucked-up ten-speeds
Sometimes they pull into the store
A six of Bud
They weave one-handed back into traffic
Sometimes I can look into their eyes
They always have that hard dull glaze
Hours of hard manual labor grinds the shine right off
Sometimes I think I see the same guy
I could be in Redondo, Hermosa, Torrance, Venice
It doesn't matter
I always see that same Mexican guy on the battered
    ten-speed
When I look at him I think of overcrowded apartments
Too many days and nights of never enough
Too many mangled hands
Too many lies and broken promises
That keep you hungry and hanging on

▼

I sit at my table and listen to the noises outside. City sounds. I can imagine a new kind of jungle complete with its own animals, habitat, and laws. The way one pusher whistles to another, each has a different sound and pattern. Like birds in trees. The police choppers, the motor scooters. The arguments, the fights, the gunshots. The eventual siren. The cacophonous blend makes me lock my door and keeps me up at night.

▼

When I was seventeen, I went to Spain. Nothing adventurous, just a school trip. I stayed in a hotel with a few hundred other bored, horny students from all over the USA. It was as if I never left home. It was a big party where everyone got drunk and nobody got laid. One of the cool things I did besides barely escaping getting raped by these drunk Spanish faggots at the Don Quixote was to go to this bullfight. It was me, the students, and all the locals. The locals didn't like us one bit. We always wanted the bull to win. We booed when they stuck the poor bastard with all the knives. There were three fights in all, and they all ended the same way. They would make a big deal of killing the bull slowly, and then the matador would put the sword through the bull's neck and kill him. They would drag the dead bull around the ring. Maybe to rub it in or ensure that the matador got laid. The last fight was the best. The moment came when the bull and the matador were looking into each other's eyes and the sword was about to plunge. The bull pulled to one side and swept his horn up and ripped out the matador's kneecap and chucked his ass up into the sucker seats. All of us Americanos were on our feet cheering like crazy. The locals were booing at the same velocity. They sent in another guy, and he killed the shit out of that bull. They dragged his ass around the ring three times to let everybody know that you can't win when you're alone scared and crazy, pitted against a bunch of men with swords who aren't drunk and who need to get laid.

▼

The boy in the chip shop wasn't fucking with me. He was just standing there waiting for his order to come up. He was pale and lean. Nervous face. Acne, that gross facial hair that resembles some kind of fungus. I watched him lean against the counter tapping his coins. Like I said, he wasn't fucking with me. I had this overwhelming urge to kick his ribs and head in. I have no explanation for this. I just stood there and looked at his midsection and imagined myself kicking. I could feel the ribs against the toes of my shoes, just like that dude's head I kicked in Florida. That was the hardest I had ever kicked anyone in the head. I had no animosity toward this boy in the chip shop, no hate, nothing. That's why I was standing there wondering what my problem is. The boy eventually got his order and left the shop. I can still imagine myself kicking his body across the floor of the shop. His body twitching and convulsing with each kick.

Driving home I imagined the car in a terrible accident, where the driver's head was smashed into the dashboard. I thought of his brains and teeth mixed together with the food we had just bought. I could almost smell it. The smell would be like the one I caught while I was crawling around the site where Katherine Arnold blew her brains out. There would be smashed bodies, steaming food, and blue lights of the sirens bathing the wreck in rhythmic passes.

▼

I don't want a shoulder to lean on. I don't need it. The whole idea of "Someone, that special someone!" is for me a load of shit. I must be fully contained. No leakage, no spillover. Dependency is weakness. It's such a lie. Lying there in bed, in your lover's arms. *She's behind me, she believes in me!* No one is behind me. I am behind me. I believe in me. I don't need any support group to keep my head together. I know what I have to do, so I should just shut up and do it.

▼

Walking down Main Street in Venice. I watch all the people go in and out of the stores like gerbils in a cage. There's always people eating in the window seats of those restaurants. I look at them. They look out at me and they look away with a troubled frown. I could never eat in a place like that. I would be afraid of someone driving by and shooting me. You know they always look at me when I walk down that street. I always look right into their eyes. They always look away.

Like they got too close to something they don't like. I like that. I think that's the way it should be. As I walked by that bullshit factory on Rose Avenue I looked in the back where they take their coffee underneath the umbrellas. I thought how cool it would be to go through the place with a flamethrower. Like a real sanitation engineer. Hey fuck it man, it's a pig pile, and if I don't like it I should move. Across the street from where I live there was a shooting the other night. Two girls got it on the front porch of 309 Sunset Avenue. I was out of town the night it happened. Typical luck. I heard all about how the shots woke everybody up. And I heard about how this lady was wailing and screaming all night. Fuck I wish I was here for that. I would have been laughing and partying like a motherfucker. Blasting David Lee Roth out the window. Turning on the lights, dancing on the sidewalk. Laughing in their teary faces. High fiveing with the pigs. What a drag to have missed it. The other night I was walking by the place. There were all these white dudes hanging out in front. That's strange, I thought to myself. No matter. I pointed my finger at them and said, "Bang bang," then I laughed and went in my house. I'm glad that those two got shot the other night. Now things are real quiet around here. There's a lot of pigs around now, but life is one big give and take, isn't it. Sure it is.

▼

I see why husbands beat their women. I see why moms and dads beat their kids. I see why they take oaths and break them. Make promises, forget and regret. I don't know why I didn't see it before. It's right there. In all their eyes. It's a lie. It's a lie and no one seems to mind. They find the most painless and elegant way they can to stand in line.

▼

The frail white people on the bus. They look so out of place. Mixed in like pieces of shit hanging from a Christmas tree. They're out of place and they know it too. Look at their faces. The slight discomfort, the nervousness, their thinly masked disgust. What a trip. They always look like they're being filmed by the police. I'm one of those white dudes. I ride the bus. I watch them and it makes me laugh inside. The Mexican girls with all that makeup. Big asses crowding over into the aisle. The homeys in the back smoking dope. The faceless workers and the whiteys.

▼

The ambulance came and took the bum's body away. The girl next to me looked out the window and said, "God, there's a lot of blood there." I wondered if the ambulance attendants curse under their breath when they have to haul away some stranger who stinks of his own wastes, who dies in a pool of puke, shit, and urine. I wonder if they ever take one of those stiffs to a dumpster behind a twenty-four-hour doughnut place and dump it. Or toss it over a bridge. Might be cool to dump the damn thing on your landlord's doorstep. Toss it into a swimming pool in Century City. The body is taken downtown and incinerated by a wetback who works for minimum wage.

▼

I'm never wrong inside this room. Everything I think, everything I do is right and true. Even when it's a lie, it's my room. I know I'm lying, there's no one around to tell me any different. You could tell your friends that last night you were right about everything and there's nothing they could say to prove you wrong. That's why I don't like to leave this room. Outside it's all lies. You tell the truth and you get ripped off. You can get arrested or even killed. Inside my room I can tell the truth out loud. Sometimes it's the only time I get to be real. Because out there everyone is trying so hard to get away from what they are. Reality is the terminal machine. Death-propelled. The truth is so plain that it reduces us to crummy bags of flesh. Weak and dependent. Shitting, pissing, eating, escapists. All of us, this is a drag for some. You can't rise above your asshole, you can only rise above those who think they can.

▼

I saw this dog run diagonally down the street one day. Right after it had gotten run over by a car. The dog was howling like its throat was going to come out of its mouth. Its guts were coming out of its stomach. They were tangled up in its hind legs. Made the dog run diagonally. I watched the dog go all the way down the block and around the corner. I could hear the howls for a while after that. I looked at the old black folks hanging out on their front porches. Their faces didn't even move. Now I'm sitting here wondering what kind of shit they must have seen to make that nothing at all.

▼

When I was young, I used to go to this park to play almost every day. One day I went there and I was heading toward this clump of bushes. There were all these policemen there. I knew from the TV that I had nothing to fear. I went over to where they were and asked if I could play in there. They told me to get back, and then one of the park maintenance men pulled me away and said I should play over by the swings for a while. The police didn't leave until it had gotten dark. I found out the next day that a little girl's body had been found right in the same spot where I had buried seven pennies. I dug up the pennies a few days later. I kept them because I thought they were important. Soon they were gone in the gumball machine.

▼

It was 360 degrees outside
The police had come dressed like friends
Acting like soldiers
They arrested everything
All the apartment renters
All the condo owners
The rich girls were trying to catch the pigs' stare
In hopes of getting in a quick suck behind the bushes

To avoid prosecution
The rich boys could only offer credit cards and
    their assholes
The asshole offering had worked so many times before
It was no use, we were all going in
The last thing I saw before I passed out
All the rats and roaches cuffed and walking in a line

▼

Standing in the bathroom with my dick in my hand. Pathetic slob-bering fuck looking into the mirror. Come like any other animal. Wash it down the drain. I feel mean now. I don't need the girl I was thinking about. That was a temporary weakness. I'll never do that again. I want to kill someone now. I want to see someone get destroyed, fuck that. I want to see a whole lot of people get wasted. I catch myself. Almost punched a hole in the wall. I killed romance. That shit was all right when I wasn't wise to the ways of the world. Now it's nothing to me. No girl can make me lose it. I must have been out of my mind. Stupid child. No more. It's just a place to put your dick as if you had no brains. Getting all bent out of shape. I tell you though, it's the lies that I couldn't deal with. Having to lie to not be alone at night. Lying my god-damn head off just to get laid. I can't do it. I'm glad that I don't feel the need to do that shit anymore.

BANG!

Most of this book was written in Los Angeles in 1988. The neighborhood I was living in disgusted me. It was filthy, garbage was strewn everywhere. It was a failure in human engineering, and I was stuck in it. Taking the public bus and getting out in this nightmare made me mad. I would sit for hours in my small room with all my worldly possessions gathered around me and seethe. I wrote a good part of the book while listening to the music of Black Sabbath. There is a piece in the book called "Knife Street" that was the warm-up for a piece titled "Everything" that appeared in the book *Eye Scream*.

I used to love you
I still do
So selfish
I love the old you
The you that didn't shoot drugs
The you that didn't get beat on by men
You laugh in my face and call me a fool
But it's true
I still love you
Sometimes, I can see the old you
When your eyes flash
When you look almost alive

▼

He sits in the folding chair
He stares at his hands
All the scars
Fist to face
Fist through glass
Fist through wall
Fist
Fist
Fist
Where to now?
Glory is an echo
He listens to the others tell their stories

They all sound the same
He thinks to himself:
Rehab isn't a road, it's a treadmill
He looks at the men he's sharing the wagon with
Faces hollow
Seen ghosts
Seen Vietnam
Seen Korea
Seen Beverly Hills
Seen too much
Too many times
They sit in a circle
Confessing
Coming clean
Wagon wheel
Lonely, holding on
Still addicted to addiction
The fluorescent lights make them look injured
Soon, time to go home and wait until next week
Get back together and sing the old songs

▼

Awoken from a dream
He looks out the window
Three a.m.
What happened to the last two years?

▼

Running away
Curling up
Hiding
No use
Just abuse
He conceals his pain and horror

Life could be so great
Without them
He got raped
By his mother's boyfriend
You think I'm joking
I wish

▼

The disease died
Brokenhearted
There was no one left to infect

▼

There was a time
When things weren't so
And the air was
And people were
When you could go about at night
And not hear
Gunshots

▼

27 to life
Staring him in his face
Hanging out with him in his cell
Following him to the shower
Putting him to bed at night
He's got a lot of brothers
Friends as a gesture
On the edge of violence
The thing that keeps everyone together
He doesn't want to be a faggot
It's hard
No woman in seven years

What the hell was it like?
How did it feel?
There they are
The walls
There it is
The time
There it goes
Life passing

She was raped by her uncle
Her father left home
For another man
She is confused
She is sixteen

He never told anyone about the beatings
The time his father broke his arm,
He yelled so loud,
That the neighbors called the police
Now he lives with strangers
They're all right
He had the closet door taken off its hinges
He doesn't let anyone touch him

Listen!
Hark!
Machine-gun music
In the sky
Police chopper
Electric warrior
Round up from above

Random gunshots
Somewhere in the palm trees
I sit in my hole
Safety in #1
At night LA glitters like a woman
Who got punched in the mouth
And got told to get her ho ass back to work
Listen!
Hark!
I think I hear an angel!
Oh, it was just a pig

▼

I'm lost. I don't understand. There are a few things that I can remember. I have dreams of him touching me. Dreams of his tongue. I swore to myself that if anyone ever touched me like that again, I would kill them. The dreams never stop. I am afraid he will be there to rape me again. I know I do it to myself. Why? Do I hate myself? I rape myself in my dreams. I torture myself daily. I murder myself at night. I let him into my dreams. I've tried to have boyfriends. I don't want to be alone. I like boys. It's hard to deal with it when they want to touch me. I know that there's nothing wrong with what they want to do, but I can't do it. They call me bitch, castrator, tease. They don't understand. I am so scared and alone. I wish someone would hold me. I'm so cold. Why doesn't anyone understand? I can't talk to anyone. Sometimes I want to die. I feel that I will go through life with no one to love me. The only one who ever told me that he loved me was him. Maybe that was why I keep having the dreams. Please God let there be someone to love me besides him. Someone on the planet to love me. I see the looks on people's faces. The world is cold and mean. People are wild and dangerous. Someone to love me. Please don't let me go through life like this.

▼

I miss you. I know that I keep saying that and I know that you're getting tired of me writing you all the time but I can't get over the fact that you're gone. I know that you only live across town but it's hard driving by that house you share with that guy and knowing that all the time he's using you. You know that he's using you don't you? You never did listen to me. I have some friends who hang out in this club that he goes to. I am told that he hands you some pretty heavy beatings. I hear that he sells you to his friends. I am afraid to go over there and knock on the door and talk to you because I am afraid he might kill me. Are you using drugs? You never needed to when you were with me. Can I see you again? Will you call me? Will you at least call me? I miss you.

▼

Everybody is somebody else's freak
Think about it
Sit at home with the television on
Watch some people burn shit down
Thousands of miles away
"Look at those freaks. Aren't they something? Must be
        rough over there."
Outside a killer is checking you out
Thinking to himself about the freak propped up in front of
        the television set
That's you
Everybody is somebody else's joke
You laugh all the time
You're always up for a laugh
Point your finger and laugh
Put it all below you
Meanwhile
The monkeys are laughing at you from their cages

From their glass boxes
You laugh back and throw excrement
You go back and forth and laugh and throw
But it gets to you
You wonder what's so funny
What's the matter, can't take a joke?
He is laughing his ass off
You do look funny with a gun at the side of your head
And his cock in your mouth
Who is the freak now?
You're one of those bad trips
One of those things you read about
Don't bite
You might get shot in the head
I don't know if you get what you deserve
All I know is that you get it
Sleepwalker with the "boob job"
Yeah get one of those
You'll need it
Otherwise fuckhead won't fall in love with you
When he grabs the top of your head
And tells you to get busy, just think of it as an investment
Get yourself well-oiled
For the lifelong sellout
Drive down the boulevard
Look at the young boy working the corner
Look and laugh right?
It's not you
You couldn't touch a reality that fierce to save your life
Look at the freak
Don't look for too long or he will rip that smile right off
        your face
Hand it to you
And then he'll start laughing

You're a ripe apple on a low branch
You're a fillet in a shark tank
You were born human
Perfect for gang rape
Mutilation
  Prostitution and glory
Everybody is somebody else's excuse
Perfect
All you need to get by
A point man
So you can have a reason to point a finger
To be able to escape yourself one more time
That wasn't me
I was drunk
You know how it is
That's not my fault
I was in love at the time
The pressure of the city made me do it
I took drugs to get away from my father
I drank to get away from my boss
I go to the bar to loosen up from the hassle at work
I hit my wife
Because the car wouldn't start
Because our son won't listen to me
It's not me with the problem
Someone else will take care of my sins
Some medicine will be invented
Someone on television will say something
Everything will be all right
And since I can stop anytime I want
Don't tell me how to run my lie
I'm free
I heard that in a song on the radio
The cesspool of love

Festering swamp
Hear the blues song
The one about the man sitting alone in his room
Waiting
Hoping
That maybe she will come back
It's because of her all this pain
All this sweat
Like heavy thoughts
Like:
I don't want to live
I can't live
There is no sunshine
There is no life
There is nothing
Without her
So when that woman comes staggering back in
There will be a hot fist of love
Waiting
It's nothing but the blues
Keep your blues to yourself
Unless you want every pore, every hair, every thought
        you possess,
Bought and sold at the speed of light
Blood, dust, and an empty six
Spent shell casings
A broken television
A bent spoon
Dirty sheets
Broken glass
The smell of rotting beer
Stale sweat
Dreams of nowhere
You want mercy?

A break from the plague?
Arms to hold you?
A kind word?
Then get out of the 213 area code
It's all the blues around here

BLACK SABBATH

So much litter out of place
It's time to put it in its place
A mind is a terrible thing
A dream is flashing like a polished weapon in my mind
To the summer ambulance
Siren songs
The two girls
Drunk
Fighting outside the club
Broken glass under the crime lights
Fuck these streets
And the bastards who put them here
All these experiments
Like how much blood will it take to drown you
All the while I know
That I am a hero in the making
A walking legend
Superstar status is my domain
If I had a car big enough,
I would drive all of you right off the edge
But there is not the time to play games
I walk the streets looking at you
Listening to you living your garbage cowboy coward
        fantasy
This place is going to look a lot different
After I get done decorating

Too bad you won't be here to see it

I am an angel

I am a soldier

I am on a mission

No one knows but me

The streets talk to me

The sidewalk looks up at me and makes faces

It mocks me

When I breathe in the stench fills me

Tries to consume me

Tries to destroy me

It will not destroy me

I am here to clear the air

Look at this place

Look at the filth

Look at the decadence

It forces you to pick a side

Either you destroy it or you become it

Every moment of the day it stares you in the face

Taunting you

Destroying you

And you let it

Tag

You're it

You're shit

It is too late for spiritual awakening

Fuck that hippie shit

It's too late for social change

You can't educate a flock of sheep

Can't you see that's what they want

They want you to turn away

They want you to lie down

Like a lamb for the slaughter

Like a chump for the sellout

There will be no revolution

There will be no uprising

There will be no race war

How could anyone be that stupid?

How could anyone believe that bullshit?

What a joke

I know a lot about jokes

I see them all the time

I spent years with some living jokes

You should see them now

Fat

Stoned

Cowards

Living death

Men of action turned into weak pieces of shit

They could get my respect again

If they shot themselves in the head

At night I walk the streets

I take mental notes

I take inventory

The filth

The garbage

The stench

Liars

Freaks

Clowns

My mission becomes clear to me

My life focuses into a laser beam

My purpose

My life

My vision is pure napalm

I am here to clean

There is only one way to clean

You have to incinerate

You must cleanse with fire
You must turn disease to ash
Or it still lives
Things have gone too far
The strong are destroyed by the weak
Decadence has set a precedent
It has become a way of life
Not the way of my life
Shit is shit
I am here to burn it
Can't you see?
I am beyond your timid lying morality
I don't believe in equality
That is to say
That I don't think that if you're alive
That's all you need to get by
The man who sells drugs,
Is not equal to me
The man who rapes his son is not equal to me
They cannot hide
Guilt trips will not shield them from me
I don't believe in human rights
I think you have grown fat and evil
Hiding behind your human rights
Reveling in filth
The balance must be brought back
When I walk the streets in my neighborhood
Drunks come staggering from bars
Guns go off
Police helicopters fly above
Yet nothing happens
Some show
Let's cut the drama
Get rid of the display

The ritual is nowhere
It's hollow
The nights are made of tin
Cheap
Bitter death
I will show you my world
I will bring it home
My beauty
The summer nights of fire and truth
Can you see it?
A dark hot night
The whine of engines from above
The tree line explodes in fire orange
The air fills with the smell of gasoline
The air strike
Like a flower erupting in rapid birth
Filth turned to ash
So beautiful
Decadence lies bleeding
As I walk and plan
I hear angels singing
Black Sabbath songs
The soles of my shoes are thick
Keeps the blood and urine at a distance
The mind I occupy is iron
My time is now
I see them
Maybe it is you who I see
Singing the song of the loser
Your endless, diseased song
The end is coming
And I am the one who is bringing it
I am the punch line
I will defoliate before it's too late

You spend millions on rehabilitation
Rewashing the brainwashed
There's no such thing as rehabilitation
How big does a lie have to get before even you can no
  longer avoid it?
You shit in your bed
You wait for someone to come
And clean it up
Well, here I am
Ready to throw out the baby with the bathwater

ONE FROM NONE

I wrote this book while on the road in 1987. I spent most of the year playing shows and recording. A good part of that time was spent in Europe. The book's title reflects what I think of myself. I have always felt that my greatest achievement was to survive my upbringing. The greatest lessons I ever learned, I learned on the road. The scars on my skin are my road map.

At some point they show their true colors
After the breakup
After the trial
After the contract is signed and broken
Their true colors stink
These days
I find it hard to get along with them
I want to push them until the colors come out
And sometimes I hate them so much, I push and see
I do the same to the ones I like
The ones I don't care about
I smile at real nice

I closed my door
I saw the world frowning at me
I sat shut away from their downward-spiraling universe
I stared at the walls
My universe frowned at me too
Shut away
Turn away
I want an eject button I can push
So I can get out of myself
When my universe frowns at me

▼

All my war stories are old
They hang like old clothes in the closet
No one wants to hear old war stories
It's all I have right now
My mouth flaps dry in the air
I am in this room pacing the floors
Sun up sun down grinding my teeth
Jumping at shadows waiting
I don't want to think about that old war anymore
It's driving me up the wall with bad insanity
I need new war
High on war

▼

All the beaten-down men got on the bus long before I did
I look at their cheap clothes and run-down shoes
Their bags of junk
Their faces look like they're going to drop off their heads
And hit the floor
Most of them are holding transfers
It's late
Look at these guys riding into the night
Like a sad song played out of a cheap radio

▼

I hate to feel need
I look at her and I need
I feel it burn
I have a black gift
I heal myself into a mass of scar tissue
Unparalleled in insensitivity
I numb myself to myself

Instead of listening to my need
I don't feel the cuts and I can't taste the blood
Like having a headache
Blowing your brains out to stop the pain
Stupid and gutless
But it's easy and it hurts so much
That it doesn't hurt at all

▽

Stop the headache
Cut off the head
Stop the bleeding
Drain the body of blood
Stop the war
Kill both sides
Stop hunger
Starve them to death
Stop crime
Put everybody in jail

▽

He sits in his room night after night
No one comes over or calls
He makes no sound
He looks at his hands
He looks at the floor
He listens to his breath
He doesn't look at the clock
Time doesn't matter
His hands don't matter
He doesn't matter
He pays no attention to his thoughts

▼

There were things I wanted to tell you
I couldn't get it together
I couldn't get past your eyes
After you were gone it hurt to have kept quiet
So easy to not say what you think
To not do what you want
Hard to take rejection
Easy to hurt someone else and not know it
Easy to make it hard

▼

They will try to destroy you
At all times on all levels
All the things that go bump in the night twist your balls
Listen to how they talk
Sounds like trash falling out of their mouths
Every sound, every motion wants a piece of you
You must:
Disown
Disavow
Discard
You must break it over your knee
Dislocate
Look at all the animals looking at you

▼

Big Larry the black fag
We used to hang out at the parking lot
I would watch him park cars
We would hang out on the avenue and talk
So much bullshit
Sometimes all we could do was laugh

He would sometimes reach over and grab my dick
I would say get off me you big black fag
We would laugh like shit
He would look at me with these watery eyes
He would say:
White boy, you got no box, you got no ass
What are you going to do?
I didn't know
I asked him why the hell he didn't like women
He laughed so hard he nearly fell off his crate
He said that there was something about that big old piece
Just hanging there, really did it for him
I told him that women were what was happening
He laughed hard as shit
Asked me how the fuck I knew that
I didn't know shit about women
Much less anything else
All I had was a milk crate under my ass
And this big black motherfucker grabbing my dick
I told him that I was with women all the time
He laughed so hard
I thought his eyes were going to fall out

▽

I met a guy once
He had been locked away in solitary for a stretch
When they came to let him out, he didn't want to go
He liked it better in there
Said it was a world that he could understand and control
Sometimes I think it would be better to stay in a cage
It gets hard to take the shit that these fakes put across
They should be careful
Someone might take them out of the picture
Just for a laugh

87

Or because they have the blues
The world is big
You see how people react to the terror
The size and the noise
Freaks them right out
They wish for the cage like I wish for the cage
Sometimes I want to kill you
Make you wish you gave me the cage
Before one of your pigs takes me out
I am going to take a few of you down
I have the blues from the size and the noise
Where's that cage

▽

I have come back to you swinging man
I left you in that room years ago
I went out into the light and looked around
I have come back into the darkness
To bask in your rancid creaking rhythm
I can hear you swing back and forth
I can see liquid dripping from your mouth
Sticking your tongue out, making fun of the world
I see why now
They make me feel like they made you feel
Hollow and alone
Emptied and gutted
I must tell you right now
Silence is the most powerful sound I have ever heard
The things they said feel good
Don't
You could never fit in
So you made your own place
That's what I need to do
I feel pushed out of everything

I wish I could have seen you kick out the chair
It would have been great to see your eyes
But then again
That wouldn't have been too good for you
The best things are done alone

▼

Take my hand
Come into this dark room
Get down on the floor with me
Let's get slain
Lick the sweat
Taste the blood
Hear the sound
For once
For real
I need something real from you
I want you so bad
I want to taste you
I need to feel your teeth in my flesh

▼

I took you to you
That's what you wanted
I think I did a good job
You got mad when I left you there
You cursed me
For the stench of your trash
Well, it's all you now
Sooner or later you'll see
The sun shines outside the sewer
It's easy to come away empty-handed when you don't
        reach out
It's hard to believe you when you say you're choking

When you have your hands around someone else's throat
It's all you and you now
If you lean too far to one side, you will fall
You'll have to pick yourself up off the floor of your soul
Scar tissue is stronger than normal flesh
It's all you for you now
All things inside
The poison
The medicine
All in you for you

▼

When I look at you
I want to destroy your smile
It sits on your face like a lie
You look good
I want to know the truth about you
I want to get close to you
When I do, you see that I see through you
Your heart beats like a small bird
You know me well
That's why you can't handle me
It hurts me to act a fool
Pretend I don't see you for what you are
All of you keep me on the outside
I want to believe your lies
Turn myself off and feel you
But I can't stop seeing through
All of you

▼

He sat in the dark room and waited for her
She was not his friend

He tried friendship for years and knew the truth
He wanted someone to be nice to him for an hour
He was lonely
It made no sense that someone would find him attractive
That someone would want to be with him for what he was
In his business everybody wanted something
There was always an ulterior motive, a game being played
There was something wrong when someone was nice to
        him
And they weren't getting paid
Every time someone wanted to shake his hand
He wanted to say:
What are you after?
How much do you want?
He was not a bad person
He just couldn't identify
He sat and waited for her to come
She was a whore
Not off the streets, she was high-class
His manager got her for him
There was a knock on the door
He opened the door and she came in
She looked at him and smiled
She looked down at a card in her hand
Asked if his name was Frank
He nodded
She went into a speech about the things she wasn't into
Rough stuff, anal sex, S&M
He nodded
He spoke:
It's hard for me. I'm not used to this. I need you to be nice
        to me for a while. I want you to pretend that you
        know me and like me. You don't have to take off your

clothes unless you want to. Maybe you could just put
your arms around me for a while. Could you do that
for me?
She put her arms around him
He closed his eyes
He felt good
She looked over his shoulder at the television
She almost started to laugh out loud
She wanted to ask if she could light a smoke
What a crack-up, this rock star
Her little brother had all of his records
If he knew what he was really like, he would throw
     them out
After a short time he pushed her away
Gave her a wad of money
Said: It's all there, thanks
Get out

They don't lie a lot
They just don't tell the truth very often
Truth does not mean much to them
You can lie to them, or tell the truth
Makes no difference to them
Walk on them if you want
Eat with their forks
Destroy them for the hell of it

Animals in pain
Sweating and screaming
Sweating and screaming
Bullets blowing brains across apartments all over town
The janitor hangs himself in the basement

Had a falling-out with God
Leaves a note saying he was sorry for his life
Hot night breaks jaws
All is fair in love and hell
If you don't like it, crawl on your hands and knees
And stick your head in the oven
Breathe deep
Dying in rooms
Crying out from plaster tombs
Heroin worship
Nightmare in the womb
Sliding down the icy spike
No way but out

In New Jersey she said:
"It's always been a dream of mine to have you inside me"
In Rhode Island six people came and no one clapped
In Pittsburgh she said:
"You're the most gorgeous man I have ever seen"
In Minneapolis the pigs arrested Joe
In Des Moines she said:
"It's so exciting when you come inside me"
In New Brunswick he said I was a hippie
In Birmingham he said I was
"A talentless jerk that stole freely from bad sources"
In Madison she said I was a typical asshole
In Washington I quoted Hitler and made her cry
In Athens I tried to fuck behind the police station
In St. Louis she said that she hates all men
In New Orleans he said that someone was coming to kick
    my ass
In Pensacola she walked away from me, wordless
In Daytona Beach she said I was a pig

In Miami bugs crawled on my face and I couldn't sleep
In Jackson she said:
"It's hot and things move slow around here. That's why we
  fuck a lot, fight a lot, eat a lot, and drink a lot"
In Philadelphia I fucked in a men's room stall
In Columbia he said: "White power all right" I said: "Heil
  Budweiser"
In Vermont I saw him get hit by a car
In Albany I saw him get taken to the loony bin
In Boston she said that her friend hadn't washed her shirt
  since I sweated on it
In Lincoln twenty people came and they all sat in back or
  left early
In Memphis he pounded the stage with his brass knuckles
In Hoboken I spat puke for the last three songs
In Chicago I spat puke for the last four
In Cincinnati I spat blood
Here in LA I wait to go

▼

People get lost
The alarm clock goes off and someone loses his way
All of a sudden five years have passed
Same job
They look at themselves in the mirror
Can't understand where it all went
A dirty underhanded trick
Someone gets lost and destroyed
People walking the streets like dumb animals
Smart enough to be cruel
Handcuffed to the television set
Another beer can opens
The sun goes down on another day

Self-destruction slow and complete
What nasty things we do to ourselves

I get calls from crazy girls
Late at night
They sound like they're calling from another planet
The other night one calls from some bin in O.C.
She tells me that her parents put her there
They no longer want to see her
Her older brother told her that she is ugly
She believes him
She starts to cry
She says that he goes out with a girl that got named
Ms. Huntington Beach
She asks me if she is ugly
I tell her she's not ugly at all
She says that her brother is a big fan of mine
And he wouldn't believe that we are talking right now
She tells me that she lives in a ward
A lot of other kids around her all the time
A tough weird reality
Almost thirteen years old
She asks if she can call again sometime
I say sure
She says goodbye and hangs up
I stare at the ceiling and try to fall asleep
I feel so lonely right now

1:22 a.m.
Phone rings
Long distance

She is off medication
Nervous about starting up with the new shrink
Trying to get her friends off drugs
"She works her ass off all week. Gets her pay on Friday
     and it all goes up her nose. She's trying to quit but
     it's hard."
She says that all of last year she was on medication
She sat in her room and stared at the wall
Her family pretended that she wasn't there
She goes to bars to be around people
She can't be alone for too long or she starts to slip
She says she is coming out to LA
She sounds like she's talking in her sleep
I tell her that I have to get up in a few hours
She gets mad
She tells me that I'm trying to avoid her
She calls me a few names and hangs up
Another night warped

▽

She calls me from a bin out in the sticks
Tells me all about getting strapped down
Tells me that she's getting better
She can't feel it now
But they tell her that she's getting better all the time
I think of her as she speaks
Shitting her pants
Men in smocks putting electrodes into her head
I think about lab rats
The smell of shit
All these people getting better
Bright lights
White sheets
This stranger

BLACK COFFEE BLUES

I wanted to make a book that would be a good travel companion like Henry Miller's *Black Spring* was for me in the summer of 1984. The book is made up of short stories, journal entries, essays, and a record of dreams. I finished the book in 1991 and did the rewrites in 1992.

124 Worlds

#29: We walk down the street debating. Should we take a cab, bus, or should we walk to the graveyard? I say that I don't mind walking. She says she doesn't think I'm up to it and hails a cab.

We get to the graveyard and walk through the gate. I feel hesitant. Not because I have a problem with walking past a bunch of stiffs, but because I think that some kind of custodian or cop is going to come out of the little shack at the front and give us shit about what the hell we were planning on doing in there. I could see it plain as day, some fat piece of shit pig,

"What do you think you're going to do in here? You're looking for a place to screw aren't you? Yeah, I figured as much . . . you little sluts. You think you're going to go into one of those mausoleums and screw your little goddamn brains out don't you? Well you're not. You get the hell out of here before I kick your shit all the way down to the station. I see you looking at me fella. Go on, try something. I want you to. I'll hit you so hard your mamma will get a black eye. Get the hell out of here you little shits." Something like that. We go past the gates, no one comes out. We walk down the uneven, cracked pathway.

Whole families lined up in rows. Some stones just say BABY. Small stones with numbers are all over. These are plots for sale. I think of a man walking down the path with the caretaker after they have had a cup of coffee and a few laughs. The man looks down at a stone and says to the caretaker,

"Here, this is the place. Is this taken? I want my body put right here. Still open? Great. How much? Oh great. Yes, I like the way the sun catches it. Not near any trees, good. I don't want any birds getting my stone dirty, not that I'll know anything about it. That's a joke. Yes, I believe that you've heard it all before, but yes, I'll take it."

If I were going to pick a place where my body was going to rest for eternity, I would want to be really sure of the place. I mean *really* sure. I would set up a tent and camp out at the spot for a few days. I know that it would look a bit strange, like if there was a funeral nearby and all these mourners filed past my bright orange tent. I'd smile and wave as I tended to my franks and beans cooking on the Sterno stove. I would stick out without question, but at the end, I would know for sure. I would walk up to that caretaker with a steady eye and a voice that defined conviction.

"Yes sir, that's the grave for me, you betcha. Where do I sign?"

I would mean it and he would know it.

I suggest that this place would be a great golf course. It has a pond and everything. It would take a mighty golfer to be able to get through the course, what with all the stones in the way, a real challenge. I mean come on, pro golfers must get bored of these tournaments. These big-ass fields, every once in a while an alligator or something. Imagine the fun these guys would have playing through a mausoleum. What if a golfer's ball landed on his long-lost uncle's grave?

Okay, my dad used to walk his dogs on this golf course on the weekends. The course was huge. The dogs ran around and had a great time. The dogs were faithful and good. They would see those balls flying through the air. They would retrieve them and place them like a little pile of quail eggs at my father's feet. From hundreds of yards away, I could see golfers shaking their fists. Although the distance was great, I could still hear what they were saying. A lot of shit about, "Goddammit, shit, dogs . . . my ball!" My dad would laugh his ass off. At times like these, he was almost human.

We walk over to a mausoleum all decked out in iron and granite. The room inside is bigger than a lot of apartments I've lived in. She thinks that there might be passages underneath it. I ask her what she thinks a bunch of dead guys are going to do with secret passageways. I can see them all down there laughing,

"Haw, haw, our wives still think we're dead! Hey Moe, pass that over here. Haw haw . . ."

You never know, so I go over and put my ear to the door and listen for sound, the sound of a stereo, the sound of bowling pins . . . Nothing, not a sound.

We keep walking. I trip over a wreath and knock it over. I pick it up and put it back on its stand. I read the name on the stone.

"Sorry John, I mean, Mr. Garland."

I walk away and look back. The wreath has fallen over again. I know that if there really is a hell, I'm going to be there and old John Garland will be pissing on my head from a cloud on high.

We have walked all the way around, and we're close to the gate again. I look over and I see what looks like a television antenna poking out from behind a stone. I walk over there and check it out; it's just a wreath stand turned over. That would be great, to see a pair of rabbit ears clipped onto a stone. A repair guy hooking the grave up for cable. *Hey, we got big-screen TV, grab a shovel and come on in.*

There's every type of stone you can think of in here. I point out one that looks like a big ebony dick. She looks at me and starts laughing. I suggest that some of these people should have gotten their loved ones to put some fancy custom neon work on their stones— that would really stand out amongst all the gray and black.

We get to the gate. I hear some voices. I look over and see three guys in workman uniforms leaning up against a truck. They are passing a joint between them. I tell her that David Lee Roth's grave will have a full bar and a merchandising booth. We leave the graveyard.

#30: He had the day off. He sat in the room. That's what he did when he wasn't at the job. The job made him hate, made him hate endlessly. Made him punch the wall. Made him keep his fucking mouth shut. It felt good to grind his teeth. He would walk home from the shift, hoping that someone would fuck with him so he could use his fists.

It was the day before Christmas. Like many Christmases past, he didn't send or receive presents or cards. To him, Christmas was another day. Just another day to be followed by another one. He knew they were full of shit because they needed a day of the year when they could be nice to each other. They couldn't just be that way. They needed an occasion to come out of their holes and be human beings. What rotten shits they were. He knew this. It always boiled down to money for them. There was no escape. Life was waiting for the next shift to start.

He remembered the Christmases of his youth. He was living with his mother. She would get him some presents and never let him forget for a minute that he was a pain in her ass. She would pull out the plastic Christmas tree from the closet and put it up with the same lights from the year before. It was a sad ritual. He remembered how she always had a cigarette hanging out of her mouth and she would tell him that he had better appreciate this shit. She put "goddamn" before everything she said. Goddamn presents, goddamn toys, etc.

He wanted to tell her that he didn't care about the tree and the presents and could she not be so nasty all the time, that she was scaring him and he hadn't done a thing to deserve it. He didn't make up Christmas.

Opening the presents was a drag. He knew that she really couldn't afford the presents and buying them made her angrier than usual.

"You better enjoy that one. I paid a lot of goddamn money for that."

She would light up a cigarette and watch him like a hawk. He did his best to look happy when he opened the presents. In truth he had no interest in them. All he wanted to do was kill her. He could tell by the things that she got for him that she didn't know anything about him. It was like having a crazy woman paying your rent and buying you shit and telling you that she wished you didn't exist.

At Christmastime, his mother's mother would call. Grandmother was a drunk. He met her a few times and she was always fucked up, slurring her words, makeup on all crooked, falling over chairs, laughing. They would get on the phone, and his mother would start screaming, her cigarette ashes falling all over the floor. Finally, his mother would slam the phone down and start breaking things in the kitchen. He would run to his room and hide.

A few days later he would be sent over to his father's house to visit and collect presents that had been bought for him. Sometimes there was a Christmas tree, but most times there wasn't and that was a big relief. His presents were always in the closet next to his father's boots. The presents were never wrapped. He could tell that his father didn't know him at all. His mother would give him a box of cigars to take over to his father for a present. Father would look at them and put them on a shelf and not say anything. His father would watch some sports game and fall asleep in front of the television with a lit cigar in his hand. He would watch his father sleep, debating if he should let the cigar burn his father's hand. At the last minute he would gently remove the cigar and put it in the ashtray.

Later on there was the overcooked dinner served up by his stepmother, a terrifying and unpleasant bitch. She would never use sugar. She put artificial sweetener in everything. The meal was dry and neglected, a hateful heap of shitty food. He would get a sharp poke in the ribs from his father signifying that it was time for him to say something nice about the meal.

"Real good ma'am."

His father would look at him and nod. She made it clear that he was a pain in her ass. He couldn't wait to leave. She scared the shit out of him.

He would go back to his mother's house with all the presents from his father. His mother would pull it all out and look it over, muttering as she went through the lot. "Goddamn, he really is a goddamn slob isn't he? How do you work this goddamn thing . . ." She would force a moving part on of one of the toys, breaking it. "See? This god-damn stuff is cheap. You see what a cheap bastard he is . . . Christ."

He would pull the presents into his room and put them in a pile in the corner. He rarely played with the things that they bought him. He was scared to break them. She would hit him. Call him ungrateful and threaten to have the police come and take him to jail forever.

"I'm thinking about calling the police and having them take you away. How would you like that?"

Whack.

"How," *whack,* "would," *whack,* "you," *whack,* "like," *whack,* "that?"

He sat and thought out loud.

I should have let you burn your whole fucking house down Dad, just what you needed.

Another Christmas going by. He sat and watched the snow fall by the window. Nice view from where he was—another apartment building. He could see a few Christmas-tree lights blinking. The occasional head pass by. The heater was making small rattling sounds like it was shivering.

"Yeah, you and me both pal, ha ha."

Tomorrow another day off. Another day to wait until the shift started again. The shift would always start again. Any time away from the job was just the spaces in its big teeth—little gaps in which you were allowed to breathe, lie to yourself, and make yourself think that you were alive. They had you coming and going. They had you. There was nothing but the shift and the apartment. The work and the wait. He spent his off time resting, soaking his feet in hot water to keep the swelling down. It was endless. The room was poorly lit. There were three sockets in the ceiling, but he never replaced the bulbs after they burned out. He was now down to one. Darkness came. The snow kept falling. He sat and waited for the shift to start.

#34: He watched a lot of television. He didn't care what was on, he was picking up information. It was all recon. Every hour that he watched, the more he knew about them, about how they worked—

their patterns. The more he knew, the easier it was going to be to take action when it was time. He was on a mission that was classified. Protocol demanded that all details of the operation be kept out of general circulation. This was, after all, a matter of national security.

At work, all his fellow employees thought that he was crazy, but they liked him because they knew that it wasn't every day that a top agent used a dish-packing company as a cover. This was fine with him. He used this to work inside without raising his profile. Easier to get into their lives and see how they ticked. The more information, the better.

Back at the house, he watched the television nonstop. He had the notebook open and took notes furiously. The woman in the shampoo ad would scratch her ear the same way every time. In fact, her movements and speech patterns were so precise that he could swear it was the same ad every time. He made a note to get all possible information on lifelike robots. That was another thing he knew about her—about them all.

"They lack any kind of style, definitely a cult of personality. It's easy to see that they are used to lying and getting lied to. In fact, from my estimation, they use lies as their primary means to exchange information. When dealing with them, use lies to befriend them. Employ the truth to confuse and debilitate them . . . must get more information."

Years went by. People at work would ask, "How's the mission going Larry?" He would tell them that he knew of no such mission, that even if he did have any knowledge of any so-called mission, he wouldn't be at liberty to disclose the details of such a mission, even if it did exist. The piles of notebooks grew higher.

He found a new and fantastic place to pick up information: the library. They were always whispering in there. They must be exchanging secret lies. He would go into the library and pretend to look through the books. He even went as far as to get himself a library card. Every once in a while he would take out books to make them think that he was a fan of literature. He usually selected books that he had already read so he would be able to answer questions in case the librarian attempted to spot-quiz him. Keeping all the bases covered is a principle detail in top security work. You have to be sharp and at your best at all times.

#36: They were on the couch watching television. He had his arm draped over her shoulder. They watched a program about a group of young lawyers full of compassion and human values battling for the rights of society's underprivileged. A young man had been accused of raping a woman. He was in court now, trying to plead his case. The girl on the couch said, "He's guilty."

He asked her how she knew, thinking that perhaps she had already seen this episode.

"I know he did it. A woman can always tell. We know how men are. Yes, he definitely did it."

He looked at her.

"What a load. I know how *women* are. They say that they want it, but if they don't like it or they get pregnant, they yell rape, and the guy goes to jail. It's a pile of shit I think. If they didn't want men coming up and trying to get next to them, then why do they wear the clothes that they do? It's a mean, fucked-up game if you ask me. Women have men by the balls and sometimes the weaker of them loses control after getting their dicks teased through the roof."

She looked back at him like he had just dumped a bucket of llama shit on her head and asked for a dollar.

"You think it's okay for some guy to do what he wants to a woman? That the clothes she wears are an invitation for gratuitous sex? If that's your attitude, I'm leaving right now. Men are pigs!"

"No!" he shot back. "That's not what I meant at all. I don't think some guy can do what he wants to a woman. Come on, what do I look like? Damn."

"Okay," she said, "I know what you mean about the teasing thing. I hate to say this, but me and my friends used to do it when we were younger and not as classy as we are now. We used to get guys all hot and bothered and see how far we could go before it got too heavy, and then we would leave. It was fun for a while, but I can see how it would drive a man wild."

He reached down and cupped her breast. She looked at him and smiled. He kissed her and worked his hand into her shirt. He got his hand into her bra and outlined her nipple with his finger. With his other hand he went up her skirt. He had his hand in her panties now and was running it through her pubic hair. She slowly removed his hand from her shirt and held it. She took his index finger into her mouth and ran her tongue around its tip and looked into his eyes. She took her other hand and placed it on the bulge in his pants. A commercial came on. An ad for milk.

A beautiful girl drank a glass of milk, licked her lips and said, "Ummm, yummy."

The beautiful girl smiled and the ad went off. She squeezed the bulge and said, "Ummm, yummy."

She started unbuttoning his shirt, kissing the places where the buttons had been. She dug her tongue into his navel as she undid his belt. She pulled his cock out and started talking to it.

"Hello handsome, you look so good I could eat you like candy. I bet you taste so good. You're so big and strong. What's a poor girl to do? I can't control myself!"

He could feel her breath on his cock. She looked up at him and smiled. He closed his eyes and let out a long sigh. This was going to be great. She gave his cock a slight tug and laughed as she got up.

"That's the kind of stuff that we used to do. God, weren't we mean? Those poor guys must have hated our guts! Well look, I've got to go. Me and the girls are going to go down and see that new Joe Cole film. Have you ever seen him? He is so hot. All my friends want to rip his clothes off! If any of them call here looking for me, tell them I'm on my way. Bye!"

#66: A dick thing. She promised to call me after she got back from her trip. I waited for her because I wanted to see her badly and was looking forward to it. Ten days after her supposed return to the country, she still hadn't called. Now, if she was blowing me off, she could have at least had the guts to have called and told me. I call a few numbers looking for her. Finally I reach her. She seems surprised to hear from me. I ask her why she didn't call me. She gives me a noninformational answer. I know this girl very well. I have known her for years, and I know when she's lying. She is not good at it either. So I have a little fun and ask her some rapid-fire questions about things that she should be able to tell me immediately. She can't get answers very quickly. Of course she can't, she's making them all up as she goes. Being insulted hurts, especially when it's over the phone. Have you ever felt so powerless as when you're trying to deal with something like this over the phone? I know! It makes you crazy. So we finally agree to meet at a restaurant. We can't meet at her new place because "it's being painted." That's nice that her new man is painting the place for her. This is days away from now. I called her later this evening to try to talk to her because it was getting impossible for me to get anything done around here. I called and got a nice deep male voice on the answering machine. Now I don't get into revenge and all this heated-passion bullshit, but you know sooner or later I will run into the two of them and it doesn't matter how big or tough this guy is. Chances are he isn't as fucked-up crazy and as ready to die as I am. If he is, well all the better. I want her to see me mutilate this guy for the fun of it and also so she can have a good horror story to tell her children years from now.

#70: He would go to those dances. He could never get the nerve to ask a girl to dance. Like he would really know what to do when he got her out on the floor. He had tried dancing alone in his room and had gotten so embarrassed that he just had to stop. He watched them though. If you could get points for being attentive, he would have cleaned up. Women were so mysterious and full of shit. He wouldn't have a clue what to say to one if he ever got the chance. The dances went by and he went to almost all of them. He would find the darkest part of the gym and watch them with his back to the wall. He saw a girl who was doing the same thing he was. He checked her out: She was pretty enough. A few times she caught him looking. She was looking at him too after all. He looked at her again and she waved at him. His entire body shuddered. He knew what he should do, and at the same time he knew he didn't have the balls to go over and say hello. He was so shy he could barely answer to roll call in class. He looked down at the floor trying to appear unconcerned and even bored. When he looked up again, she was there in front of him. His heart started pounding. He thought he might choke. She introduced herself. He managed to get his name out as well. They both agreed that these things were stupid and that they were both there to see how stupid their friends could be and how stupid it was to dance, etc. They decided to try it as a joke. You know, like "Here, eat this pound of lard, but only as a joke though."

They went for it in the dark corner of the gym. It was a slow song, something by Three Dog Night. The singer shouted over the music.

"Look at this! We have all the boys against one wall and the girls against the other. Why can't you all be like THOSE TWO OVER IN THE CORNER?!!"

He felt his dinner rising up. They broke apart. She ran off. He never saw her again.

#83: I was going to shoot her in her living room. I knew it. I had it all in my head. Earlier that morning, I had been there and picked up the rest of my stuff. I felt like an asshole picking up my shit and putting it in a plastic bag while she watched like some mother. I could see that she didn't really want me to go. Perfect. Keep them hanging on so you can hurt them later. If they forgive you once, they'll keep forgiving you. You can do any damn thing you want with them. This woman pissed me off. I thought I was above falling in love. I was always the player, the mindfucker. I was damn good at it too. I used to take a real pride in seeing how far I could take these stupid bitches. I loved seeing them cry. This morning it was me who was the one crying. I asked her how she could turn me away like this. I figured I would plant the guilt seed in her tiny mind so I could rake her through the coals later on. I could see it almost work. She tried to stay strong.

"Why don't you grow up and be a man for once in your life? Cut out the dramatics."

I felt my whole body tense. I was going to break her neck right there, but that would be too easy. In this life, I strive for control at all times. She made me almost lose it all. I'll admit it, I loved her.

Hours later I was on my way back to her place with my gun in my pants. I got to her place and knocked on the door. She didn't open it up but instead pushed the mail slot open and told me that she was busy and would call me later. So busy that she couldn't open the door? What the fuck was going on in there? I told her to open up. I wanted to give her something. She told me to put it in through the slot. I said okay. I opened up the slot and looked in. She was standing right in front of me. I fired three times. I hit her in the stomach at least twice. I turned and split. I walked back down her street toward Sunset Boulevard. I felt nothing. I passed an apartment complex. There was a man standing in front of the small pool right by the fence. I stopped and stared at him. I don't know why. Finally he smiled and said, "Hello, my name is Paul."

I took the gun out of my pants and shot him in the stomach. He fell to the ground. I walked away. I didn't run. I don't know why. I don't remember feeling anything. I went home, made some dinner, played some records, and fell asleep. I went to work the next day. That was six months ago.

#92: He stood behind her for the better part of an hour. She barely moved. It was as if the television had some kind of magic hold on her. He watched the back of her graying head as it gently nodded with the canned laughter.

It was the end of all time. It was the end of all struggle and all sorrow. No more lying awake at night thinking about the job and money.

Numbers! How many hundreds of hours had he wasted thinking about money and little numbers in little rows so nice and neat? Numbers weren't anything! What a revelation so late in the game.

What was real life like anyway? Did he ever really live? Was there ever a moment when he wasn't in fear of losing something? Had he wasted his life away? He thought about the lines in his face. Sixty-four years—was that old? Too late to start over again. He would look at all the women on the street and know that it was too late to even think about doing anything.

He looked down at her head. He called her name out loud.

"Ellen."

She jumped slightly and turned around in time to see him shoot himself in the mouth. It was the end of time.

#99: At this point you have found the note and you have found my body as well. In the envelope with this letter, please find the three hundred dollars in cash. That should cover the cost of cleaning the room of the mess that I have now made of it. I think there's a cleaning company that specializes in getting blood and gunpowder out of rugs and walls. Check the yellow pages. There should be some money left in my account; please use it to dispose of the body. Anything that's left over, please pay any outstanding bills that come up in the next few weeks.

I know what you're thinking. If he's dead, why the hell would he care if the bills are paid or not? Well I do care. I might as well be responsible for all of this.

You should have seen me here wracking my brains (ha ha!) trying to find a way to kill myself and dispose of the body at the same time. I wouldn't like to be looking at this scene. Sorry, I tried to do something with a little bit more style and flair, but at the time, my mind was troubled. Now it's all over the room, ha ha.

I suppose you want to know why I did it. I couldn't find anything that meant anything to me. Money, women, sex, love, fame, friends—

none of that could hold me. I think it's all a bunch of shit. So much lying involved to get any of it happening anyway. When was the last time you got a date with a girl and didn't lie every five minutes? Right, well I got tired of the lies. If you tell the truth too much, you'll go broke!

At my job, I felt like a fucking robot. I can't believe I stuck with it so long in the first place. Isn't it the stupidest damn thing you can think of to do with your time? Get up, get dressed and go there to take it from some asshole. Go back home and get ready to do it all over again the next day? Not me. Not anymore. Look at all of our friends— if you can call them that. The only time they're not bitching is when they have just found a new way to fuck someone over. Otherwise, they're the same predictable mean-assed bunch, just like all the others.

I don't mean to come on all heavy, but I felt like a hamster in a cage. Running for the food, hitting the treadmill every day.

It was an insult that I could no longer stand. The things that I considered "good"—good torture is what it was. Good sado-masochism. Nothing more. Life is death in slow motion. It takes years. They give you the poison slowly so you don't even taste it.

So look, don't get all bummed out with this okay? I am where I should be. It was coming to this. I saw this coming years ago. It was just a matter of time until I got the courage up to give up the poison. I don't want you to feel that you have to do this. If you can deal with life's bullshit parade, then more power to you.

Again, sorry for the mess.

Black Coffee Blues

March 4, 1989. Vienna, Austria. 7:59 a.m.: It rarely gets better than this. I'm in the breakfast room of this old hotel. The gray light of the Austrian morning puts a soft cast on the empty tables that surround me. Across from where I'm sitting is a long table of food: eggs, cheese, bread, rolls, butter, jam, milk, orange juice, muesli, and a large pot of coffee. I am halfway through the first cup; it is awesome. There are beads of sweat developing on my brow.

I have stayed in this hotel before, in 1987. The band was playing across Europe, a ten-week tour. The table we sat at is to my left. What a great, mighty morning it was. We ate so much food that I think they were going to throw us out if we so much as even looked at the food table again. It was fantastic, an exercise in overeating, "sport eating" we used to call it in Black Flag. After we had eaten much too much food, we made sandwiches for the road, put them in our pockets, and exited.

I have finished the first cup. I ask the friendly young woman if I can have some more coffee. Her reply endears her to me until check-out time. "Yes, of course," she says. She understands. The second cup has arrived.

This hotel is across the road from the train station. In 1987 I walked the streets here on a night off. I went into the station and watched an amputee try to sleep on a bench. He was rousted and expelled. I watched the whores work the boulevard in their thigh-high

113

white plastic boots. Last night as I was getting back from the club, I thought about taking a walk down to where I saw this beautiful blond whore hold up the side of a building. She was a hot icy sex-merchant machine. Last night I thought about her as I stared into the darkness of my room. I wondered where she was—maybe still out on the boulevard, maybe dead. Was she still as pretty as I remembered? Is anyone? How memories lie to us. How time coats the ordinary with gold. How it breaks the heart to go back and attempt to relive them. How crushed we are when we discover that the gold was merely gold plating thinly coated over lead, chalk, and peeling paint.

She comes forward, a pot in each hand. "Would you like another cup of coffee?" she asks.

"Yes, please." I reply, through clenched teeth, trying to pull my right hand from my leg, which is gripping it so hard I might be cutting off the circulation. She pours it. There it sits, black and ominous, a slight oil slick at the top. I drink. Smooth—like death.

Today I go to Budapest, Hungary, where the idea of coffee is but a joke. Hard to find and when you score, it usually tastes like instant that has been stored and aged in the bladder of a goat. I see why they drink so much booze.

As I drink, I think of her, the beautiful whore. Since I saw her, she has probably sucked ten kilometers of cock, gained an incredible insight into the frailties and insecurities of the average male, seen enough to know that she's seen too much, and knows enough to know that sometimes it's better not to know it all. You brave, beautiful sex beast. This third cup is for you.

Excuse me, I must be on my way.

March 6, 1989. Linz, Austria: Staring at cup #3, not so hot. Not half as hot as the waitresses in this place. Same girls as last time. They act the same way too, cold and distant. Tonight feels empty. Spent the day driving through the countryside of Hungary and Austria. I don't know, something in this place is pulling me down. The waitress is wearing perfume, it smells like something wonderful. Good thing the coffee is here to blast me through. Sometimes you hit these situations where all you can do is endure, take it minute by minute. It's good though, to be in this room full of voices and not be able to understand a word of what anyone is saying. I like this lean feeling that moves relentlessly through me. Sometimes I feel like a perfect stranger, like I was born to be forever isolated from them. Do you know what I'm talking about? Totally alien. Heavy coffee blues #3 is hanging in there, staring up at me. People all around me talking. I'm on another planet. I don't feel lonely, just anxious and confused. People staring. I hear my name start to pop up in their conversation. Forces my eyes to the paper, to the coffee, the oily black eye of Truth!

For the life of me I can't figure out the women here. Are they made of wood or ice or a combination of both? I observe them. I don't talk to them unless one of them asks me a direct question; otherwise I have nothing to say to them. Who is *them*? *Them* are them. *Them* are everywhere. I don't understand them. I used to think I did, but now I see that I was wrong, I was fooling myself. All the hours I spent fooling myself. Everybody fools themselves sometime. The better of us spend less of our waking hours doing this I think. There is however a lot to be said for those who are good at being foolish. They get all the headlines.

March 7, 1989. Linz, Austria:
Alone in a room
R.E.M. playing on the tape deck
Staring at the floor
Single bulb stares down
Waiting for sleep
Waiting for the brain to pause
Hours ago I was in another room
Talking in front of a bunch of people
Now I'm here
No one knows
So what?

I can stack hundreds of nights like this
Like bricks
Build it higher and higher
It's what happens anyway
So what?
It takes no guts to do that
I have found it takes a lot of strength
To endure myself
It gets harder all the time
I don't know
If I'm getting smarter and stronger
Or better at fooling myself

March 8, 1989. Dortmund, Germany: Do I have a mind left? How many cups has it been? Why am I doing this to myself? I staggered into the breakfast room half an hour ago, half a day ago, half an hour, half a day? A while ago the coffee lady gave me a lot of shit because I poured the coffee myself and didn't let her do it. All I could do was smile, look away, and repress the urge to rip her throat out. The rain is falling in Dortmund. It rained last time I was here.

Something Selby said to me yesterday about romance made me start thinking. Right now the coffee is on, the black blood of the almighty coffee god is surging through me. I can do nothing but give myself to the storm.

Romance? Shit, there's this girl I used to see in LA. She was always giving me shit about my total lack of romantic attitude. One time I told her that love and romance had been beaten out of me. Sure, it was one of the stupidest things I have ever said in my life, but I thought it would have great impact on her, a great foil for one of my typically male hang-ups. She never let me forget that one. She would ask, "Why don't you send me flowers sometime. Oh wait, it's been beaten out of you, so sorry." Well it's 1989, I am twenty-eight years old, and sex is not a new experience for me. At this point, it's bio-mekanikal. Perhaps I blew it somewhere along the line.

I had a brief, fleeting brush with romance a couple of years ago. I had dreams about her, I wrote things about her, to her. I didn't even know her name. She was working at this place that I used to go into a lot. At that point she was perfect, she could do no wrong. It was great, a total nonreality. ROMANCE. Eventually I got together with her, and for a short while it was great. I went on tour somewhere, wrote her all the time, called her twice from thousands of miles away. Her response was always the same, it was like I was calling her from right down the street. She couldn't care less. When I got home, she had written me a letter. It said that she didn't want to be with me anymore. I found more interest in working hard than in following the whims of nonbusiness-related or nonmusical relationships.

The next song I wrote was about the distance I felt when I thought about that girl. The song centered around the lines, "The closer I get, the farther away I feel." I was thinking that all the time I was with her, I worked hard to put that out of my mind. Romance passes the time.

Selby said that he wanted some romance in his life. He said he enjoyed sending flowers and cards to someone. There's nothing wrong with that I guess, besides that's Selby talking and he is the man. There's this girl I know, she sends me flowers and cards and all kinds of shit. Of course I throw them out immediately and think of all the things I could've done with the money she spent on all that garbage. After we fuck, she disappears into the bathroom. Minutes later she reappears with a damp washcloth and wipes my cock off. Isn't that nice? The Hallmark greeting-card company should make a card for that one, with a nice one-liner: *You're so beautiful when you're wiping the juice off my spent cock.*

Maybe I have become burned out. A typical male, a mean-assed slothful fucker, a real American beauty. It's a form of blindness, Vaseline on the lens, no problem. I know you're laughing now, thinking that I am a total bastard. I am the last man, the unromantic one, the one who sees it all as a big-ass biology party. Well okay. Maybe someday I'll snap out of it, but for right now . . . make mine schwarz!

March 10, 1989. Berlin, Germany: What goes best with a cup of coffee? Another cup. This morning's pot has its own burner, it sits faithfully to my left. A few hours from now I will be on the road to Köln, Germany.

Today's sky is gray. I am alone in the breakfast room of a large hotel. I ate with Selby this morning; we have been doing this the last few days. He is such a great man. It's an honor to be on the road with him, to be around him all the time, to see him work every night. It means a lot to me—everything.

Ah yes, we drink the coffee and we feel the isolation settle in. Picture yourself at the table, staring absently at a crack in its surface. Your eyes a vacant lot for all the garbage and all that is lost and thrown away. All the people you knew, past experiences, ten lifetimes of gray skies, a planet of rainstorms fill you. You are totally alone. You take a long walk through yourself without moving. You don't remember when you sat down. Time doesn't exist for a little while. The isolation, the isolation that we all feel. Sometimes it's so clearly defined that it becomes another entity altogether. It sits across from you and shares the empty space of shattered time. Freedom can be a vacant lot. It fills you with nothing and then leaves you to figure it out. Isolation keeps me together. All the hours spent in the van staring at the passing road. I wrap myself around myself. Isolated parts starving for isolated parts that are starving. We can only get so close. In this truth there is a rough, lean beauty, a pure line. Even when together, we are apart. I think that there are moments, instances of power, of time outside of time. Moments that are truly larger than life.

At first I had problems with the isolation. I didn't understand it as truth. I fought it within myself and I tore myself up inside. Once I saw and understood the isolation, new doors immediately opened for me.

The end of the line defines the line. At the end of the line, there you are alone. Life was a flash, a handshake in the dark. In the lonely room packed with people, there they are, there you are. Truth screaming in your face. Sometimes the night is a sharp punch in the guts.

March 20, 1989. Amsterdam, Holland: Tonight is crawling by like a well-fed roach. Alone in my hotel room. Cheap town Amsterdam is. Hash-dealing freaks staggering, their sales pitches mixed with coughs that rattle. One guy followed me into a bank. I contemplated a shot to the head, but you can't be doing that in a public place. Don't want to get into it with pigs in a place like this. That would be something though, to dump a Dutch cop. The hotel here serves up awesome coffee. I'm seeing the light. I am feeling the great weight. I have been coming to this hotel since November 1985, when I was speaking at the One World Poetry Festival. A lot of cool people were there. Jeffrey Lee Pierce, LKJ, Z'ev. They were so great. One morning I came into the lobby and there was Mufti from Einsturzende Neubauten asleep on the floor, waiting for a room to be opened for him.

Tonight is a night off. It's getting on near midnight. The moon is full and shining down on the canal in front of the hotel. Good to be alone. Sometimes I wish the night would last forever. Daylight brings the static human confusion overload. Been having a hard time keeping from caving in on myself. I feel so hollow. I don't want to be with someone else. That's just another nowhere, another gesture, a lie. Sometimes life is such an old joke. Another night in some hotel room in some city in some country somewhere. I chain-smoke nights like these. Small lit cubes these rooms. The nights are the stitches that hold me together. All the faces have fallen away, I see no one in this dream. Isaac Hayes on the tape deck singing "Walk on By." I used to play that when I felt lonely. Now when I play it, I hear it differently. It's not as good. I have to get out of this room and get some air.

March 21, 1989. Amsterdam, Holland: Walking from your hotel to the city center without getting hit by a car, bike, or streetcar is something of a triumph. I wonder how many tourists have been done in by the flying Dutchmen of Amsterdam.

I bet the residents of Amsterdam have a love/hate relationship with tourists. They love the money that they bring into the town, and they hate their rudeness just as much.

This morning when I was walking to the record store, I heard a group of young men speaking English. They had surrounded a large group of pigeons and were kicking them to death. One said, "Look at them there eagles!" Another said, "I wish I had my twenty-two, I would blow them all away!" I tried to look as Dutch as possible as I walked away.

Tourists buying blocks of dried dogshit thinking it's hash. Running back to their hotel rooms and smoking it up, thinking that this city is so cool to be able to buy this stuff right there in the street. Some Dutch guy with a pocket full of guilders laughing his ass off, thanking the USA. He sees a dog taking a shit at an intersection and says in his best Southern Californian accent, "Hash dude, awesome!"

The Dutch have mastered the deadpan reply. That's the one where they make you feel like an incredible asshole. No matter what you ask, you will be answered as if someone is reading to you from a book on Russian history. The more energy you put into a question or a greeting, the more you will be halted by slow, measured speech, which often contains better grammar than you will ever possess. If you make a joke, the Dutchman will retreat ten big steps down the hallway of ultra-infinite cool.

Back to the subject of the homicidal tendencies of the Dutch roadways. One thing I have noticed about the drivers. They have their eyes keenly and intensely focused on everything except what is directly in front of them. Today I heard a lot of beeping, resulting in bellows and shouts in French, German, English, and Spanish, but none in Dutch. Yup, tourists all. Be careful carefree travelers, it would be such a shame to send you home to Carbondale, Illinois, in an American Express Euro-Fun body bag.

March 22, 1989. Nijmegen, Holland: Powering some B-grade coffee in a graffiti-covered backstage room. Cold in here, raining and dark outside. This place reminds me of this place I played in Australia a few months ago. There was this dressing room with all these dead cockroaches on the floor, their little wings scattered all over. Tonight the roach wings flap in my ear—crunchy brittle, flying low, writing blues songs effortlessly. In the other room, the club is showing a live video of Black Flag. I hear the song "Slip It In" pound through the wall. Life pushes you around, gets you all caught up, confuses and trips you. Nights like these, passing the time, waiting to get onstage and bleed in front of strangers. That's what I do.

When I go on tours outside of the USA, the term "back to the world" keeps coming up in my thoughts. When I come off a tour and have to deal with people I haven't spoken to in months, it becomes clear that I have nothing in common with them at all. It's as if I have stepped off a spaceship and the world outside of the tour is some alien planet. All I can do is be as cool as possible for as long as possible and get away as quickly as I can. I have nothing to do with them and the world they live in. The only place to go is back on tour, back to rooms like these. Here is better, just getting on with it. What else is there? Nothing. Nothing for me at least.

April 1989. Montreal, Canada: I can't find her. I keep looking. I'm tired of feeling above it all. I want to be taught a lesson. I want to know if my heart can be broken. Is it hard as iron or am I a gutless wonder? I want to meet a woman who will make me stop and listen to what she has to say. I want a woman who will make my jaw drop in awe. A woman who has little time for me. One who does not throw herself at me. One who respects herself, who has a sense of herself. Where is she? I wish she were here right now. I am in a hotel that also serves as a place for whores to take their trade. When I came in, I saw this young man being led in by a whore; he looked a bit scared. The man at the desk looked at the young man like he was just another sucker. What a fucked-up room this is. Have a long way to go before this thing is over. Should try to get some sleep. There's a woman screaming in the room next to mine.

October 10, 1989. Toronto, Canada: After shows I sit on the floor sweating. Sometimes there's steam coming off me. People come up

---

and talk to me. I'm not much good at this point. All I can do is pretend to hear what they are saying to me. The last thing I want to do is talk. I have nothing to say to anyone. I figure I said it already. The people who want to talk to me are usually friendly and really cool. Hell, they came to the show and they thought enough of what was done to come back and talk about it. That is something that I respect. Sometimes there are too many people, like last night. It's easy to lose your temper. After playing hard, you might want a minute to rest. I sit still, arms wrapped around myself. There is no time when I feel more like the total embodiment of all that I do this for, to be total and to embody the number one. At this time, I see clearly. All things have been stripped away. My body is full of pain, and it feels good. It is the reward for having reached beyond myself. I learn the lesson. I stare perspective in the face, and it stares back. We lock in total agreement. Sometimes after a show I can barely get up to change, but I know that I am stronger than I was a few hours before.

November 4, 1989. Leeds, England: Walking the wet streets in Leeds. Goth-rockers, dipped in black leather. Sad, sexless, miserable. They walk bandy-legged across the park. This city has been slapped in the face with a coat of gray poison.

Last night a kid came up to me and told me that he'll have to walk twenty-five miles to get home because his ride left him behind. He said he didn't mind and told me to keep coming back.

Walked for hours, got a haircut, lied to the lady when she asked me about the tattoos. Had tea in this shopping mall. Old women, fat legs and folded faces. Fried-food diet for five decades, lard in the blood, silt at the bottom of the brain. Chew the water and don't breathe the air.

Walked by Chris's old house, 52 Harold Mount. The place where we wrote all the stuff for the *Hot Animal Machine* album in October 1986. There was a beautiful blond-haired girl sitting in the kitchen where I used to sit at six in the morning, desperately trying to write songs.

Damn these days off. Give me work so I don't have to constantly consume myself. I turn corners, I keep seeing myself mirrored in the bricks. This city fills me with an alien strain of stagnating, suffocating sadness and regret. A pinpoint on the map, mental quicksand. Trudge through the park, cold wind mixed with tiny rain, like getting coughed on by a corpse. Sure I'm good, good at fooling myself so I can sidestep despair with the grace of a matador. I can wear a weary smile and carry it off quite well. Like all human insulation, it's cowardly and sometimes downright mandatory to get through some of the shit that gets thrown your way. To be able to pull away from a night that's reminding you of all the things that trip you up. I know you know what I mean.

November 6, 1989. Brighton, England: Brighton beach full of peoplelike organisms. Sitting in a food shop waiting for the tea and veggie burger atomic greaseball dinner to hit the table. Cold outside, Clash tape playing over the sound system, tape is full of dropouts. Sounds like Joe Strummer is going through a phase shifter. The others ran into Paul Simonon the other night in some curry place near our hotel in London. The PA in the club where we are playing tonight is a toy. The stage is tiny and the backstage area is small and cold. Welcome to England. It could be worse. I could have to stay here another day. With any luck I'll be out of the UK soon. It's funny, every time I come here I swear that I will never play here again, and then we get the offer to play and I always say yes. What the fuck, a gig is a gig.

November 14, 1989. Somewhere in Germany: Walked the streets today. Day off. Day off from what? Posters for *Last Exit to Brooklyn* are up. They look great, way to go Selby. Sat in a café tonight, breathed in secondhand smoke, listened to the talk I didn't understand. Wrote a song called "Loneliness Is a Crushing Wheel." Now I'm in a hotel room alone. Roy Orbison burning cold blue on the tape deck. Tried to write a postcard to someone. Gave up after three lines, have nothing to say. I hope I don't dream tonight. Sometimes you can get so far in yourself that you don't know who you are. I try to shake it off by walking. The sound of my feet and the sound of the cars passing brings me back to life. In these rooms, it all closes in on me. Lonely as hell, makes me swallow all the good and the bad at once. I face myself, endlessly analyze, rip apart, and mutate. No dreams please.

November 16, 1989. Geneva, Switzerland: The DJ is playing Bad Brains over the PA. The song "At the Movies" comes on. I remember when I sat in Paul Cleary's car and Darryl played me a demo version. That was 1980, I think. The song "I" rolls by and I remember watching them work on that in Nathan's basement. What do you do with your past? When I sit in the van for hours at a time, I walk backward through myself and think about the things that have happened. A word that I despise comes into my thoughts, that word is *regret.* I hate that one. Regret is an ugly and destructive luxury and it must be avoided at all costs. Today I thought about all the years on the road with Black Flag. The road has a way of turning me on myself. The road keeps coming back in my face. Confusion, comparison, they trip. I find it hard to deal with my past. Sometimes I feel like locking myself away so I won't have to see faces and places that remind me of faces and places. It plagues me, like playing someplace for the fifth time. On this tour, I played a place in Amsterdam where I turned twenty-two on-stage. Sometimes it's hard to convince yourself that you're not an idiot.

November 20, 1989. Frankfurt, Germany: Bitterness—when everything seems like it wants to see you die. You bump your head on self-doubt. Despair runs circles around you, flashing its teeth. You recoil with bitterness, you feel dizzy and sick. You feel the sickness of the entire world coursing through your body. You become filled with pure hatred for all that is. You find all things poisonous. You reel like an ocean of nausea. What brings this bitterness?

I find much bitterness in myself. My desire for great heights brings me crashing down to the terra firma of reality. Expectations I had for myself, thinking that bullshit was real, expecting more out of people. Our shortcomings leave me splintered and alienated. Entertaining my archenemy, hope. Judging others, making them adhere to my strict value system so that I can accept them instead of letting them be themselves. These things have sent me staggering into the darkness, lungs full of bitterness.

The desire to possess, the will to lust. These things have brought me countless nights of bitterness. Example: I am sitting in a club waiting to play. A beautiful woman walks into the place. Her beauty intoxicates me. She walks by me, and the same beauty that intoxicated me moments before now infuriates me. I have made her beauty my problem. Beauty can fill one with loathing. How convenient to put your need on someone else's shoulders. The smell of a beautiful woman's perfume is enough to ruin an otherwise perfect day. It's also easy to hate someone for their virtue or talent because it makes you feel small—bitter to the core.

Bitterness is the core joy of self-pity. Bitterness reflects the result of when expectation meets reality. You wallow in the self-inspired swamp of your misery. A great way to meet yourself!

Bitterness due to overload, too much. Perspective and reason can become blurred or lost altogether. Bitterness from fatigue. On tour I get asked the same questions every night. I get tired of answering the same thing. Like if you had to say hello to every person who passed you, you would get tired of the word and tired of people. You might even start hating their guts for no good reason. You could start hating people for their good intentions. That is the time you need a definite attitude adjustment.

It's easy to become so full of shit that you become deaf, dumb, and blind to common sense and good reason. I am constantly working to rid myself of the bullshit. I win some and lose some, but I keep working all the same. The coffee in this place is hell, and we don't go on until 1:30 in the morning.

November 28, 1989. Zagreb, Yugoslavia: It's almost dark now. All the stores are closed. I was told that it was a holiday today. Few people on the streets, mostly soldiers walking in small groups, their long green coats flapping in the wind. The city looks strange to me. A block of buildings, ancient, ready to fall over, faces a row of buildings all shining glass and neon. The streets look tired, looted. Spray paint scars the fronts of the older buildings. This place looks like a frozen ghost town.

Exhaustion was what I wanted to get to. Thirty-six shows down, ten more to go. Exhaustion has found me. Every morning I wake up tired. I keep myself to myself during the day. Time usually spent in the van watching the scenery pass by the window. I don't want to talk, and the rest leave me alone to my thoughts. I keep my energy for the show that night. The only thing that makes all of this worth it—the chance to play. The music is the reward for feeling like you have carried someone's luggage up five miles of stairs.

December 16, 1989. Los Angeles, CA: Pathetic. In 1987 there was this woman I was down with. It was the first time in a long time that I had been into someone, and it felt great. I was out on this tour, and she called me and asked if she could come visit for a day or so. I thought it would be great. I was wrong. She flew out to the city where we were, and I hardly saw her most of the day because of sound check and all these interviews and then stretching before hitting the stage. After the show, she and I got this hotel room. We were in there and all I could do is stare at the wall. I was tired from playing, and my mind was on the road. I tried to find words to tell her that I was burnt. I didn't pull it off. She got pissed off with me, my silence and my limp dick. The next day she told me to fuck off, and she left. After the show that night, I was in the parking lot looking at these pictures of her that I had. I started to cry. I was so mad at myself. I looked up and saw all these people gathered in a semicircle staring at me. I didn't hear them come up. I must have looked pretty stupid. What the fuck was I supposed to do? I walked through them and tore the pics up and threw them into a dumpster. I walked back to the van, and there was this guy from the local newspaper wanting to take pictures of the band. Must have looked like I was stoned, with the red eyes and everything. I got over it after a while. Since then I haven't let anyone get that close to me.

December 20, 1989. Los Angeles, CA:

> Don't hold on to time
> It moves with or without you
> It's like trying to hold on to a passing train
> Don't hold on to people
> All you do is hurt yourself

I come back from a tour, a dull roar in my ears. In my mind I play back the last show. How I walked off the stage, never told the audience that it was the last show on the tour. It's none of their business. I remember walking up the stairs to the dressing room. While I walk, I remember the ends of other tours over the last nine years. I enter the dressing room. There's no one there but me. I drink from a bottle of water. My sweat is turning to ammonia. I can smell it, I stink. Two girls come in and try to talk to me. I tell them to get out. Two days later I'm back in my room, jet-lagged from the Frankfurt-to-LA flight. I feel like talking to someone. I feel a vacancy. I don't know what to do with the night when it's gig time. After fifty shows in sixty days, it's all I know how to do. I'm lonely for the tour. I miss the van and the road and the smell of the gasoline. I look at the floor and I feel like shit. Finally I come to my senses and let it go. When I let it go, it lets me go. When it's over, it's over. Let it go or it turns on you.

> Don't attach
> Don't hold on to anyone's anything
> Throw out memories
> Pull them out like bad teeth
> Don't attach
> What was, was
> It's not easy to face

February 12, 1990. San Francisco, CA: Oh yeah: We got to get that one on tape. We have to make a document out of that thought, a monument out of that tomb, a hero out of that corpse, a lifestyle out of that criminal. Yeah we got to get the awesome picture of that. Quick, get the light just right. Damn, we blew it. We had it right there and we let it go . . .

Oh no: Sitting on the front porch, a whole mess of time on our hands. So much damn time that we had to get up at the crack of dawn to start plowing through it. So much of this time stuff did we possess that we had to stay up till near four in the morning on foot, skateboards, and bikes trying to chew our way through it. Steaming down endless cracked sidewalks and pitted streets. The median stripes radiating death and abundance under the relentless inspection of the crime lights that hovered above at iron tree stamina straightness. We were hypnotized by the neon, rust, and the raw fact that we were alive right then, righteously so. We were as alive as the power lines crackling. Alive like the dictionary's definition of the word *explosion*. We were blind and full of shit, but we were alive. Throwing off ballast, insults, clumsy threats, promises, and other taunts at Death.

Oh well: Here I am. Looking down, looking back, looking for broken pieces to put together. Making out like a desperate detective trying to find out where it went. Looking high and low for clues. All the while, Time is doubled over with laughter. "LOOKING FOR ME?!" Now I know. All time happens right now. The finger is pointed at me. There is only one direction.

February 20, 1990. 3:36 a.m. Los Angeles, CA: Can't sleep. Got my mind on my mind. I think I think too much. Been thinking about my friend, the hotel room. I feel more at home in those than I do here.

Sure would be good to get back out to Europe. Been thinking about it ever since I got back here. So great to be in a room full of people and not have to know what they're talking about.

Tonight I fill the room with thoughts. I push out the unmoving air and replace it with my thoughts. Shifting rain, heat lightning, red neon shining on a wet sidewalk. Rain falling on the roof at 3 a.m.

September 4, 1990. Munich, Germany: In a restaurant, eating alone on a night off. All around me, talk and laughter over the music. Body is in pain. Too much road in the last nine months. The time passes so quickly. I stare at my calendar. Third trip to Europe this year.

The road keeps me alive. If it weren't for the constant motion and work, I would have blown out years ago. It's the only way to get rid of the pain that follows me. I am not an artist. I am a reaction to life. I know that I'm not as strong as life. Perhaps that's why I drag it kicking and screaming down the road. It's my life but it's not. I can control it to a certain extent. The parts I can't control rip me up and keep me moving. I want to get old on the road, disappear without a trace. Take years to learn and unlearn, to learn to forget. Impossible for me now, a challenge for later on. You can go as far as you want on this motherfucker.

September 11, 1990. Bordeaux, France: Night off. Hotel room # I've lost count. The bed takes up most of the room, hard to walk around. Smash my eyes out. Eight-hour drive, maybe they'll fall out on their own. This endless trail of lit-up boxes. *Bonnie and Clyde* overdubbed in French on the television. If I could remember what your face looked like, I could better imagine what it would be like to touch you. Hours ago I saw you in my mind. It was just a flash, couldn't hold on to it. Days go by without name. Tuesday could be Friday—dayless, dateless. Coltrane playing on my tape machine. Coming up on midnight. Your eyes . . . I have been trying to remember what they looked like when I stared into them. Exhaustion turns everything into an endless expanse of road. I'll take it though. Short tour, long tour, whatever. I was thinking the other day when we were at some gas station, how great it will be to tour this coming winter. Touring by myself in the cold, it's a great test. The guys in the band don't like it because they say that it makes their hands cold. It's okay though, I like touring on my own better anyway. But the bottom line is, I'll take a tour anytime, anywhere, hot or cold. Canada. Hell, even Italy. Even England, and that's saying a lot, seeing how crummy it is there. Anywhere is better than my room for more than five days straight. I wonder if you like me, what you think of me, what you think of everything. I wonder what your hair smells like. How it would feel on my chest. I should have smashed that piece of shit in Pisa the other night. Should have taken that bottle he threw at my head and shoved it down his throat. Someone told me how they saw Michael Stipe catch a bottle in the face in Vienna, Austria, in the same club that I played with Black Flag in 1983. Things are different there now. It was enjoyable smacking those three guys, not to mention cutting that guy's head open with the glass a while ago in Vienna.

Chris and I walked to a post office today during a rest stop. We asked for stamps for mail to America. The man laughed at us. If you saw the river and the bridges and buildings, centuries old, you might think that a postcard to a country of hotheaded murderers is a joke. I might be able to convince you to get together with me. But even if you wanted to, it would be a bad idea. I don't work well up close. I am abusive and I don't know when it starts or where it comes from.

Must keep moving. These hotel rooms are good—no one knows where I am. I would never want to hurt you, but I know that I would. I wouldn't know when to stop either, happens every time. Better off on the road. Happiness chokes me. There's nothing I could tell you that wouldn't turn you away. I can cough and spit out thousands of miles of black pavement. Miles of stinking men's rooms, a planet of stench. I don't want to alienate you. Years ago I would have been able to get around all this and get to you. But now, I'll take the long tour, the short tour, winter, summer, bus, train, plane. Motion is a disease. A beautiful plague. A fever that burns my dreams.

September 18, 1990. Frankfurt, Germany: Waiting for the flight out. Outside on the street, the drunks argue and laugh. The *haupt-*

bahnhof is a few blocks away. The junkie dead collect and drool. Tonight I was on the Autobahn. Clear night, stars, pine trees. Motion is all. I am hooked. Those truckers, the hard faraway look in their eyes. I know this is where I belong.

October 5, 1990. Somewhere in Georgia: Big moon on the rivers we cross. Roads full of debris and sadness, old music shifting on the radio. The smell of gasoline on my hands. The woman at the diner said that all the other employees were either in AA, NA, or were "drug fiends." How many times down this road? Station to station of exhaustion. Keep moving fast enough, enough of the time without looking back. You won't see the pieces of yourself fall and shatter. Crackling voice on the phone reinforces the distance. One ear to the receiver, so you're already only half-listening to the voice talking to you from the other world. The world that isn't addicted to motion. Miles go by, stare at the cracks in your hands. Smell the gasoline, fall into yourself further. Roy Orbison was on the FM tonight. "Oh, Pretty Woman" doesn't do anything to me anymore. That was over with fifty thousand miles ago. The truck stop near the river with the beautiful Indian name. The man inside fixing CB radios and telling jokes for the truckers gathered around him, watching him work at his folding table. Country music, stale lights, dry air. Later on the moving road, the desperate mortal artery. I watch the Road Men slam by. Sitting high up in their mad cubicles, shielded by glass and steel. Enshrouded by dead insects and bird blood. I see the tail end of a truck pull away, OVER NITE across its back. We're all going to die out here—in transit.

October 9, 1990. Tucson, AZ: The man with the swastika tattooed on his chest helped us load our gear into the shitty club.

"I'm glad you guys don't have much stuff. Just as soon as I get your stuff in, I can go home and get my dick sucked again. This place used to be a shit country-western bar. No one ever comes here."

The Southwest is filled with sadness. The sun takes so long to set. Seemingly motionless it hangs, painting everything with deep resounding sorrow. It mourns the earth before finally dropping out of sight. Rolling along the 10 West, every town looks like a ghost town. Like they built them so they could have a place to leave. So many dead ends. The heat paralyzes, holds everything in its grip. These shitkickers, they have eyes of stone that fix upon you with a vise grip. They stare right through you like a hot moving desert night stares through you. A fat man staggers through the dressing room.

"Yeah, it's dead out there tonight. Deader than hell. Almost as dead as when John Doe was here . . ."

Drinking, smoking, broken knuckles, jail time, tattoos, missing teeth, motorcycles, poverty, and violence. America's glittering hollow dream lying on its side. The oasis dried up a long time ago. So much sadness out here in this sand-and-cactus sprawl. In less than an hour, we go onstage to shoot electricity through this empty desert night.

October 29, 1990. Leitham, NY: In a cold beer barn. When we came in, we saw this big barrier in front of the stage. We asked the man if he could remove it. The guy said no because it keeps the people off the stage and that's good for the kids because the bouncers beat the shit out of them any chance they get and that's the way it is. The barn is out on a small highway in the middle of the sticks. Danzig played here last night, and they only drew a few hundred people. This place reminds me of the places I played when I was in Black Flag. Cold rooms in the middle of nowhere, staffed by nasty coked-out, jaded burners. This whole place is cold. The toilets don't work. The walls are covered with moronic displays of sexual frustration. This is the kind of place that would make you miss your girlfriend if you had one. Makes you think of your room at home and makes you want to be there right now. Three or four nights in a row in places like this and part of you dies. Like you could ever hope to translate the boredom and depression that a place like this generates. The attraction I have for these places I will never understand. Perhaps it's because it's so far away from their world that I feel like I can breathe. In a place like this, I know what the deal is, I know my place. There is purpose and pain. Without movement, pressure, and confrontation, life is an embarrassment.

June 18, 1991. 8:28 p.m. Los Angeles, CA: Motion sickness. I've got it bad. Been home for a few days and I never want to see another one of them again. They call on the phone and it's torture. The only thing that makes sense is to get back out there where anything can happen. The tour of Europe was good. I'm okay when I'm out there. When I'm here, the voices get me. I can't take them. The guy from a band called Pantera called me today. How the hell he got my number I'll never know. What the fuck is my problem? I had to do two interviews the other day. It was like getting teeth pulled. It was never this bad before. The phone has become an enemy. I am complaining like a child, but fuck it, it's the way I feel right now.

The night is here and I'm playing Sonny Rollins and Coltrane. It's getting better by degrees. Slowly the pieces are settling and I'm not wishing I was going 150K an hour down the Autobahn. Motion sickness gets you coming and going. Makes all the words come out strange and fucked up. Makes me unable to deal with the reality of these people that don't travel 600K a day. If you don't do it, then you don't know how to deal with someone who does and vice versa.

Let's not talk when we meet. We can nod and move on. There's no need for words, smiles, or questions. Life is in passing anyway. All in passing.

SEE A GROWN MAN CRY

This is collected work from 1988 to 1991. Pretty hard stuff. My writing always reflects what is surrounding me at the time. In those days, there was a lot of pressure and stress in keeping the band going and keeping the book company together. The writing was the stitching that kept me from exploding.

Fuck it

Life is an embarrassment

Every breath threatens to pull your pants down

The lies are stacked in obscene piles

Makes me think of a dead man

Swinging in an apartment by an extension cord

The note in his pocket reads:

I stopped it, it did not stop me

I'm not going to grow old

I'm not in love with this heap

I will stop it

It will not stop me

Language falls out of my mouth

Ritual habit

Love hates

Truth lies

Blah blah blah

The convenient torture methods

Stacked layered and crammed into every pore

Until you're forced to stand next to yourself

On bended knees

With all the smirking clown faces

Without motion and confrontation

Without my hand around life's throat squeezing

Forcing definition from this diseased confusion

Life is an insult

So fuck it
I'm taking it down the cinder trail
And I don't want to hear about
What you think you stand for
Because it's nothing
Furniture, boxes, bonfires, lists
A cast of renters
The embrace, the kiss, the long look
Falls to the floor on death row
Life is an embarrassment

▼

Some things are too embarrassing
I could never tell you
I could never tell anyone
How much I think about you
How it scares me
Every morning as insomnia's grip loosens
I stare at your picture
I think of your painful shyness
Your ravaged self-opinion
Your incredible beauty
How drawn I am to you

▼

You are the reason I don't want to die all the time
When I am with you life is worth living
Time away from you is strange and full of pain
When I look into your eyes
I can see how life has savaged you
It's ok if you fall
I will be there to catch you
Anyone who would want to hurt you
Would have to kill me to do it

I will never be able to pound words into lines
To match the velocity of your presence

▼

I will never let you know how much you hurt me
No, I will never tell you
The last few months have sent me into myself
It's not easy to forget you
Time is healing me
I keep my feelings to myself, it helps
I don't understand you or your kind
I end up getting myself messed up
I can't take any more beatings like this

▼

In dead hours
Sitting in my room
Face in my right hand
Music playing
Thinking about him
His hands in your hair
The scent of your skin
Making his eyes close
Your breath on his neck

▼

As she becomes
Away
I watch myself try to hold on to her
I have never known a pain like this

▼

When you go insane there will be nothing
When you go insane there will be no one

Nothing to hold you
No one to love you
No one to talk to you
But it won't matter
It won't matter if the walls are gray
Or that time is hollow and lonely
And passes whistling and hissing like wind through
     high weeds
I'm laughing and shrugging all the way to death
I've never known a moment of real life
Watch me as I run mindlessly and directionlessly
Forward

▼

If I thought it would help
I would stay with you for as long as it took
I would show you something different
That I was telling you the truth the whole time
As it is right now
I have taken all I can
Your shallowness has thrown me into a deep hole
It would be better for me to hate you I know
But I can't
I try but I keep thinking of you sitting alone
Seeing yourself as pieces of broken glass on the floor
Your inverted rage is hard to be around
Good luck

▼

My loneliness is so large it has outgrown me
It walks beside me, a wasteland that keeps in step
Sometimes our shoulders touch
It feels like teeth sinking into my flesh
A new and strange stretch of desert opens before me

▼

If you want to hurt them and their children not yet born
Tell them the truth always
When you meet them
Stare deep into their eyes
Take those who wish to dominate you
Turn the game around and play it on them
Don't spare them a thing
Make sure you tell them about the blood and the pain
They can say what they want
You will trigger all their responses
It's all blood and death from here
You won't be kept waiting long

▼

To take a step into this vast emptying desert
This lit-up hope-filled expanse
This space that reduces us to the truth
To embrace this life-extinguishing process
To constantly fuck with death
To live through this slaughter without killing yourself first
Here is dot dot dot

▼

For me it's the ever-widening shadows
A silence that steadily increases in volume
Separation from myself
So that I walk alongside my body
I hear their voices like wind in high grass
Darkness is rushing forward

▽

If I could I would melt into your arms
I would fall like ten dead languages
I would not front
I would not lie to you
I don't think I could lie anymore
I have grown too old for such youthful pursuits
I want to love someone before I die
Hurry
It won't be long now

▽

All we do is eat sleep and worry about the rent
Somewhere there is real life
And those who live it
What about the rest
Paralyzed by television and police choke holds
Alas
Life widens and grows distant

▽

The loneliness that the world generates
We keep it going all night long
Waiting for a dull moment, or a lot of dull moments
To sneak away from the pain
During these unmoving silent nights I feel its
        crushing wheel
Is there anyone in the world who I can know?
I am tired of knowing myself so well

▽

I am immune
Too exhausted to notice

Too paranoid to sleep or wonder for too long
Too self-abused and withdrawn to help myself
Real life doesn't come close to this

▼

Love heals scars love left
We're all hypocrites
Searching desperately
Before our ability to attract
Takes too much effort to use
Or disappears much to our horror
We die trying to impress each other
I'd rather be respected by a bolt of lightning

▼

I like my world
Right now it's all I can stand
Get too close and they'll take you to the bottom
They fuck me up
I go to the store and I have to listen
It's a nonstop tragedy
The night is here though
No gunshots
I wish the sun would take a vacation
Leave me in darkness for a while
Let me heal
Let me try to figure out why I'm fucked up

▼

I'm obsessed with documentation
I must record every drop
I have good equipment
I don't miss much
It's a sickness

An obsession with contempt for life
We all need a sickness to live
A way to show our fear of death
I've got hours of conversation trapped
Pages of words in lockdown
Video on double life
Doing forever
Don't end up in this place

▽

It's all important and meaningless
Depression drives a car into my back
It gets worse with time
Sometimes I can barely speak
The phone is almost impossible
I tried talking to a woman tonight
In the first thirty seconds I wanted to get away
Tour starts in a few days
Start the tour or kill me
At this point I'd take either one

▽

Don't come close
I'll hurt you
It's all I know how to do
I can't translate the pain into words
That don't cause pain
Don't tell me you love me
You'll make me think of my mother
And 1,000 broken windows
Years of knotted screams into the bed
So much hate it would break your ribs
I put the miles through my eyes
I slam silence into my brain

Anything to get away
Walk away from me as fast as you can
Never speak of me or to me again
It's too late
For all that
Death is the only shadow on my road

▼

Men hugged him
Women asked him to come home with them
The money rolled in
He was so lonely it was pathetic
If they knew how he lived they would laugh
Sometimes he saw it all as punishment
Never escaping the humiliating inferno of his parents
The parents are gone now
Now he gets paid to humiliate himself
He constantly disgusts himself
In the name of telling the truth
Loneliness and alienation choke him
He tells people to stay alive
He tells himself to die

▼

I live behind a wall of scar tissue
Scare tissue
Scarce issue
I don't like to think of myself
I like lifting those weights though
I like the feeling of pain
Nothing else
I am rescued from my mind
The nights are painful again
I can't do anything with that kind of pain

It's bad
Behind the wall of scar tissue
Hemmed in tight
I don't want them to know me
I tell them everything so there will be nothing left
That's the part I'll keep for myself
I figure the deeper I get into the pain
The better I'll be at dealing with it
That's how bad I hate this shit

▼

100 women left me tonight
I didn't take it too well
I kicked myself for letting it matter
I kicked myself for letting it go so far
I lost myself in the shuffle
Now the room is cold
All of a sudden it's Saturday night
There's no magic
Too dangerous to go outside
No shit
I pride myself on being the loneliest man on earth
Damn

▼

December 19, 1991
Part of my life ended
My best friend was murdered
On my front porch
He never hurt anyone
The man who shot him in his face
Never knew his name
I am still alive
Sort of

From now on
My life is totally fucked and without purpose
Without inspiration
A mask that I will die wearing

▼

After dark I wait for something horrible to happen
I figure I'll have people shooting at me for the rest of
    my life
Like a drama in installments
Nightmares delivered to my door
Darkness comes and I wait for more horror
I figure we'll be friends for life
I'm swimming in an animal bag
Everything smells like meat
Everyone is a killer
I look at all of them now
I search out their eyes
I let them know that I'll kill them back
They take one look and they know I mean it
I lock the door behind me
Everything that moves begs me to attack it
I know how people are now
They take your money
Break your heart
Or try to kill you
Now I walk the streets like a secret animal
Some of them know
But not all of them
The one who fucks with me
Will lose his throat
He'll have no idea what he's fucking with
I live on the outskirts of humanity
I am scarred for the rest of my time here

That's all it is to me
Time left here
Time spent walking the city filth
Breathing in and out and keeping my teeth sharp
Waiting for something horrible to happen again

▼

Every slow dance took my breath away
Pinned my heart to the wall
I believed every slow song
I was intoxicated by the smell and the movement
Every one of them broke my heart a little
Now there's nothing but wise bitterness
Fatigue from seeing the whole thing
The pool of blood in the dirt
The end of real time has begun
It's all legendary from here

▼

The detectives went through my house for hours
I was at the pig station
I didn't know until later
They went through the food in the kitchen
I got back to the house and all kinds of shit was
        turned over
My best friend's blood was all over the front walk
They're looking for something to bust us for
The pieces of shit even went through the attic
They were curious as to why I had so many tapes
He talks to me and makes me think he's my friend
I look at him and know he thinks I'm scum
If I give these pieces of shit the time of day then they win
You know
There's so many pieces of shit in the world

It's amazing anyone gets by
The pigs asked if me and Joe were faggots
They were so relieved when they found out we weren't
Fuck you pig
Like I have to prove myself to you
I can't think of a more fucked-up situation
I have to talk to these shitheads all the time now
They still ask other people about me
Like I might have been up to something
I'm some kind of suspect?
Nah, but you sure are some kind of pig

▼

Joe you should have seen the tabloids talk about you
They really love the fact
That your father was married to the bitch in
    Charlie's Angels
They talk about her sorrow
How you two were so close
Like you hung out all the time
How you were 29 and in Black Flag
One of your father's piece-of-shit friends was lying
Talking a lot of shit
You looked great in the *Enquirer*
Good pictures of you and whatever the fuck her name is
I saw her at your wake
I wanted to spit on her
Your father had it at Gazarri's
All his AA friends were there
After all these fake-ass people who didn't know you
Had spoken and congratulated themselves on their acting
And talked a lot of shit about god and AA
Your father stood at the end of a line
So people could come up and talk to him

Your mother didn't know anyone there
She just stood to the side
With her husband and your stepsister
They weren't used to the Hollywood sickness
It was gross
After that we went and looked at your body
Your father didn't go
He didn't go to your funeral either
Don't know why
Maybe because there would be too many people
Too busy with their own grief
To compliment him on his
I miss you man
I look at pictures of you and I can't take it
Yesterday I wanted to crawl inside the pictures and be
        with you
I have been thinking a lot of dying myself lately
Life is pretty boring without you around
I have to tell you Joe
I did it all for you
I was hoping that if I went out there and did
        something good
You would see that you could do something magnificent
Like I told you the night before you died
You have such a great talent
It's because you didn't lie
I admire that truth
You will inspire me for what's left of my life
I see now that it might not be all that long
That piece of shit took you out
In less time than it takes to turn off a light
When I was looking at you on that gurney
That bullet hole in the side of your head
All filled in with mortician's clay

All the powder burns on your face
What courage you have to be dead like that
This thing that we all fear the most
And there you are pulling it off like it's nothing
You even had a slight smirk on your face
But you were cold and you smelled like formaldehyde
It was so hard to leave that room with you in it
It took me three times I think
I kept coming back to say something else to you
It never seemed to be enough
It will never be enough
Please come visit me in a dream soon
I miss you so much
My good friend

▼

1992 is a couple of hours away
I'm staying in someone's house
I am almost 31
All my stuff is in storage
I am single and plan on staying that way
To appeal to the more tender nature of a woman
Is a total waste of my time
What a joke
Meanest damn people I ever met
I am alone in the world and there's no changing that
My loneliness burns deep within
I don't mind because
I am one from none
My line has never been so clear-cut
Death has stripped most of the words from my speech
Talk is a disease
Action is its cure
Death has been walking with me all year

Talking to me in the night
I answer with my insomnia
Paranoia has put a hard shine in my eyes
I mix humor with my fury
Efficiency with my alienation
Beauty with my rage
The rising sun is my silent battle cry
Exhaustion is my victory
Death is that which I measure myself by
I acknowledge no peer or ally
I understand Death as master
And the definition of absolute power
My path is clear and laid out before me
The wind rushes past me
I dream of empty desert landscapes
And proceed forward

NOW WATCH HIM DIE

In late December 1991, my good friend Joe Cole was shot and killed when two men robbed us on the front porch of my place in Venice, California. As per the usual, a long tour was not far away. A few weeks after this happened I started a series of live dates that hit over 160 shows by the end of November 1992. I took my loss on the road and dealt with it. Grief, exhaustion, shock, rock and roll.

January 17, 1992. Sydney, Australia: Five in the morning LA time when I walk onstage. Eyes hurt and I want to puke. There's a dead friend in my thoughts. He'll be waiting for me in my room if I ever get through this gig. They yell and I can smell the beer coming up through the rug. Earlier today it was interviews and heat. Small hotel room and loneliness. It's what I know. It's all there is.

January 19. Melbourne, Australia: I stood up there and told them what I knew to be true. If I think about it too much, I want to scream and run away. I throw myself out like the trash in cities all over the world. The cities don't care. They don't even notice if you live there, leave there, or die there. They really don't care, they really don't. Don't let the world break your heart too many times.

January 21. Adelaide, Australia: I skipped this town with the band last time we were here because of the bullshit that went down. We were playing James Brown and Parliament, and people in the crowd were telling us not to play "that nigger music." Really great. I wonder what the show will be like tonight. I'm in the bug-spray-smelling hotel room looking at footage of a man digging up his parents in Hungary. They were executed. This room is cold and it's raining outside. The last few days have been hard. I wonder if the rest of my life will be like this. The last month has been unreal. Like walking through a dream. Later: I'm back in the box. The show was really cool actually. More people showed up than when the band played here. They were a good bunch as well. I told them why the band didn't come to Adelaide the last time we toured Australia. I told them a story about when I met Dion and he told me about touring the South with Sam Cooke. So now I'm back in the box and will be going to Sydney in the morning. I'm glad no one is here right now. I have a feeling that I will be spending a lot more time alone now.

January 26. Sydney, Australia: Last talking show in Australia. Soon I leave and the entire year starts kind of. I don't know. Everything feels new in a strange way. Joe has been all I think about. I talk at these people. I do interviews. I stare at the ceiling in my box at night, and it's all the same. Inside I'm screaming. No one will hear me or see the difference. Perhaps something strange or unsettling in the eyes will give me away; other than that, it's all in my head. I see them from ten miles back in my skull.

February 1. Trenton, NJ: Tonight was good and one of the only times I've ever felt a bit nervous about going on a stage. There were more people there tonight than when the band plays. About seven hundred. I told them everything I knew. I really like the Trenton crowd. I have been doing talking shows on that stage since 1987. After the show Death overcame me again. People were around me all talking to me at once. I did my best to hear them all and talk to all of them. It's hard after spilling your guts out for over two hours. After that, useless sex in a roadside motel somewhere on Highway 1. These nights hammer me. I wonder why I don't wake up with blood on my pillow. I figure my brain will break someday. I guess I am hanging in here because I am into self-torture. I will not allow myself to burn out. The ones who burn out are the lucky ones. Then there are the others who hang in for the long haul and get really chewed up. I know something about this.

February 13. Hamburg, Germany: Second night in this place. Played better than last night. Got taken out to dinner by people from the record company. Ate with a bunch of drunk Germans who were really cool, and that was it. The only thing on my mind is playing well. I love opening. I can't wait to hit the Chili Peppers fans again, they're so nice. Fuck this shit. Let's be honest. The Peppers are cool people and they kick the hard jams, but all I want to do is blow their asses off-stage every night and that's the only reason I'm on this fucking tour. Wish I could see more of Hamburg, but there's no time of course. Doesn't matter. All I'm good for is playing, doing interviews, and sleeping in my black box.

February 21. Hannover, Germany: A guy got up onstage tonight with a sun tattoo on his back that was bigger than the one I have. It had all kinds of fucked-up colors in it. Green, put on all crooked. Sometimes this shit trips me out to the point where I can't get myself out the door. A lot of people at the gig, and they were onstage all night. I wonder how much sweat comes out of me a year. When they talk shit about me in magazines that's what I think about. I think about all the sweat coming out of my skin and landing on the floor. They'll never know anything. Moving across borders totally unknown. I feel like I am on tour with Joe's dead body. I keep expecting to see the corpse on my bunk in the bus. I drag it with me from town to town. It's been hard doing all the press and getting asked about him all the time. I think the whole year will be like this. I don't know how I will get through it.

February 28. Innsbruck, Austria: I did a talking show here in this place before. In the bus today Chris played a tape that Joe made him of himself talking. It was strange hearing Joe's voice. It was hard to take. He was being funny as hell, and that made it worse. I sat there kind of laughing and kind of bleeding out the side. I listen to dead people on records all the time. It's not hard to take when I listen to Coltrane or someone like that, but it's different with Joe. Eventually he took the tape off. I sat in the backstage area and stretched and waited to play and wondered if the crowd was going to be the same bored-looking bunch that always seems to go to our shows in Austria. We played hard and they watched and that was about it. Went back on the bus and waited to leave. The mountains were beautiful today. I cannot imagine living in a place like this, having a view like that every day. I wonder what that does to your mind if you were born and raised in clean air and streets that were not violent. I wonder what they think of people like me who come in from a different world.

March 1. Milan, Italy: I'm glad this is a Peppers show and not one of ours. I don't have to worry about the bullshit of "Fuck we're in Italy nothing works and the crew are the laziest pieces of shit known to rock and roll." I can just go out and play and not think about the fact that every other time I've ever played here it's always been such a load of bullshit just to get onstage. I had to do a press conference. I counted the tape recorders, there were fifteen of them in all. Some others were just writing shit down on paper. Whatever. What the hell are they going to use it for anyway? I would be surprised if they can get the printing presses to work. I watch the Peppers crew agonize with the local crew people who are dropping delicate equipment and thank my good luck that I'm only in the opening band. A security guard tries to stop me on the way into the back of the hall. I laugh in his face and walk past him. It reminds me of the scene in *Saturday Night Live* when the crew comes on the set of *Star Trek* and takes down all the props and Chevy Chase tries to put the Vulcan death grip on a guy and the guy just laughs at him and says, "Back off joker." How can you take them seriously when they barely have any shit together? They make this huge arena right next to a church. The nuns won't allow much noise, so you have to run the sound at way below normal level. How typically Italian. I heard that and laughed. Perfect. Hours later we play and it's a great time. I sit on the bus, wait to go, and eventually have to leave and wait in the parking lot because there's so much pot smoke that I fear getting contact weakness by being around people who are so weak they have to smoke it in the first place. At least it's a nice night to look up at the stars.

March 5. Liverpool, England: The Peppers production guy tapes up a sheet every day in the dressing room telling stage times, after-show travel plans, etc. Today's said that the "punters are mental" here in Liverpool. The hall is freezing. I am told that even in summer the place is cold. It's got to be at least two thousand years old. Looking forward to playing. Later. The crowd was really cool. Easily one of the best crowds I've been in front of since I've been coming to the UK. Being in the opening spot is a good way to start a long tour. It's good to get out in front of an audience that is not there to see you. Tonight was one of those shows that you do and then walk away from. Sometimes the opening slot leaves me a bit unsatisfied. You never get to really expend yourself. I finish and sit in the dressing room wishing there was another gig across town. The shower room was in the front office for some reason. This shit doesn't matter. I see how tunneled-out I can be. I wonder what I would be like in the real world.

March 10. Glasgow, Scotland: I was figuring that we were going to get pelted, spat on, and all the rest. It was a great gig instead. The place is a famous venue called the Barrowlands. Real good-sounding hall. The load-in is a drag because there are several long flights of stairs and no elevator. The loaders are famous for getting gear up and down the stairs in no time flat. Since most of them are psychotic biker motherfuckers, you stay out of their way. I watched the Peppers play tonight. I have never seen anything like that. The place was packed to capacity of course, and everyone there was jumping up and down at the same time like the whole thing had been choreographed. I thought the floor was going to break. Now I'm in the dressing room, which is cold and smells, and the shower only gives out cold water. I'm not lonely because I'm not human. I am this thing that plays shows and gets it going on every night. No matter what happens to me, the music and the road don't care. The road is always waiting for me to throw up my hands and walk off. It's always trying to tell me that I never really had it, never really meant it. You have to keep rising to the occasion, that's what it's all about, you have to be ready to go without to get to it. That's why I don't hang around for the talk and adulation fests. I know better. The road watches and laughs thinking that it's going to take me out. You stick around and get congratulated and patted on the back, then you lose your edge. That's what these bands don't understand. In order to give it up you have to be pure. The impurities are what wear these rock stars down. Most of these people with guitars are so lightweight. So fake. They don't rise to the occasion. The road chews them up and spits them out. They complain about the road being hard. It is hard so you have to be hard. It's so simple. Either you go for it all the way or you pose out.

March 14. Brixton, England: Last night with the Peppers. All the Beastie Boys showed up. Now that was something. One of the only bands that matters. The Peppers guitar player walked into our dressing room and mumbled something about it being a beautiful experience playing with us. I guess he was stoned. Seems like a nice enough guy. I never said a word to him the whole tour except for hello in passing. Andrew is all bent out of shape about all kinds of stuff and asked to meet with me and Gail, and when I said okay let's talk he has nothing to say. It's always the same bullshit with him, he never confronts. Fuck it, I played hard as hell and gave it up. This has been a good tour I think. It was hard to look at all the Beasties in the room hanging out and not think of Joe and how much he would be getting off on all of this. I have to go to New York and do press for the next few days. Night after night and I'm still here. You have to keep coming back and hitting year after year. You need to be unbelievable. That's the part that a slob like Andrew will never be able to get to. You have to have a great deal of straight-up pride in what you do and realize that it matters more than sleep, more than anything. I have samurai in my blood. The hall here in Brixton is cold and the rooms smell. Some guy who we remotely know from London came in here and started to fuck the place up, and I had to throw him out. Drunks are so pathetic. I can't take them. If I know someone and they get drunk and get in my face, I no longer respect them. Somehow I can tolerate when someone in the band gets drunk because they never do it onstage, but I can never respect someone who drinks and gets drunk as much as I could some-one who is straight. If you really want to destroy, then you are straight all the time and you get it done. Otherwise you're just talking shit.

April 1. Fullerton, CA: We played outside today at Cal State Fuller-ton. It was good. A few songs in it started to rain. We kept on playing. It really started coming down. But we kept playing. I fully expected to get shocked and killed. There was a girl up front grabbing me and she had on all this lipstick so I wiped it all over her face and wiped it onto mine and went for the scene with Frank Booth in *Blue Velvet* where he's kissing Jeffrey. I was telling her that I was going to send her straight to hell fucker. We finished the gig and like rock stars left the equipment behind for the road crew and went to the Dennis Miller show where there was more gear waiting for us and we sound-checked and then played "Tearing" on the program. I hung out with Dennis on the talk-show scene for a few minutes, and it was better this time than the last time. I feel okay, nothing really on my mind. We go to San Diego in the morning for two shows. Strange day. One set out-side with people watching from all sides, no walls, the music just fly-ing into the trees and into the air, and then a television show, all in one day. Now I'm in my box waiting for the road to begin.

April 14. Cincinnati, OH: I think tonight was the first show where we broke a thousand paid in America as a headliner. I don't know if that's important, but it put some shit into perspective one way or the other. I thought we played good tonight. It was a trip leaving the place. I walked out into the cold only thinking about getting on the bus and getting some sleep, and there were all these people out there waiting to get their stuff signed and all. There were a lot of them too. I did the best I could. I'm standing there shivering with my wet shorts and the rest of my shit on the ground between my feet, and I'm telling them that I'm really cold and I have to get on the bus, and they just stand there unmoving. I don't know if they hear me or not. They just stand there with their stuff in their hands and they're not going anywhere. I did the best I could, and then I finally got on the bus and I felt like throwing up. I am not the rock-star type. I don't want to bum any of these people out. How can you *not* like them? They like you, they came to your gig. It's hard for me to not like young people, and it's hard not to like someone who likes you, even a little, even if they're strangers. That's my problem. I can't help but like these people, even though I don't know them. I think that's the part that's the hardest. I don't like myself as much as they like me. They have no idea how fucked up I am these days. How hung up I am with Joe and everything else. Some nights when I'm standing there like a cardboard cutout, I have to wonder who they're talking to.

April 21. Washington, DC: The line at the in-store never ends. Girls there since the place opened so they could be the first in line, and they didn't make it. I sign stuff and shake their hands and look into their cameras. It's all I am these days. I know nothing else. The heat at the show cannot be translated. At some point I stop being hot and become heat, and then I can play. It's getting to that point that hurts so much. I made up a song during a jam. I wished you loved me, why don't you love me? It worked itself out right there. It's raining outside, and I am thinking about how I made my escape tonight in a friend's car. At some point I have to just walk away from all the voices and questions and hope they understand. Out here is endless. They don't know me and I don't know them, and that's all the space I need. Tonight my mother hovered in the dressing room. I left and sat shivering on the stairs. I don't want to know anyone, the very idea that I know anyone at all is a lie that I will not take.

April 28. Atlanta, GA: My legs won't get loose. I do the best I can at the in-store. They give me things and I promise to do the best I can to read, listen, and use it all. If they only knew the language that I use in my brain. The language that screams with clearly formed words yet will not come out of my mouth. I stand there like some guy waiting to get smacked. I wonder if I'll ever get shot at one of these things. I hear these girls say ohmigod it's him. I realize that they're talking about me, and I want to hand them my lungs and make a getaway out the back of the store. Tonight I'll play harder than I did last night. I remember the other times we played in this town. They just stood there and watched. This time they know all the words and they move and they even sent one of their women onstage to touch the wounded animal.

May 4. Menomonie, WI: The sky is huge and filled with dark clouds. The hotel is in the middle of nowhere. I like it. They find me still. Call me in the room and ask to come over. I dodge them as best I can. I feel watched. I sit in the diner across the road and listen to the low rumbling of the truckers over in the smoking section. Better than the fire-filled streets I left behind in LA. The only break is that I get to keep moving. Have to move like I have to breathe. To those who don't feel this, no amount of explanation will make them understand. I love the big-sky country. The night air is fresh. Tonight's theater was packed. I told them the truth. I pulled out my guts, and we watched them steam in the lights. I throw out my entrails and pull them back in at the end of the night. I go back to the room and wait to move to the next city. This is fine with me. Nowhere I'd rather be than on the way to the next city. How many of their fathers blew their brains out? How many sons came back to this town from some steaming jungle with an American flag over their remains? How many rapes, how many heartbreaks? What happens in a town this size when someone is murdered? I am in a lit box with a parking lot outside the window. Across the road are fast-food places and small-time desperation.

May 6. Cleveland, OH: Flat and the dirt clings. Been here so many times. Stayed in one girl's house while her boyfriend who hated me shot junk in the other room. Another city gets stuck in my throat.

Another flesh wave stands in front of my face. Heat. I sweat through my clothes. I shake their hands. The city waits outside the doors of the venue. Another night on the trail. Another city in the life. I don't want to know them like they want to know me. It never works out. I sleep off heartbreak like you wouldn't believe. I can't translate.

May 28. Los Angeles, CA: I imagine watching myself from the back of the hall. I see a man with a bucket of his guts throwing pieces out to an audience. The bucket seems bottomless. The entrails never seem to stop coming. I feel sorry for the guy because I know that when the seemingly bottomless bucket is empty and he walks offstage to the basement and listens to the feet of the audience above as they walk out of the theater he will look down and see that there's blood all over his shoes. He'll look under his shirt and find that he has no more guts left. Confusedly he'll shake the hands of people who are for some strange reason in the room with him. He'll feel nothing for these people because he has no feeling in him whatsoever. He has no feeling of himself, for himself. He speaks thoughtlessly. The words fall out of him as he tries desperately to make these people who are saying things to his hollow frame feel at ease thinking that it will somehow make himself feel something. Soon they are gone and he stands in the room alone. He is as alone as he was several minutes before when he was in front of so many. He leaves the theater and walks unrecognized past people who are waiting to meet him. They imagine he is so much bigger than the average-height-and-build human who quickly walks by them, a broken machine on two legs. He returns to a small room and waits for sleep. The phone rings. It's someone he doesn't know who got his number. The stranger tells him that he was at the show. He asks the stranger, this person out there somewhere on the end of a curled black cord, "Was I good?" The stranger says yes. He hangs up and unplugs the phone. He feels like the only person in the world, so remote, so horribly singular. He knows that all the pain and bloodletting in the world won't get it out. He'll wake up a few hours later, and he'll be full of venom and guts and poison and he'll have to find another place to get it out before the pressure becomes too much.

May 31. Berlin, Germany: Sitting outside a coffee place looking at what's left of Checkpoint Charlie. Some sections of the Wall are still standing. Looks stupid now, like you wonder what took them so long to tear the damn thing down in the first place, and you know why, but still. Small painted versions of the Wall stand in gift shops. The sun sets and she and I talk about getting out of America alive. She lives here now and has no reason to go back. I think of America, and it becomes a horror-filled murdering plane. Blood, glass, and needles. Lies and sorrow. Larger than Death, so much larger. Seems too big to go back to, like it's the last thing you would want to do. The sun disappears and the night hovers above us. It's one of those great nights that happens around here all the time. I hear about her roommate who was from the East. Her brother engineered wiretaps on her to turn her in for the state. You have to wonder about the ones who know how to use a title to their best advantage. Like he'll never sell you out, he's your brother. Sure he will. Your brother's human. So's your mother. What about a place where you could go and pay a small amount of money and sit in a room with someone and trust them completely and then after the time was up you would leave feeling like there really is someone out there who you can depend on. You would feel good about it because you had paid for it. I don't trust anyone and I don't ask anything from anyone I don't pay. Do you? What a mess we're in this time.

June 3. Düsseldorf, Germany: My skull exploded onstage last night. I wonder if anyone in the crowd saw it. I saw bright lights and smoke. I felt my heart scream and die. It was so hot, and the weight of the music was heavy. It occurred to me that there could be music that was so heavy that it destroys the people who play it. An honor to be destroyed by music. Build the body up to withstand the music that you took part in creating. Music doesn't care. Music will rip your guts out and laugh in your face. The heat made me a visionary. I heard the dead of Vietnam scream, and I answered them with my own. No one would believe me if I told them. I looked up into the lights and felt so alone.

June 12. Florence, Italy: Shit doesn't work and you know you must be in Italy. Didn't see much of the city, didn't want to. Something about this country pisses me off. Maybe because no one ever seems to have their shit together. They get mad if you get mad at that fact. For me I don't care. I'm good at lying awake in that bunk compartment reliving death trips over and over. Making up bullshit conversations with women who don't exist. Thinking of ways to try to fool myself into wanting to live. I like it in there in that hole, that dark box. I don't have to see anyone and I can breathe easy. I have become an enemy of language. When people talk to me I hate them for using the language that brings me pain. I don't want to talk. I want to get away from anyone who wants to know me. When someone tries to talk to me I only feel the emptiness of the language, the desperation of words. The hunger of the need to communicate. I know my truth in that I know I'll never be able to say anything back to them that isn't coming from the dark room that is my mind. All I know is horror and ugliness. I'd rather keep most of it to myself. It's like diving on hand grenades. I went out earlier and tried talking to the guy selling the horrible bootleg shirts outside the show. It was a great conversation. I told him he was a fucking thief. He smiled and shrugged. I told him to get the fuck out, and he said he couldn't, he already bought the shirts. I told him he was fucking with our trip. He told me that he was sorry but this was his job. I told him I was going to beat the shit out of him. He begged me not to. I took a big pile of shirts and threw them to people in the street. He ran around trying to get them back, and I grabbed him and wouldn't let him take them away from people. I told him to look and see how happy we were making people by giving them free shirts. There was really nothing I could do to persuade this guy to leave, and

I really didn't hate him, he seemed like too nice a guy to get mad at. In the end I don't really give a fuck, but the shirts are so bad. I feel sorry for anyone who bought one of them.

June 24. Los Angeles, CA: This place is so dead except for the murderers. Whores on the corners, pigs everywhere. Burned-out buildings. Piles of rubble. Men working in the hulls of huge structures with smoke marks all over. Friend in the hospital. The city is killing another one. My room smells of Death. I can smell him in the closet. I can smell the blood. I can smell the brains. I leave soon. This city starves me for real life. It's a heartbreaker, and all the inhabitants will die horrible deaths. I will not be one of them. I am a road man and get out whenever I can. You stand around here long enough, and you'll get murder one done to you. Believe me, they're all scum.

June 30. Columbia, MO: Everyone makes me crazy and mad. The more they talk, the more I get twisted inside. I sit by myself and they keep coming up with words. I wish I wasn't so fucked up so I could talk to them, but I'm fucked up and I can't talk to them. I play an hour later and I don't know how it is for them. I know that they can't be getting the same thing that we get. If they did, they wouldn't get onstage and fuck us up. After the show I'm sitting in a place eating and a woman sits down and tells me that she likes what I do but the only thing she didn't like was what I said about pigs. She's a pig herself, and she says that she's an individual. I tell the pig cunt that when she puts a uniform on she loses all individuality. I told her that I party down when I hear that a pig has gotten wasted. I hope she goes out and gets shot in the knees by some low-rent motherfucker who laughs in her face. She really thought that she was a human being. I don't know how they brainwash these shitheads into being so self-righteous about being a bag of shit that should be taken out and shot in the face. Fuck these people. You never know when they are pigs in disguise. Fuck you, you stupid pig bitch. I hope you get Magic Johnson disease and die in some ward. I wonder how long I have left with this shit.

July 1. St. Louis, MO: I had sex with a girl in the club shower. It was good. Then we played. I think we played well. It's hard to tell when they don't let you play as hard as you can. They get onstage and they fuck your shit up. We finished the show and I sat and waited for them to leave. It was hard as usual to deal with them after the show. I can't talk and they just make me mad. After they left, me and the girl went back into the bathroom and had sex again. It was good again. She said that she was sorry that my friend had passed away. I told her that he didn't pass away, he was murdered. Whatever. The flies ate the blood anyway. I went to the back door to get to the bus and saw all these people waiting by the door of the bus. I pulled back in and snuck around to the front of the club, and the bus picked me up and we got out of there. I don't know what they get out of the music. I think about it more and more seeing how many of them get onstage and stomp on people's heads. Now I'm vacant and waiting for sleep to take me out. The sex getoff was mutual. I had to wipe my cum off the floor so no one else would slip when they came in. Another page of life has been ripped out of the book.

July 15. Los Angeles, CA: Night off in LA. Got here this morning. I don't think it was a good idea for me to come here for this one day. I feel weak being off the road. It takes so much compression to get through the sets that when I'm not near it feeling the pressure so much that I stop feeling it, I fall apart. That's how I am tonight. Sitting here in my room wondering if I'll be able to do it tomorrow night. Knowing that I have to. I was with a woman tonight. I don't think it was a good idea as good as it felt to be with her. It fucked my head up to where all I can feel is the exhaustion that makes my bones ache from the marrow out. All I can feel is the need for my body and mind to get away from this for a little while. I also know it's greatness calling, seeing if I have what it takes. Greatness is seeing if it can weed me out. My room is the siren song calling out to me to stop what I'm doing. Trying to separate the eagles from the birds. To do this you have to fly in the thin air. One cannot surround oneself with friends and feel that fake support. It only breeds a false sense of security. The only thing that will get you through this shit is to pull inward and harden and move forward. The less friends and words you exchange, the better. I have at least fifty to sixty more shows to do this year. If I don't do it just right, I'll wind up in the hospital with a nervous breakdown. This is my hardest year yet. A lot of things are going against me. It's greatness calling.

July 21. Los Angeles, CA: Hot onstage. I actually felt pressure tonight. Something about the size of the place and all, I was wondering if we were going to get swallowed up in there. Body Count was in the house. Played hard but I don't know how it went. Dave Navarro came out for the encore jam. What a great guy, good to see him again. Looking forward to getting back on the road. Something about playing in California doesn't seem real to me. So many people, they come out of the cracks, they spill over the edges, they are everywhere. I like them more than they will ever know. I don't know if I'll be able to tell them the way I want to.

July 30. Pensacola, FL: Hottest show I can remember. It was like breathing your own flesh. All I could do was try to stand. I hid from them tonight knowing that I was in no shape to even shake anyone's hand. I woke up in the parking lot of a hotel with interviews starting soon after I walked into the room. I worked out too hard. Losing weight. Nothing but that. Didn't talk to anyone. Came here and played and now I'm leaving. I don't know if the people at the show have any idea what we're about, but they seemed to like us okay. I am pounded flat and totally useless.

August 3. Minneapolis, MN: Eighteen hundred people in the big room. More than Black Flag ever had in there. I watched the equipment come in, and all I could think about was loading the gear into the small room a few years ago. Taking shit from the 135 in attendance as they got shitfaced. Tonight we played hard and it felt good to be set free from bullshit thought. Throw out thoughts that you don't need—what a great idea, what a time-waste–eliminating lifesaver. Went to a thing to meet people from BMG. Not my kind of thing. Standing around saying thank you. Thank you, I'm glad you like the way I'm fucked up. I'm not good for much, but what I'm good for I'm really good for, and that's all that matters. The rest is just bullshit.

August 12. Toronto, Canada: Woke up in a woman's bed after a day off. Back into harness once again, felt strange to be out of the zone for twenty-four entire hours. Did a small press conference and then went to the venue, to a gym, and then back to the venue. Phone interviews with Australia after sound check. Short sleep and then got ready to play. Twenty-one hundred tickets, sold-out show. By the time we went on, the walls were sweating. There were no moments when the stage was clear of people. Tonight I tried a different tack. I stood in the middle of them and got kicked around for two hours. Sitting in the bus with no liquid left in my body. Sometimes the days turn into nonevents. A day like today leading into a night like tonight where you get up and stagger around until sound check and then wander onto the stage, do your trip, and wander off again. I stayed inside the venue until they all left. When I emerged from the hall no one was on the streets, it was as if the whole thing never happened at all.

August 21, Asbury Park, NJ: Did a photo shoot for some magazine and then went to the gig. Got there late and made sound check. Asbury Park is a hard place. The club is a depressing dive, don't know how the evening will go. The boardwalk is empty with only the occasional jogger to break up the lack of humans. I got stomped on, kicked, and whacked around by people getting onstage. Managed to play anyway. I don't remember waking up this morning. I have started to think of women again. No one in particular. It doesn't matter anymore. I am thrown into the fabric of the road, and I am not anyone who anyone will ever know. When I think of other people, I know that I'm from another world. I'm too tired to think of anything to write. We played and we were good and I'm alone as always and sometimes it's hard to take. My body is in pain, I am still sitting crooked from the kick in the ribs I got from one of the people who claims to like us so much, yeah right.

August 29. Reading, England: Reading Festival 1992. We drove past hundreds of people who were doing their best to look fucked up and filthy. It looked like they had rubbed shit into their hair. We got to the compound and waited for our passes. The press bullshit never stops, started as soon as I got my pass. Talked to the shithead from *Kerrang!* and he has no idea how close he came to getting smacked like a bitch right in the teeth. He's asking me all this shit about now that I'm a big rock star he reckons all of our new stuff will suck. If I were going to interview someone, the last thing I would do is try to get on the guy's nerves. I got suckered into a tent with a bunch of people who wanted autographs. I stood behind a table like a propped-up ass-hole and signed pictures like a human Xerox machine. All I could think of was getting on with the gig. Finally I got to get ready and hit the stage. Played as hard as I could. Sure were a lot of people, about thirty, forty thousand. As far out as I could see there were people wav-ing. After the set I had to do some photos, and then I got the fuck out of there. I was amazed at how hard it was to do the autograph thing; it was unbearable. The people were cool and all, but I can't stand mak-ing people stand in line to meet me and get their little thing signed, it makes me feel like such an asshole. I'm out of here.

September 11. Brisbane, Australia: Brisbane is always a taste of the waste. On jet lag I was sleeping up until an hour before the show. I woke up in a dark room with the show yet to do. When we got there, it seemed unreal. Like this whole evening had been going on while I was asleep. I looked out at the other band and watched the stage divers push them around; it looked like the band didn't give a fuck about it either way. The people at the show were either beating the shit out of each other or beating up the bouncers or throwing up or drinking. Tonight was no exception. Not as many fights as last time. There were about fifteen hundred in there tonight; I think they all got onstage at least once. I played a little. I spent most of the time at the back of the stage keeping out of their way. What utter bullshit, having to stay out of their way. I don't care about them because they don't care about the music. So we played and I stayed in the kitchen until nearly 3 a.m. so I wouldn't have to meet and speak with drunks—they always make me mad with their slurred speech and bullshit talk. Finally we left the kitchen area and I looked on the floor of the hall. It was covered in beer cans. The green Victoria Bitter can was all over the place. Over 2,000 sold tonight. One girl told me that she stocked 2,400 cans herself earlier in the day. I'm glad to be by myself right now. I hope I don't dream tonight; the moon is full and it's shining down upon the water. I wish someone knew me.

September 15. Canberra, Australia: Today we drove from Sydney, we saw kangaroos and desert. The air is so clear here. I thought about Joe and what he might think of this scene as it flew by the window. Another night of them getting onstage all the time and me getting out of their way instead of playing as hard as I could. We played well anyway. After a show like this one I will not talk to them, I will not sign anything. I take it personally that they will not let me play hard. They don't respect the music so I can't respect them, end of thought on that. Too bad though because last time we played here I remember it being a lot better in that respect. Maybe I take this too seriously. I don't think so. Life is so short, why fuck around. Charlie Parker, Coltrane, Miles, Monk, Hendrix, they didn't fuck around. I must aspire to that weight at all times. Tomorrow is a day off. I go to Melbourne to do press. I see things differently now. Press doesn't matter, the punters and what they think doesn't matter, the only thing that matters is the music. The rest is just ego and entertainment. I think you can do a lot more if you sidestep the ego trips and the entertainment bullshit factor. The music is enough. If it's not, then you're in the wrong business.

September 21. Adelaide, Australia: For some reason they like us here. Last time we were here we played two nights and no one showed up, and this time we sold this big place out completely. Go figure. It was uphill for me. I just stayed out of their way all night. People seemed to get off on what we were doing, or trying to do. A band called The Mark of Cain went on before us; they were great. I was distracted by having to look out for people all night. On the good nights I get to go into my own world and play from in there and play my guts out. Other nights aren't as good, and all it amounts to is getting through the set as best you can and not getting hit in the head. I am alone in the box and am glad. The questions wear me out. I had to wait for a while to get out of the hall tonight. It was question and autograph time until I went and hid in the back room. After a while I hate the sound of my voice. I hate having to explain myself to people all the time. I'm wearing out piece by piece. I keep writing so perhaps I will have some kind of map to use to retrace the steps if I ever get time to go back and pick up the pieces that are scattered on the side of the highway. Blank.

September 25. Sydney, Australia: The day started out in a television studio. I didn't want to do this shit, but we were doing it anyway. It was Andrew who really wanted to do this. I knew it was going to be the same bullshit as it usually is. If every piece of equipment isn't exactly what he wants, then he throws a shit fit. He was told that the equipment for the TV show was going to be the best gear they could get, and he said that was okay. I knew that it wasn't going to be okay. I hate listening to the complaints. Of course there was the prima donna bullshit, no surprises there. "Tearing" three times and "Low Self-Opinion" three times and then on to the hall for sound check, then back to the television studio to do it again as a dress rehearsal and then through it again "for real." After that, back to the hall, a little before midnight. Stretch for a few minutes and then go out and kick it. Spit, ice cubes, beer, the endless chain of bodies onstage. A guy who would fill up beer cans with water and bring them to the front and cover our equipment with it. Can't play too hard because that would involve too much concentration and that means taking my eyes off of them for a few seconds and like the ocean, you can't turn your back on a crowd like this one. I spent the night looking out for the flying beer can or the ice or the punker. At one point I told the people up front that I wished they were all black. I knew that would piss them off, and I was right. Funny as fuck to see them get mad like that. Even with all this lightweight element at the show we still rocked out. I don't stick around after the last song is over. I get the fuck offstage. I can't be sure what they will be planning. Maybe that one shithead is waiting to throw his glass right on the last note and there I'd be standing there with a fake-ass grin on my face like a sitting duck waiting to get what I deserved for giving them an inch. So I play and split, make the hit and leave. I learned that this bunch isn't about music, so I do the trip and get the fuck out. Might be a long time before I come back here again.

October 3. Osaka, Japan: Tonight was another good playing experience. It feels great to rock hard and not have to think about getting whacked around. Some kids kept flying over the barrier, and as they flipped over, their boot tips would slam against the stage, and if my feet were there they would have been broken by now. Japanese fans are the most intense I have ever encountered anywhere. I did an in-store appearance at Tower today, and it was a heavy experience. People out of breath when they would come to the front. All of their hands were cold and wet when I shook them. They were everywhere even at the train station when I was on an early train I took ahead of the guys to go to Osaka from Nagoya. After the show we went to the van and they were there and there was one guy crying and telling me he loved me. Tonight they were in the hotel lobby as well. I took the stairs, twelve flights, just so I wouldn't have to wait for the elevator and get told that someone is sorry again. They always say they're sorry when they want your autograph and picture. They were in the lobby of the hotel when I got there this morning. It would be too crazy if you were in a big band and came here. Imagine someone like David Bowie or

Prince—insane. After the set we went and ate food in a restaurant where you take your shoes off and sit at a low table and the ladies come out with the robes on and all. It was great. If I had a real room to live in, that's what it would look like. I got a good workout in today. When I got to the gym they wouldn't let me in because I had tattoos and they had some problem with my shoes. They had a discussion about it, and they gave me a sweatshirt and some shoes that they had around. Some gym. These guys would shit themselves if they went to a gym in America. In the gym here there were no weights that were heavy. I was doing shrugs with a couple of hundred pounds to warm up, and I looked behind me and all the people had stopped and were staring at me. One guy came over with a calculator and showed me exactly how many pounds I was lifting. No one made a sound except me. They looked at me like I was some kind of monster. Honestly it felt good. The gym is the only place where I feel totally at home. People in a room sweating, lifting up shit and making animal sounds. I don't have to apologize for the way I am. I don't have to be nice to fragile people. It's the only place where I feel natural. I like working out better than sex; it's only second to music. Right before we went on, this strange thing happened. I had bought a Jane's Addiction bootleg CD in the store underneath the club, and I had the DJ put it on. I was standing in the hall and the CD came on. At first it was just the sound of a huge Jane's audience waiting to see the band. The bass line for "Up the Beach" came on, and the crowd went nuts. Every time I ever saw them that's the tune they opened up with. For a split second I thought I was at Lollapalooza. It was an intense flashback. It only lasted a fraction of a second, but it was intense. I'll have to tell those guys about it if I ever see any of them again.

October 10. Honolulu, HI: I go to the toilet and they come in and start the talking. We're in a toilet and I have to answer questions. I am a fucking idiot for being in a place where this can happen to me. They yell, we play, what the fuck. I had a great time tonight. They threw ice and yelled the stupidest shit I have ever heard, but they stayed offstage and that was great. The guys always want to touch me. After the show they find their way backstage and put their arm around me. A woman keeps patting me on the back, and she tells me that from what she heard me say tonight she thinks I would be an interesting person to talk to. I just stare at her until she leaves. What did I say tonight? I asked if there was a difference in the smell of rape and normal sex. That I didn't want to unite with anyone because humans smell like blood and brains. I am the Death Star, and everything that comes out of my mouth is from darkness.

October 25. Tucson, AZ: I don't know if they know. The sun sets and I sit outside waiting for the sound check to start. Small groups of youths come up to me and stand around like I am some museum piece or wall hanging. One will speak and I will stare and use one-word answers. One by one they will go away wordlessly. I don't know if they know. Pain is the only thing that will tell you the truth about yourself and the rest of them. The pain shot through my body like electricity tonight. After the show I sat in a puddle of my sweat on the floor of the arena. People looked over the barrier and yelled shit I couldn't understand. I felt like a boxer. I don't care what they yell. I'm just an animal. Just meat, experienced meat. They don't know that underneath my skin the pain is screaming the truth to me. So loud that it shuts out anything that they are yelling. Pain is my friend because it has never lied to me. It never leaves me for long. When pain is with me everything becomes clear and life has meaning. I know something about myself. I see deeper. Pain makes me stronger. Fire fills my body. After I get dressed I walk out and talk to people from some radio station. They are alien to me. Pain is the great isolator, the almighty truth teller. Fuck spirituality. It's all in the flesh and how much you can take. You want to transcend? Burn.

October 31. Indianapolis, IN: Happy Halloween. The crowd looked the same as always. Kicked it as hard as I could. Now I am the hole. After the show I sat shivering in a corner and shook my head no when they came to interrogate me. They take and take. They can't get me all the way. You finish playing your guts out and you're sitting there steaming and they will come up immediately and start in with the questions. I get sick of my mouth. I get sick of answering endless questions, some nights it's all I do. Scratch, pry, dig, scrape. Sign this. Wring his bones until there's no juice left. No. You won't get me. The radio guy comes out of nowhere and tells me he has some people he wants me to meet. I tell him that after shows all I want to do is kill people. He goes away. They have no idea. You work with people for years and they have no idea what's going on with you. You just go on talking hoping that somewhere someone gets it halfway the way you meant it. Wince when they don't, run and cover when they do. Some Nation of Islam guys were here tonight. They were an intense crew to say the least. Immaculately dressed with bow ties and full-length leather coats.

November 1. Chicago, IL: We get to the venue and there are kids outside waiting for something. There are no tickets and they stand there in the pissing rain all day. Hours later sound check starts. Tonight they're up close and they throw Oh Henry candy bars and tell us that we suck. We play hard and I can't tell what they're saying. The bass player pulls one of his infant attitude trips for the encore, and no one kills him. That's it. It's a good thing that I do this for myself because if I were an entertainer I would be looking for their approval. How fucked up is that. They would hand me my head. Steve Albini is at the show tonight hanging out with the opening band I guess. I never met the guy before but once read an article he wrote that put me down. I am considering breaking his face up for him, but when I move in on him I see that he's just a skinny punk. It wouldn't have been a good kill, so I let it slide. He'll never know how close he came to getting his face fucked up in front of his friends. After the show is over I leave the venue to get some food before we leave for Toronto. People are outside waiting in bad weather. I sign whatever they got and do my best to be nice to these people knowing they have no idea how much

I want to puke my lungs out of my body when I get asked to sign an autograph. I go to the restaurant up the street, and people put pieces of paper in my face as I'm eating. I get on the bus and we leave.

November 10. Raleigh, NC: Played hard as possible. Ran out of time before we got to finish. Showered and got out of there. I don't know what else happened, been playing hard to the point to where it blasts out the rest of the thoughts that I have. After the show was over I sat on the bus and waited to leave. People looked inside for a long time. I felt like I was living on display. It was good to leave. I am falling apart in some ways.

November 19. Dallas, TX: It rained all day, and I watched the men load the gear into a fucked-up old wrestling arena. I sat in the bleachers and thought about how many times people had sat there and yelled for one redneck to rip the head off another redneck. Water was coming in through the roof. There was a hole in the floor right in front of the stage. A girl I know came early to talk to me, and I was lame and had little to say. I felt like a jerk sitting there not being able to say anything. I don't get along with people as well as I used to, it's like I have turned into another person. Right after Cypress Hill finished, the barricade was broken almost immediately. Great to see it handed piece by piece across the front of the stage. After a long time and a lot of people onstage talking to the crowd telling them to get back we finally got to play. Our set was cut to forty-five minutes. We pulled off a few songs and did the best we could to get the crowd to be cool. It was like one of our regular shows, people all over the place. Other than that it was a good night. The Beasties were great as usual—it's great to see them every night. I didn't have to talk to too many people after the show, and that made things pretty easy to deal with. I find it hard to say thank you over and over. It makes me want to rip my lungs out.

November 25. San Francisco, CA: They threw large plastic containers of pepper, garlic, you name it. There were about four spices thrown up there all in all. Missed my head a few times close. I caught one. I spent the gig watching the crowd, inhaling pepper and waiting for the next projectile. I got hit in the head with a coin. Good shot. Tried to play with all I had but couldn't because of a few pieces of shit in the audience. Play all year and it comes down to your last show and they shit on you all the way. It would be nice to have a way to shit right back on them. It would have been so great to have found the guy, imagine the hospital bill. So like Iggy once said, "You're paying five dollars and I'm making ten thousand, so screw ya." I hopped a ride with the crew bus and wound up at the airport in LA. We saw Ray Charles, it was cool. He was being led by this guy. They were walking real fast. I took a cab to my room. Sure was a good year for playing. It was great playing with the Beastie Boys and Cypress Hill. I wish we were playing tonight. I don't know what I'll do with myself.

GET IN THE VAN

This book contained all my journals from my days in the band Black Flag. The highs and lows of a band on the road are detailed with no sugar coating. It took me four years of typing the journals in and gathering all the pictures to put it all together. It's a good adventure story about brave people with conviction and diminished social skills.

September 11, 1981. Devon-shire Downs, CA: I learned what hard work was with Black Flag. I thought I had worked my ass off before doing minimum-wage work. For this show we put up flyers for days on end. Start in the morning and come back at sundown. One day Greg and I went out to put some up on telephone poles around La Cienega and Sunset Boulevard. We were across the street from the 7-Eleven on La Cienega between Santa Monica and Sunset. Greg was telling me about the pigs in the area and how the last thing you wanted was to get caught. Right after he said that, we got nailed. The pig gave us so much shit. For some reason he let us go.

I ended up going out on flyer patrol with Mugger. We would make a combination of white glue and wheat paste. One guy on lookout, one guy slapping up the paste. One layer on the pole, put the flyer on, and then another coat of paste. After that all you had to do was let the sun do the work. These flyers would stay for up to a year. You couldn't get them off. We would pick a main street and put up flyers for miles. We went to UCLA, the Valley, everywhere. This was just for one gig.

One day we were putting up flyers in Hollywood and we walked through a supermarket parking lot. We saw this guy putting his groceries into a gray Mercedes. Someone had spray-painted a big swastika on the guy's hood. I just kind of stared at it. Mugger went off and started laughing his ass off. The man shook his fist at us and drove away. Mugger and I had no hair on our heads. He probably thought we were skinheads getting off on the artwork.

I learned a lot from Mugger. We went flyering up around West-wood. We were hungry all the time and never had much money besides bus fare. We went to a Carl's Jr. and each got a small salad plate. The place had one of those deals where you get to fill the plate but you don't get to go back for seconds. I followed Mugger's lead. He put the plate on the tray and proceeded to make the entire tray into his salad plate. It was a mountain of food. Awesome. I did the same. The manager saw us and he didn't like it, but I could see immediately that he wasn't going to do shit about it. We were too fucked-up-looking. Covered with paste and dirt and sunburnt. Our bucket of paste and backpack of supplies. Forget it, not worth it. I learned that you can get away with a lot of shit if you just do it like it's all you knew how to do. Mugger told me about times he was living on the streets and was reduced to eating dog food out of cans put on white bread. He said you balled it up and ate it as fast as you could and tried not to taste it. All this was new to me.

Finally the gig came. I hoped all the flyering was worth it. It was a great bill. Fear, the Stains, and Black Flag. I can't remember who was onstage at the time, but at one point someone shot tear gas or Mace into the crowd. People were on the ground holding their faces and screaming. I carried a few people to the bathroom and got them under the sink. Finally we got to play. A few songs in I looked out and saw this brown shape in front of me. I was thinking to myself how strange it looked and what was it doing suspended in the air like that. A one-quart Budweiser bottle bounced off my hand and went under the drum riser. Tough crowd. The PA company normally did country and western gigs. There was no way they were ready for this audience. I broke one mic and went to get another one. The PA man gave me one and gave me a look. A kid landed on one of the monitors and stomped on it on his way offstage. The PA man came out and started yelling at the crowd and looking over his monitor. He was immediately show-ered in oaths, spit, and cups. He looked at me and said he was going to turn off the PA. Chuck told him that his PA would be destroyed and he would get his ass kicked by the crowd. All this was true. He looked at us and called us every name in the book and went back behind the monitor board and remained there glaring at us for the rest of the gig.

In the fall of 1981 we recorded the *Damaged* album. The building where we did the sessions is now gone.

The guys did the songs without me and I did the vocals later on. It was amazing to watch Ginn in the studio. He was relentless. So much energy. He would tape the headphones to his head for overdubs so they wouldn't fly off. Robo always wore these bracelets on his left wrist, and the drum mics would pick them up. It became part of the sound. You can hear it on the record.

Chuck and Greg coached me on the vocals. I needed all the help I could get. I would sing as hard as I could every time. I didn't know anything about pacing myself. Chuck walked me through the break-down section in the song "What I See"; I couldn't come up with anything. It must have been funny to see me work hard instead of smart. We did a version of "Louie Louie" that was never used. The guys did a strange jam at the end of it until the tape ran out. I heard it back once and never heard it again. I don't think it was even mixed down. I did the vocal for "Damaged I" in two takes. It was just me winging it like I did it live. After the second take Spot told me the first one was the one and I was finished. We used a different version of "Rise Above" than the one we recorded for the album. Several weeks before we went into the studio to record what was going to be a single. "Depression" and "Rise Above" were the two songs. We never released the single. I guess Greg liked the version from this session better, so we used it.

We did the record fairly quickly. I remember the vocals for "TV Party" taking a long time because there were so many parts to do.

It was fun to work with Spot at this time. Spot was the band's producer and soundman. He produced several records for SST. He was one of a kind. He would go in and play Greg's guitar so Greg could hear it at the mixing board. He could play any Black Flag song, no problem.

I never thought Spot liked me. I got that feeling as soon as I joined the band. I had a feeling that I was intruding on some imagined territory. It was just bullshit. Years after the band had broken up I wrote him and asked him what was up, and he told me that in his opinion, I had ruined the band. Whatever. Listening back to the records he produced, I think he ruined them. It doesn't matter at this point.

It was the best time I ever had doing a Black Flag album. The rest were hard to get through for a number of reasons. Financial stress was a twenty-four-hour-a-day reality for the band. We were up against it for the entire time the band was together. There never was any "sellout," any "rock star" bullshit. People would sometimes talk that shit, and it was always so funny to us.

Soon after the recording was done we set out on the first tour with me singing. It was amazing to me. A few months before, I was working behind the counter at a straight job, and now I was hitting the road with the baddest band in the land.

June 27, 1982. Asbury Park, NJ: One long day. We got pulled over by the police on the way into Asbury Park. The pigs made us pull the van onto the grass median strip. We were ordered to stand outside and not move. In our hurry to get out of the van and do what the fuckheads wanted us to do, no one woke up Emil, who was still asleep in the back of the van. They were crawling through the van, and I guess they stepped on him or something, but they scared the hell out of him and vice versa. They freaked out on him. The poor guy wakes up to New Jersey highway pigs screaming in his face. We finally get to the place. I sat out front and watched three fistfights take place in front of me. Hours later we're about to play and I have to run out and get something out of the van. I get can't back in because the door guy doesn't believe that I'm in the band. I can hear the band on the stage. He let me in and said that if he didn't see me onstage he was going to take me out and beat me up. A few songs into the set I saw him come in and check. I love this town.

June 10, 1982. Buffalo, NY: The club owner said that we had to play three sets. We played for most of the night and did every song we knew and just took breaks every thirty-five minutes or so. It was pretty much like a regular night. I got pulled into the crowd at one point and some guy was trying to kick me in the skull. A road-crew guy took him off me. After the show the guy was hanging around the parking lot and some guy walked right up to him, stabbed him in the stomach, and walked away. At first no one knew he was stabbed, including him. He was so fucked up. Finally his shirt began to turn red and blood started going down his pants. He got in his car and drove away. It was a strange sight.

June 25, 1982. Lawrence, KS: I learned a powerful lesson that day. We were pulling into town and we smelled smoke. The bottom of the van was on fire. We all got out and backed away from the van and watched it burn while backing slowly away. There's no gas cap on the van and we knew that it could go up any second. Dukowski grabbed a towel and got underneath the van and started trying to put the fire out. He yelled for us to help him. All I could do was watch. Mugger ran across the street to a gas station and got a fire extinguisher to help put it out. Dukowski's forearms had burning oil on them. He must have been scared shitless, but he saved the van and our equipment and he could have been killed. All I did was stand there. I felt bad. Later that night a pig came into the gig and told us to turn it down. He looked like Don Knotts and we didn't turn down and we kept on playing and nothing happened.

September 1, 1982. New York, NY: At this gig some huge guy jumped off the stage and I watched him land on top of this girl. From where I was, it looked bad. I met her a year or so later. I remembered her. I asked her if it hurt when that fat piece of shit landed on her. She showed me her glass eye. The guy took her eye out with his boot. I didn't know what to say. What do you say? "Sorry about that. How about a free shirt?" She said not to worry about it and walked away.

September 12, 1982. Montreal, Canada: We played with Discharge and Vice Squad, two big punk-rock bands from England. I remembered the singer of VS from the show in Leeds back in '81. It was good to see them opening. The Discharge guys were cool. We played hard and my right knee, which had been giving me trouble for the last few weeks, finally gave out. I had a piece of cartilage floating on the side of my knee that I had to keep shoving back into place with my hand during songs. We had to cancel the rest of the dates.

The next few days sucked. Our van broke down somewhere in Canada. We camped out in a gas station waiting for it to get fixed. The attendants must have thought we were crazy. We slept in the van and hung out in the parking lot for next to three days. My knee was fucked up and I couldn't go anywhere. The record company we were dealing with at the time eventually sent us some money, and we managed to sell our van and buy another used one. We rented a U-Haul trailer to put the backline into. We set out for LA.

It was good in the back of the van. There was room for everyone. We had never had so much. It was cool until we hit Des Moines. It was raining in sheets like some movie scene. I was looking out the back at the gray sky and all that rain. All of a sudden the U-Haul became smaller and smaller. The trailer did a spectacular flip over the railing, flew through the air, and disappeared. It nearly took out a car on its way. We pulled over and backed up. The damn thing was way down in a ditch partially submerged in water. My knee made it impossible for me to do anything. The rest of the guys slid down the grassy bank and opened up the little doors at the back and started to pull the cabs out. They tried to drag them up but slid back down. All the while, the rain was relentless. Some of the cabs were too damaged, so we left them. We left the U-Haul down there as well. We loaded all the wet gear into the van and went to some roadside place. We called U-Haul and told them that their shitty hitch had cost them a trailer, and we gave them the approximate location of the thing and that was that.

The van that we took on the tour and ditched in Canada didn't belong to us. It belonged to Saccharine Trust and they had lent it to us. We had some pretty bad news for them when we got back to LA a few days later. Another tour over. I had surgery done to my knee.

October 23, 1982. Redondo Beach, CA: This was fucked up. We got the call to play a party at this place near where we lived. It looked like an old recording studio. None of us knew the guy or any of his friends. We just showed up with some of our friends. The setup was good though, and it looked like it was going to be a good night. The guy pulled out a large bag of cocaine and threw it on a table. It was a lot of damned dope. We just kind of looked at these people doing drugs, and we just kept playing. A few songs later the police came busting in and all these people just kind of disappeared. In about a minute's time it was just us, the police, and this big bag of coke. One pig comes up to me and asked why I'm sweating and out of breath. I told him that I've been playing. He shined his light in my eyes and looked at me all hard while his buddy pounded his stick on a chair next to my leg. Eventually they let us go and we went back to SST. I never found out what happened to the guy with the coke. A few weeks later, I was in a burger place up the street from SST. One of the pigs who busted the party came in and spotted me. He stood over me and hit the seat with his stick like the other guy did at the party. He stood there until I left. I didn't get to finish my meal.

February 15, 1983. Hamburg, Germany: On a day off in Hamburg. Didn't do much. Some guy came to talk to us. Me, the guy, and Dukowski went out and walked around. We got on this train and the guy told us that you didn't need a ticket unless you got asked to show yours. You could risk getting shit, but if you went for it, you could ride for free. We went for it and it was fine. On the way back we ran to catch the train and we all got on except for the Duke, who had to pry the doors apart. This little boy comes running up to him and starts trying to push him out the door. The little fucker is yelling loudly and causing all the people to look over at us. Right then a pig came over and took us out at the next stop and proceeded to give us a lot of shit when we couldn't show our tickets. We tried to play it like we were stupid American tourists, but it didn't work. He knew we were sleazy. He kicked us out. Other than that I ate a lot of oranges and slept a lot. I needed it.

Greg went off on the guys who were running the food store below the hotel. They were trying to rip us off and I didn't think much of it because I expected these guys to be sleazy, but Greg was so pissed. He and Dukowski started eating food out of the refrigerator and yelling at the guys. The guys behind the counter knew they were busted and had no choice but to let them do it. They looked at the rest of us and realized we would have beat the shit out of them. There's something about your eyes when you haven't eaten for a while and you've been fucked with by skinheads that just says don't fuck with me.

February 19, 1983. Munich, Germany: Been driving since 8 a.m. It's now evening. Last night was pretty wild. The Minutemen were great as usual. Three songs into our set, I got hit square on the forehead with an unopened can of beer. Good shot. I grabbed a mic stand and begged the guy to come and get killed. He ran out of the place. The rest of the gig was a lot of sweat and smoke. These people seem to smoke as much as they breathe. At the end of the set the PA got turned off and we did "TV Party" without it. The crowd joined in. After that we got some food and slept in some freezing rooms. We had to double up in the beds. There was no hot water.

February 23, 1983. Italian/Swiss border: The Italian border is on strike. They don't want to let the equipment van through. They threatened to beat up Davo. Last night was real cool. When we got to the club, there were all these kids there. We pulled up to the front door and they started rocking the van and pounding on the windows. I thought they wanted to kill us. I was getting ready to get out of there as best I could without getting hurt too bad. When we got out of the van they all started hugging and kissing us and giving us presents. A lot of them had Black Flag logos painted on their jackets. They thought that the Minutemen were Hüsker Dü.

After that, a lot of people started coming to the place and wanted to get in for free. The owner went outside and told them no way. The kids started throwing rocks at the club's windows and started fucking the place up. In the main office they had a video camera set up, and we watched the whole thing from inside. The police came and started kicking ass on the kids. A couple of hours later we got to play. It was wild, to say the least.

So tonight, if we get out of Italy, we play Geneva. After tonight we have a three-day space-out. The drive here was amazing. I have never seen castles like these before. I've seen some in England years ago, but they weren't like these. The Alps blow my mind. Everywhere you look, looks like a postcard. Tonight's crowd will be the basic German type I bet. We were spoiled in Italy, all those people being so nice to us and all. Now I guess it's back to the hostile shit.

I wonder what we're going to do for the next three days. We have no money to stay anywhere. By now I'm used to this, but in Switzerland? What will this be like? The next three days are going to suck. Davo has to drive back to the border to get some paperwork filled out that they wouldn't do the other day. What a waste of time. You should have seen these assholes, fat pigs. One of them tried to buy Dukowski's watch.

Denmark is a two-day trip from here. That's the next show. Food will be hard to find. Tonight's crowd is coming in, not many of them either. They look like the basic punker type.

Later: At the hotel. We played real tight. The toughest skinheads were total chickenshit. A guy threw a cup of piss on Dukowski as he left the stage. Duke went berserk, man, it was wild. He started wrecking the dressing room. I have never seen him like that before. I have never had a cup of piss thrown on me either. I gave it all I had, but it's hard to dig all the way in with a bunch of gluehead punks casually spitting on you. Some dick spilled his beer all over my bag tonight. All my stuff is wet. I wanted to kill the guy, but he was a friend of the promoter. Me and Dukowski packed up all the food that was left in the dressing room. I made myself a sandwich for later. Who knows when the next meal is coming around this place.

February 24, 1983. Geneva, Switzerland: Still in Switzerland. Hanging out in some punker squat. Tonight we will stay here and then we will go on to Denmark. The people in this shithole are gross. All they do is rip shit off, get drunk, and listen to shitty punk rock.

Dez had some fun with one of the punkers. He put a ZZ Top tape into the community blaster. All the punkers started yelling at him. Dez told them that the tape was the new Exploited album. The punkers were stupid, they all believed him. One guy started crying, no shit.

These days off are bad for us. We lose our momentum. The last few days have not been all that great. I liked Berlin the best so far. I like the desperate shows the best. I don't play good unless I'm pushed. I know that sounds stupid but it's true. The more bashed up I get, the better I play. One of these days someone is going to get me good and that will be it.

February 27, 1983. Osnabrück, Germany: Richard Hell played here tonight and let us and the Minutemen open up. We went off. I got all cut up. I bit a skinhead in the mouth and he started to bleed real bad. His blood was all over my face. While we were playing D. Boon was in the crowd and gave me a glass of beer. I broke the glass over my head. I am all cut up. Hell went on and told the crowd that Black Flag kills. No shit. I took a bath and had to wash myself three times to get all the dirt and glass out of my skin.

May 14, 1984. London, England: Played the Marquee tonight. Me and Bill are on fuck-everybody mode. We came here two times before and got fucked with by these assholes, and now they can go get fucked. Before we went on we made the DJ play ZZ Top's *Eliminator* album all the way through. He apologized to the audience because he hated them. Figures the piece of shit has bad taste in music. It saved us from having to listen to some weak punk bullshit.

So Bill and I are backstage stretching and Gene October comes in. He's the guy from Chelsea that kicked me in the side and talked the shit about the band in Leeds in 1981. He wants to use the bathroom. Bill looks at him and asks me if this is the guy I'm going to kill. I say yes. Bill looks at me and says, "Kill him now. Kill him now." Totally deadpan. October freaks and starts blubbering a bunch of shit about how he always liked the band. We started laughing and told him to get lost. What a piece of shit. So many people should just get killed.

It was hot as hell in there. I passed out in the middle of one song and climbed up Greg's leg and kept going. We played well. People seemed to dig it. Doesn't matter if they did or not. During the breaks in the beginning of "Slip It In," Bill was standing up and screaming, "Fuck you, you limey pieces of shit!" It was great and it made me play harder. Fuck these people.

June 12, 1984, 4:28 p.m. Berlin, Germany: In the hotel. Gig was cool except for the guy who punched me out. This big guy was up front and just hauled off and whacked me one. It didn't hurt really. He put me on the floor but I got up and kept on playing, but now I'm a little fucked up. Robert Hilburn from the *LA Times* was there. He liked it. He's doing some article on European bands or something.

When we were loading out some guy took off with one of Greg's guitars. The fucker just grabbed it and ran up the street. We were told he was probably a junkie. I barely saw the guy, it happened so fast.

I don't talk to them much anymore. I'm in my own world. There are six of us in one room. We are on top of each other. I spend as much time as possible away from them.

I had to do photos with the *Times* photographers. We did shots at the Wall and Checkpoint Charlie.

We're playing here again tonight, some small club. I hope that the guys from Die Haut come to the show. One of my favorite bands. They live here. I have a black eye from last night. Fuck it. Three more shows on this one and then most of them fly back to LA. Me and Greg stay to do press.

I did something funny today. I picked up on a girl and didn't know it. I came into the lobby and saw this gross American guy talking up the pretty girl behind the desk. He went away, and when I went up to get my key I asked if it was fucked to have to be nice to people like that when you really want to smack the shit out of them. We started talking and I told her we were playing at this club tonight, and she asked if she could go. I figured that anyone could go and told her of course. I told her that we would put her on the guest list. I thought nothing of it. It's not as if we know anyone here. She shows up to the gig all done up and excited to see me. At the end of the show she's trying to get me to come home with her. Whoa.

I think that Black Flag has reached its high point. Thinking about it, each record sells less and less and we can't outdraw shitty bands in LA. I think that the new songs bum people out.

December 22, 1984. Canadian border: At the border office trying to get into Canada again. Apparently our papers are not together. The promoter from Winnipeg is being called now. The temperature is 20 below zero. I got freezing cold running ten yards from the truck to the customs building. Now people have decided that this is the time to lose ID's and equipment lists. The Chicago show was one to remember. Some people were not too happy with the ticket price the promoter slapped on. They took out their grievances on the security and the band. The shit bums me out. I hate having to listen to the bullshit. Trying to get left alone in the dressing room and these people come in, sit down, and make themselves at home. The head security comes in to talk to me about all the shit that went down. I need this? No. Fuck you. It's nights like this that make me act the way I do. It makes me want to run away and hide. I'm sick of people. Drunks yelling my name, spitting on me. I don't need it. Some guy jumped onstage, kicked me in the side as he jumped off. Just another night. I hope we get out of the cold tonight. It will kill us if we don't. It's funny, I'm watching myself come to the end of my rope. It looks pretty ridiculous. I think I'm losing my crackers. A lot of things that are important to me aren't anymore. I wish I had something in my head, but I don't. This has been the usual for a couple of weeks.

December 26, 1984. Edmonton, Canada: At the hall. Got here last night. Took us about twenty-four hours of straight driving to get here. Still freezing cold outside. Maybe tomorrow will be warmer. The show in Winnipeg was okay. Lots of "we have been waiting years to see you, you assholes better be good" and shit from the audience. It's hard to find any quiet anywhere. I'm constantly around people who talk a lot but say nothing. A sad case, the singer in St. Vitus brought his woman on tour. I asked her what she does for a living. She said she "watches the house." She said that it's okay because Scotty makes enough for them both. She doesn't want Scotty to go on tour because she doesn't like it. What kind of shit is that? She wants him to quit. What a drag. It's no real concern of mine. But still, what a drag to go out with a ball-and-chain woman. Tonight we're playing in a roller rink. It's cold in here. Load-in highlights: I carried in the soundboard, an all-metal case. My hands froze to it like a Popsicle. Oh man, that shit hurt.

Show was so-so last night. Lots of stupid punkers at the show. I told them that Jello was a narc. A government-paid agent—that bummed their lives real bad. Some people beat up the van, busted out the headlights, ripped off the windshield wipers, sideview mirrors. That's why I don't like you. That's why I don't answer your letters. That's why I don't want anything to do with you. I'm getting sick of Canada. I don't like stupid drunks and subzero temperatures. After tonight there's only one more show. Vancouver. Vancouver is drunkville. People make me sick. I am burning out. I'm getting the lumps in my throat again. I ran out of the medicine that the doctor gave me. I'm having trouble sleeping. I can only manage about four or five hours at a time. Something will give at some point.

July 23, 1985: At some guy's house in Kentucky. Can't move my neck. Can hardly move anything, headache. Just woke up. A lot of people at the Jockey Club last night, a lot of stupid, ugly, drunk people. Emphasis on stupid, drunk, and ugly. This fat skinhead boy nearly bought himself a ticket. He fucked with me, and then after the show I was sitting in the alley and he comes up and acts all tough, walks away muttering how he's going to break every bone in my body. I told him he better start breaking because fat skinhead talk is shit when there are only two of us in the alley. He still didn't deal. I wish he had been stupid enough to fuck with me. Fat boy, I would have kicked your ass so hard you wouldn't even know how to piss afterward.

Last night they threw beer cans, cups, ice, spit, fists, all of it. How can I respect them? Why would I treat any of them as human beings? I am losing my patience with these "people." A guy fucks with Greg all night, then comes backstage and wants to hang with us. I learned something last night. I now understand the "two-way street" concept. I hope the next asshole who wants to waste my time doesn't. Enough of this, I shouldn't let some belligerent drunk idiots get me in a sour mood. Not after sixty shows in sixty-four days.

August 7, 1985. Omaha NE: Now in Omaha on a day off. I cannot believe some of the places that we end up in. Right now we're at the promoter's lake house. The place is huge. He has a boat and takes everybody waterskiing and stuff. Ratman and I have our own room. Not bad.

I broke my right wrist on a guy's head last night. I have broken this wrist about six or seven times before. This is fucked. I will not be able to do anything with my right hand for several weeks. What a fucking drag. My hand is hurting so much I can hardly think straight. I guess I won't be doing any load-ins for the rest of the tour. What a trip. I'm sitting on this big porch facing this big old lake. The sun is setting, the waterskiers are ripping by. It's like a scene out of a movie or something. I should have cracked that man upside the head with the microphone.

August 27, 1985. Reno, NV: A fast rundown of our show in Reno. No frills or extras. Ready? Go! We arrived at the place, a skating rink in the middle of nowhere. Tom Troccoli's Dog goes on first. Near the end of the set Tom is pulled offstage, he falls and breaks his leg on the skating-rink floor. Later on, Black Flag plays. Our set is stopped by the police. A boy was in the crowd with a knife, he stabbed two other boys. They are taken away. The boy with the knife is apprehended and taken away. The set resumes. Two songs later, the set is shut down for good by the pigs. I go to the dressing room. Two plainclothes pigs are in there with one of our road crew. I am told to stand against the wall. I do it. The male pig stares at me, I hold his stare without moving. Finally he squeals: "You better smile more when you come into my town." I just stare without changing my expression. The female pig asks me some questions. I ignore her. They both give our road-crew guy a lecture about the pot they found on him. They tell him that pot is a felony in the state of Nevada. Finally they are called away. They get up to leave, the male pig says to me, "You better smile more or stay in LA." I just stare at him as he leaves. I hate pigs. I don't smoke and I don't need to get busted. Next time someone lights up some of that lame shit, I'm moving out of the room. This is the second near-bust on tour and I'm sick of it. That's a night in Reno.

I overheard these boys talking in the men's room. They were doing crystal meth and tequila. They were talking about how all the boys are pussies because they don't do this or that or some bullshit. There is nothing. The world is a gross place.

We drove all night to Palo Alto, California. I did an interview with the local paper there over the phone. SST called me and told me that *The Village Voice* wants me to write for them. I wonder what they want me to do. I am tired. I'm taking aspirin before I play now, it helps the after-show headaches a little. The equipment is being loaded out and I am waiting to leave. I'm not much good for load-out with my broken wrist. This trail has no end. There is no one anywhere. I don't think I'm human anymore.

January 25, 1986. Miami, FL: At a Denny's. Drove all night to get here. Last night I watched skinheads beat people up through the first two bands. The rented security made no attempt whatsoever to stop them. Later on, Black Flag's set started. It was cold outside, we were all in sweatpants and shit. We were playing away and everything seemed to be going fine. That didn't last long. People started grabbing me and trying to pull me in. One guy kept punching me in the knees. I let him keep it up for a while, and then I clipped him in the head with the mic. Not hard, just hard enough to make him notice that he's wearing me out. He kept it up, so I wound up and belted him with my fist and the mic. His nose broke and his face was all bloody. Another guy started in on me, and I kicked him in the face. Steel cap in the face, felt like kicking a melon. People kept getting onstage, and Rat Man and Joe kept throwing them off. I started to notice that now people were getting onstage for the direct purpose of fucking with Joe and Rat. They were trying to pull them in. The guy whose nose I broke was now standing in the middle of the crowd with his arms outstretched so he looked like he was nailed to a cross. His headband looked like a crown of thorns; the blood trickling from right below his eye looked great. Old JC is alive and well in Tampa.

During the second-to-last song of the set, some skinheads pulled the cords from the stage-right monitors. Rat Man went to go see what was wrong, and they got him. From what he says, they got him down and started to kick him in the head. He told me that he was trying to crawl up the stairs to the stage and they kept dragging him back down and kicking him. I didn't see anything except for Rat getting back onstage with his face all mangled.

We stopped playing. The insults started in seconds. I could feel balls of spit pelt me from all over. People started to chant "Bullshit" over and over. I just sat down behind the amps and listened to them: Black Flag sucks. Fuck you Henry, you pussy. We want our money's worth. Play more you faggots. Henry you suck, I want my money back. Rock stars. Take the money and run.

After the show was over the pigs came, and all they did was stand around and tell us to hurry up with the load-out. The skinhead guys were just standing around right out of reach laughing. Rat swung at one of them, and a pig told him to cool it or he would take him in. Rat looked so bad. His eyes were shutting and his lips were split. It didn't even look real.

They are pieces of shit. They can't hurt me, they just make me stronger. If they all die tomorrow, so what. I don't know why they come. I don't know why we come. They bitch and insult and try to hurt me. That's cool. They make me what I am. Everything all those journalist pigs say about me is true. I didn't make the shit up, I learned it from them. If they get all mad when they get it back, when they get themselves mirrored back at them, they won't have anyone to blame but themselves, and that's when I start smiling. From now on I don't trust any of them. Not in any town, any country; they're all the same. They are capable of fucking me up. I would like to see some bad things happen to them too.

January 27, 1986. Gainesville, FL: Today is a day off, kind of. It's about 8:30 p.m. and my day off started about an hour and a half ago. I got myself a single hotel room. I wanted to check in about eight and a half hours ago, but I had to wait for everyone to go do their thing—that's the way it is when you travel in a group. The show in Miami was okay, about nine hundred people came. After we finished the set I wanted to start from the top and do it all over again. We won't be back there for a long time. The next night (last night) was Orlando, Florida. Our first time there. About an hour after the doors opened, Joe and some of the others said they recognized some of the fuckers who kicked Rat Man's head in the other night in Tampa. We knew they were not there to see Black Flag. We all got ready. I was happy they were there. I was hoping they would start something so I could crack one of their skulls open. Joe was happy, he wanted a piece of one of them too.

Joe and I were at the soundboard keeping an eye on things. I turned around and they were all standing right there. I turned around and just stared at them. I couldn't help but start laughing. I wanted to kill them so bad I could barely keep my seat. I just stared at them, and eventually they went away. By then the security was hip to what was going on. They wanted a piece of them too. A Cuban bouncer came up to me and said, "I hope one of those faggots starts some shit." Then he pulls out this stiletto and flicks the blade in and out. "This is my last night, I don't give a fuck." All the bouncer guys got into it and started to stare at the skinheads. One went up to them and said, "If you start any shit, you're all going to get hurt, then you're going to get thrown out."

We played our set. They did their normal thing—cheap-shot people smaller than they were. They tried to give us shit, but they were too easy to cut down. I did some good one-liners. "Well you know what they always say, if you can't do it yourself, get about ten of your friends to help," etc. Some skin yelled out suck my dick Henry. "Of course I won't do that. I know how you skinhead guys are into boys and shit. I'm different. I like girls, I'm funny that way. But hey man, if you guys like to suck cock, that's great. Good luck and bon appétit."

I did a few more raps that went along the lines of some people here are almost ready for the army except in the army you can't be overweight and you have to work out a lot. I know how that would be a bit of a strain on your Budweiser routine. Some skinhead girls were flipping me off; I just waved and said, "Hiya Fatty!" After people started laughing at them too hard, they just kind of stood there, except of course for the occasional cheap shot.

Some guy yelled, "Disappointment, big time, Henry! I want a refund!" That made me think. If the crowd disappoints me, I should charge admission for them to get out.

Well, that's Orlando. The skinheads were lucky to have the sense to go home. I don't think they knew what they were in for. All of us had hammers, pipes, etc. If you fuck with one of us, the wheel comes around. No, I would have no problem crushing one or five of their skulls. Their lives are meaningless. I would enjoy watching them twitch.

More and more I start to question why I am doing what I am doing. Greg does not like me at all and thinks that I have ill feelings toward him. There's no convincing him otherwise. I respect Greg more than anyone I know. He's incredible, all of us in the crew are constantly amazed by his playing and his presence. He's totally nonstop. He makes me and Dukowski look like bums, no shit. I think that Black Flag is his second-string project, Gone being his first. I think the other members of Gone know that. You can see it when they deal with the rest of Black Flag. It doesn't bother me, they're incredible musicians. I think they give Greg a run for his money. Gone is the tightest, most together band on this tour. They are always working on their music. I watched Greg play bass for almost five hours straight the other day. C'el doesn't even look at a bass until it's time to play; it shows too. It embarrasses me sometimes. I don't know what I can do. What am I going to say? "Hey C'el, what the fuck, don't you like playing?" I don't know, it's hard to find people who really want to go out and do it. C'el is a cool guy, but I don't know if he's cutting it. I hope he comes around. I don't think he will. That's just what I think. I would love nothing more than to be proven wrong. I think his woman in LA is giving him lots of shit about being on tour. I had that happen once. One time I was in England and I called this girl I was going out with at the time. She hung up on me from six thousand miles away. I fooled around with different girls all the way back to LA.

It is becoming very important that I keep to myself around the others. I'm a jerk when I enter into their conversations. I'm not human anymore. When they spit on me, when they grab at me they aren't hurting me. They're just gouging and defiling my flesh. When I push out and mangle the flesh of another, it's falling so short of what I really want to do to them.

July 12, 1986. Hermosa Beach, CA: Been here about two weeks. I've been doing okay. Feels strange being in one place for so long.

When the tour ended, I felt like I had stepped off a fast-moving train. You look behind you and it's over. It's so over with that it's as if it didn't even happen. So much for glory.

I feel somehow cheated in a way, it's hard to explain. It's just over. "You did your time, now get the fuck out of here." I don't think I can explain. I feel empty, restless, and out of place. I have had a hard time sleeping. I can manage only a few hours at a time. You figure there's going to be some movie type of ending to the whole thing, some big climax, but there's not. It's just over and everyone goes home, promises to keep in touch and never do.

I have been doing some writing and reading. I did two shows of my own, one at Be-Bop Records, another at UCLA. I thought they went real well.

The door to the shed had a seven-foot pot plant growing next to it when I got back here.

Thanks Pettibon, that's all I need. Funny guy.

Fuck it, I don't feel like writing anything. Life has slowed down to a crawl. Without the tour I don't know what to do with myself. I feel like getting in a fight or slicing myself up some.

Later that summer, Black Flag broke up.

EYE SCREAM

I started work for this book in 1986. I wanted to take in America and expel it onto the page like Henry Miller did in his book *The Air-Conditioned Nightmare*. I worked on the book for years and finished it in the early nineties. The manuscript sat for a few years as I debated whether to put it out or not. In 1995 I did the final rewrite and it was released the following year. I've included the complete intro to the book.

**got it from you. Your head-
lines and head lies.** Your hate
mail and red tag fire sales. Your
justice and your jails. Your corruption that never fails to spit in the
face of the one who knows but cannot say, who has no voice, no
options, no choice. The one who has to pay the price for your greed
and pride and all the fear you hold inside. Your stereotyping paranoid
claustrophobia. Your no-minded logic defying homophobia. It's been
going on so long. So here's your authentic American blues song. I got
it all from you. I pushed back. Back back back my back against the
wall. Paranoid I'm not. Understanding I am too much to the point to
where it went too far and it went to where it hurt and scarred and
bruised and charred and took life away and put horror in its place.
Here's your ugly face. Face it. Here's your darkness slice. Here here
here it is. Here's your human race. Your rape scene siren lit gyneco-
logical boy meets mutilates meats meats meats girl—girl destroys
herself in the wreckage of her mother's cowardice—boy destroys
himself acting out imagined male imperative that father or lack of
instilled.* You can get raped and killed here. Addicted and imprisoned. Saturated and intimidated. Isolated and condemned. You might
not get what you deserve but you'll get something that'll hurt. That's
a brain-splattered guarantee. So don't come crying. Don't come dying.
I don't have a doorstep left for you to bleed your case upon. You broke
it into pieces and threw it at my head. You win. Don't come to me look-

* After they start raping they're no longer boys.

ing for answers. Your street is my street. I hear the same gunshots and share the same held breath. I'll just tell you to duck and vote NO YOU BASTARDS. I'm warning you this last time; that which stands still gets victimized or worse.** It's the way of the residents and the dead presidents. The future's on hold. If you have a problem with something you read in this book, write an angry letter but address it to yourself because I got it all from you. Hit the streets begging, for tolerance not money. Instead of rest and relaxation, here's some mutation and mutilation. Here I come. Running at you with the Anti-Life.

—H Rollins. Sworn Anti-Man

** *Evolution has a price.*

Fear

The man was a boy once. There is a room. Square. A bed, a table, and a chair. A single bulb hangs from the ceiling. A man sits in the chair. A naked woman walks into the room. He takes his clothes off and they have violent sex on the bed. She remains passive and wordless for the length of the act. After the man ejaculates, he takes a large knife from under the bed and stabs her several times in the face, ribs, and stomach. He stops when he is out of breath. He gets up and puts his clothes back on. Moments later, the man's father walks into the room with a baseball bat. He hands the bat to the man. The man bludgeons the father for several minutes. The father's brains are all over the floor. The man drags the father's body into the corner. The man's mother walks into the room. She hands the man a gun. He shoots her in the face until the gun runs out of bullets. He drags the body into the corner and sits back down in the chair. It starts again in ten minutes.

Soundtrack for the rest of my life. Summer. Heat and damp, night and day. You can't escape it. You sleep and sweat, you fuck and sweat, you think and sweat. The smell of your two bodies fills the air in the room, and the moisture holds it and makes you relive it over and over breath after breath. You die without going anywhere. Stomachs slick and rubbing together. Cum and sweat. Wet hot greasy necks trying to break themselves. All the sucking and smacking sounds. The sound of teeth clicking. Makes me think of what it would sound like to

207

hack a human to pieces. Stabbing the chest cavity. The sucking wet sounds it would make as you stabbed. The heat works on your brain. You're living in a fucking monkey house. The heat bends everything. The heat beats down with lead gloves. You understand the monster.

Gunshots as poetry. The man in the sedan cuts off the cab driver. The cab driver beeps his horn and the sedan's window unrolls and a pudgy hand comes out and limply flips off the cab driver. The cab driver gets out of the cab, his face streaming with sweat. He tries to get the man in the sedan to come out of the car so he can beat him up right there on the median strip. There's nowhere for the sedan to go. There was an accident at the intersection, and traffic is at a total standstill. The cab driver stands outside the sedan looking down at the man inside. The man is looking straight through the windshield trying to ignore him. The cab driver's hand turns into a solid rock, and he starts to punch the sedan's window with steady pounding thunder. After a dozen blows or so, the window splinters and cracks. Blood streams from the cab driver's knuckles. The man in the sedan looks like he just ate a big plate of his own shit. The cab driver looks at the small crowd that has gathered to watch the confrontation. He looks in at the man again and slowly goes to his cab, gets in, and waits for the traffic to clear.

Animal act. I can't talk to you. When you call me my throat starts to close. You ask me what's wrong with my voice, and I tell you that I'm a little tired, hoping that will mask the fact that I want to slam the phone down and rip the cord out so it will never ring again. I don't want to go into the parts about wanting to see myself dead and the part where I wake up almost every night now in a total panic. Telling you doesn't do a damn thing for me. If I did tell you, you would try to say something to make me feel better and that would just make me tell you to shut the fuck up you stupid bitch what the fuck do you know about me. You would say something about wanting to touch me and that would make it worse. It's the thought of someone touching me that makes me want to hack their arms off so they won't try to reach out to me ever again. I wake up in dread. I think I'll choke one of these nights. All I can think about is Death. In the middle of the night I fear it. I really do. I don't want to fuck you because you're a human being. You've got the human stink all over you. When I fuck, I know that I'm just following her fucked-up footsteps. I'm just hopping in the grave with her. I try to form words to fool you into thinking that I'm fine so you'll stop talking to me. But really, all I want to do is scream and break things and kill.

The sidewalk spits in your face. It occurs to me now that I have never been the same after you left me. I feel humiliated and empty. I feel like a fool. Somehow I think I should have seen it coming. I have been with other women since you, and it's been such a waste of time. I used to laugh at people who said that when their hearts were broken they had a hard time finding someone they could be with. I never thought that would ever happen to me. I had contempt for anyone who ever cried or wasted time lamenting over a relationship gone bad. I don't laugh anymore because I would only be laughing at myself. The whole thing has had a bad and long-lasting effect on me. I like to spend more time alone than ever before. I have immediate dislike for anyone who says they like me. I reject people's advances with a knee-jerk speed that's disturbing. And if you were to call me right now and tell me that you want me back, I would tell you to go fuck yourself. Not because I hate you but because I don't want anyone to be close to me anymore, not even you.

Larry über alles. Movie Idea: Larry is thirty-two years old and works at an office in a low-level position. He is overweight and has a low self-opinion. He lives alone and doesn't do much on the weekends besides watch television. When he watches, he doesn't pay attention to the show, he just passes time. One day at work he hits upon the idea that he should kill himself. He goes out and buys a handgun. He sits with the gun at home looking at it, pulling the trigger down on empty chambers. He looks over all the bullets in the box that he bought. He picks one. This will be the one that he kills himself with. He carries it around with him. He puts it on his desk during the day and talks to it occasionally. For the first time in his life, he feels alive now that he has plans to end his life. For the first time his life has direction. It occurs to him that he better look good when he goes out. He signs up at a gym and starts to work out in earnest. As the months go by, we see Larry lose body fat and become more muscular. He starts to cultivate a healthy amount of self-respect and people around him start to notice. Women smile at him when before they never noticed him. All the while he talks to the bullet, which is now shined to perfection. He flips it in his hand when he talks to people. Someone asks him about it, and he tells them it's his lucky charm. Months go by and Larry is looking good. He takes his lucky charm and shoots himself in the head with it and leaves a good-looking corpse from the neck down. The end.

The great explorer broke down and abandoned his search. Humanity had spat in his face too many times. He turned it around and killed three. Moments before the gas, we hear his antispeech. My mother's mother drank herself to death. It all comes running out of me, this black water. I see her on the floor, the way they found her days later. She had started to decompose. Her body in a frozen crawl, turning black, fluid leaking through the cloth of her nightgown into the floorboards. From the position of her body, it looked like she was trying to get to the phone. My mother's father drank himself to death. He died down in the cellar. He lived alone. By the time his body was found, he had exploded. You never escape me. I have you with me forever. You will never escape my eyes. You will never escape my voice. I have you in my spell for the rest of your life. You will never forget the way I speak to you. I can see the room the way I want it now. The two of them are on the floor. The two corpses, oozing and putrescent. My mother is on the couch looking at them and crying. Her tears are made out of wood and coal. She has never had a real feeling in her life. She was never really alive. She sees everything through the eyes of a dead thing that has never seen the light of day. She sits on the couch looking at the dead bodies, the two dead drunks. She thinks, *They used to fuck and I came from this. I came from this filth.* She sees what she is now. She wants something to take her mind off of herself. She looks around the room for a man to fuck. She throws a leg over the body of her father and attempts to have sex with it. I come into the room and see them all on the floor. I kick them. Mouthfuls of black blood come flying out of my mother's mouth. While in my holding cell, I have thought of nailing her hand to the floor and kicking her until she explodes. So many times I have killed her for all the times that she made me feel dead like her. I come from death. I come from darkness. I am the most alive and brightest-burning thing there is. To you, I am a superstar. I overcome myself by incinerating myself. Her bloodsucking vomiting body is convulsing under the weight of my vision. You will never forget my voice. Okay, I'm ready. Let's do it.

Now it can be told. The man goes to the television station and waits in the parking lot for Jerry Rivers, the television talk-show host, to get off work. Eventually Rivers comes outside and starts walking to a sports car. The man walks stiffly toward him and does his best to impersonate a harmless, starstruck fan. The man asks for an autograph. While Rivers is signing a piece of paper, the man pulls out a length of pipe and bashes him in the head as hard as he can. Rivers falls to the ground and starts convulsing in mute stupid animal panic. The man kicks Rivers's head until his brains and eyes come out. You should have a piece of wire tied around your dick and be led out into traffic and then shot at a red light. Put that in your book. Go fuck yourself. Go march in a parade. I'll be the one in the crowd who opens up on all of you with a machine gun. I won't miss. After I get to you, you will only be recognizable by your dental records.

Friend. You can fake them out so easily. You can lie with a smile, and they'll tell their friends that you were so cool when they met you. You can almost make the words come out of their mouths. You want to compliment them and ask them the answer to easy questions so they'll feel that you are stupid and they are smart. It's a great way to make someone give you what you want. Make them think that they're in control. All the while you're laughing behind your eyes calling them every name in the book. Be careful though. You don't want to come off as patronizing. You see those shitheads on television talk shows do it. I saw some piece of shit talking to this very corny actor whose name I won't mention because I don't want him to sue me, resulting in him getting his kneecaps broken. Anyway, I wondered what in the hell you could say to this guy that would be a compliment and also be true? "I think your wife's mustache is funny enough, but tell her not to take her clothes off in films anymore. It puts me off my food." No, this is national television. The ass-kisser complimented the guy on his new piece-of-shit movie that he did and got him to open up and say the stupidest shit. Another way to make people work for you. Agree with everything they say. Don't let them catch on of course. They will tell others how cool you are and how you two really "connected." People are such suckers. That's how serial killers get away with so much shit. A guy pulls up in a van and tells a girl to get in and go for a ride. She gets in and the guy rapes her and throws the body off a cliff and drives home. Easy. The pigs found her a year later with the ice pick still in her head. Basically, you want to make a person feel good. When they feel good, they think that they're powerful. When they're under that delusion, play 'em like a fucking video game. Hack them up, pull their teeth out, drive them to tears, make them fall in love with you, just for something to do. When they love you, then you get them to take out all the money in their bank accounts and give it to you. Then you tie them to a chair in their living room, cover them with gasoline, and torch them. Keep telling them that they're great and in charge of their lives. It's what I did to my parole officer, and it worked out fine. More later. Bye!

Weapon. Don't tell me that you love me. I'll start laughing in your face. You don't want to make me angry. Shut your fake-ass mouth and get the fuck out of my face before I hurt you. I don't want you to love me. Don't feed the bullshit machine, there's already enough in it. You think that no one can live without love? You're wrong. You have inflicted enough damage into me. I'm still trying to get the glass out of my guts. It's unbelievable to me that I haven't killed you yet. It's because of you that I won't hesitate to take affection and use it against the one giving it. You should see me in action. I should have a fucking sign around my neck. DON'T PET THE ANIMAL. I can't help myself. When a woman tells me that she likes me, I hate her immediately and only want to fuck her and leave. I'm at the point now where I don't even want to fuck them. I just want to scream at them to get the fuck away from me. So next time you see me, don't say a fucking word and just keep walking.

Cancerous fire-breathing bitch. In the first scene, he comes home from school and finds his mother in the living room standing rigidly with her hands on her hips. She opens her mouth to speak, but her mouth keeps opening well past the normal width. She exhales and at first all you hear is the sound of someone getting their skin torn off their back. Her throat expands, wide, wider. A fully developed fetus complete with afterbirth comes shooting out and lands a few feet away from the boy. She wipes her mouth off and lights a cigarette and kicks the fetus. She starts to speak, it sounds like a dozen beer bottles caught in a lawn mower. "Your fucking father is late again with his fucking check! I fucking hate him. He ruined my life. Look at me. Do I look like a mother to you? Jesus fucking Christ . . . oh goddammit." She bends over and retches. A large steaming mass of blood and tissue falls from her mouth onto her shoes. She looks up at him. "I hate you. I fucking hate you so much!" There is no second scene.

Could it be I'm falling in love? I'm in a hotel room on the second floor. It's 6:04 a.m. I am awakened by the sound of the sliding glass

213

door to the balcony being forced open. I quickly exit the bed and pick up a ten-pound barbell from the floor. The door slides open slowly. I am waiting with the iron plate. The intruder comes in. I bash the intruder as hard as I can in the head. I turn on the light. It's a man— Caucasoid, medium build. He's dead. I pick up the body and throw it off the balcony as far as I can. The body falls onto the sidewalk. I wipe off the handle of the door so his fingerprints are no longer there. I wash the barbell plate off in the tub. In the morning a policeman comes to the door asking if I heard anything strange last night. I tell him no and show him the earplugs that I sleep with. He tells me that they found a body in the parking lot and they're looking for leads to see if anyone might have seen who dumped it. He thanks me for my time and leaves. It's great. The lady behind the checkout desk says that the cops think the stiff got dropped off by a car in the middle of the night. She says that kind of thing happens out in these parts. I got to kill somebody and get away with it. I feel great. I mean, wouldn't you? You're like me. You know how many times you've fantasized about killing someone and getting away with it clean. You've always wondered what it would be like to kill somebody. In your mind you've killed so many times it's not funny. You've killed your parents, lovers, bosses, etc. You know that if you ever did, you would feel like the most powerful person in the world. I bet you've come up with ways to do it and not get caught. That's the only thing that stops you—fear of getting caught and doing time. That and guilt of course. I feel fine. I don't care about human life. You're all strangers to me. You're all *its* and *them*. Fucking insects, that's all you are.

Kicking the pigskin. I saw the pig in his car. I was crossing the parking lot. There was no other way I could go. The sidewalk was blocked by construction. I didn't want to walk by a pig car with a pig in it. You never know what could happen. Pigs are weak and they lash out. I walked by the pig car as quick as I could. I tried not to look in at the pig, but I had to so I would know if I had to run. I wish I didn't look. There was some boy sucking on the pig's dick. I shot the pig in his mouth. I will never forget the look on that kid's face when he looked up at me from the pig's lap. His face was covered with brains and cum. It was then that I recognized him. The little shit lives three doors down from me!

Urban contemporary blues. I called and called. She never picked up the phone. All I would get was her answering machine. I would leave thirty-minute messages telling her how much I loved her and missed her and would she please come back to me. The days passed like glass splinters under my skin. I couldn't understand for the life of me why she wouldn't at least talk to me. She had dropped me so abruptly. She had never told me why she had started going out with this other guy. I thought things were going so well. I stopped calling her. A few months went by and I thought I had it beat. You will call me a damn fool for what I did next. In a fit of romantic rage, I cut off my ear and sent it to her. I figured that she would at least call me or something. Maybe she would see that I was the one who truly loved her, because you know, I did. Do you know how hard it is to cut off a human ear? It's hard as shit. I had to do it in the mirror. I nearly chickened out halfway through. The pain was beyond belief. So yeah, I sent her my ear in the mail, first class. A week later, I got a slip in the door that said I had a parcel waiting for me at the post office. I went and got it. It was my ear. The envelope had a sticker on it that said RETURN TO SENDER. NO LONGER AT THIS ADDRESS. UNABLE TO FORWARD.

War on our shores. I want to impress you in hopes that you might trust me. I want your trust more than anything in the world, more than I want to live. I run my hands up and down your beautiful body. You show me all the scars that your father put on you. All the cigarette burns and bite marks. There are so many of them. You've been hurt so many times. I touch the necklace of human teeth that hangs around your neck. The teeth are yours. He pulled them out of your head with pliers in the basement every Sunday until you had no more left. You can't stop feeling his hands on you. You thought the scar tissue would dull the pain, but it didn't. I know you could not possibly have killed him enough times in your mind to have him dead in your dreams forever. I know this. I feel the same way. I will be the one who will always love you no matter where you are. I will be the one you will remember as the only one who didn't bring you pain. I take you to a large walk-in freezer. I take you on a tour of the hundreds of corpses hung up on hooks. All of them my mother and father. Killed so many times, so many different ways. You see many similarities. The father with the hook through the neck, face beaten to an unrecognizable mess, entrails. Killed so many times. Trying to take the pain away. Blinded by scar tissue. Aren't we all. I look at you to see if I can detect anything in your eyes. You look at me and I can see that you trust me. You see that I'll never hurt you. We drop to the ground and fuck on the floor under the slowly swaying feet of hundreds of broken-knuckled aborted screams. Your scars make you look better. I know you're real.

Flame on! A pig got torched on Lincoln Boulevard. Cuffed to a cement light pole and lit on fire. Funniest thing. That fucking arrogant pig was giving me shit all the way up until I lit the match and threw it on his pointy head. "You're in shit city, asshole!" Etc. The pig was vainly attempting to affect what is called "command presence." CP is being able to take total control of a situation immediately. You see it when pigs stop people for running red lights and parking violations and shit. They make it sound like they're invading Poland or something. It's all acting. I don't take pig talk lightly, but I take it for what it is. So imagine what the fuck that looks like when the pig lights up the night. Screaming, and straining against the cuffs, trying to suck his dick so he could have a man in his mouth one last time. His uniform burns off except the belt. Appropriate too, as a lot of cops leave their belts on when they fuck each other in high school parking lots. How did I get the pig's cuffs? Pigs are stupid and go for most lines. You can take one to the top of a tall building and tell him that there's a stiff dick and a Mexican to beat up at the bottom and they'll jump down there as fast as they can. Why does this shit surprise you? You have this world around you and you still insist that you're different from the rest. You act like you're shocked, but inside you wish for more murder, more catastrophe. If they could have executions of death row inmates on pay-per-view, it would be the biggest moneymaker going. The country's money problem would be over in a matter of months. Why do I do this? Why am I burning? Why do I pull fire from the sky? Why am I a living explosion? I will never stop. It will come like a volcano. At the end of the line, the questions will all be theirs. I'll leave with ashes on my face and my hands empty.

Fat loudmouthed has-been, no one wants to fuck you. The thought of prison keeps you safe from me. So many times I've looked at you and imagined snapping your neck or just leaning over the counter and stabbing you in the throat as you ring up my food, you piece of shit. I think about it all the time. You're safe though because the thought of prison freaks me out. The idea of going to prison for the rest of my life because all I did was kill you makes me sick. I would want to dig you up and kill you again if that were possible. Take your corpse and bash it with a hammer in front of your grieving parents just to hear them scream in horror. That's the only thing that keeps the streets in my neighborhood safe. I take it out any way I can. I kick animals any chance I get. I crank-call the parents of old girlfriends telling them that I have the bitch in my cellar and I'm killing her slowly with tools. Pulling her eyes out with pliers, that kind of shit. When they scream, I tell them to shut the fuck up. The mothers always believe me. I hang up and punch the wall and imagine her face. I'm always calm when I see you though. You never see this side. You never will. I can look right at you and make you think that I am an oasis of understanding and kindness. Looking at your believing eyes and tender expression makes me want to spit on you. You should be killed all the time. When one of you is nice to me, all I see is a throat to be cut. It makes me hate you. I can barely restrain myself from killing you. When you try to touch me, I want to vomit. It makes me want to break your arm. Prison keeps me from killing you. I can't live in this world. I think I was put here just to burn. Everything hurts. Daylight, voices, the stench of life. It's all repulsive. The thought of spending the rest of it in a human zoo keeps me grinding my teeth. If I thought I could get away with it, I would. I would kill all the time. Every chance I got. Men, women, makes no difference. I don't care if I know them or not. Any living human besides myself will do. It's the only way to ease the pain. I know that I will not be able to fight off this urge forever. It's too fucking strong inside me. When I kill, there will be no guns used. It will be all knives and blunt instruments. How good would that feel, to work someone over with a pipe until the body has no bones that are whole? You could really sleep well after that. Knifing someone until you had no more strength. Leave the bodies in places that are heavily populated. Leave a body hanging nude and battered from a basketball rim. I'll never get caught. I'll never stop once I've started. I know it will be too good.

Human video shithole machine, get another nose job. You think you're on your way, but you're only on their way. You're playing your game, but really you're playing their game. You want the house on the hill. They move out the old fool and throw in the new meat. The masters own the game, and they move you into the well-worn slot. They feed themselves on your blood. They stay young. You get worked. Look at your fucked-up face and tell me I'm wrong. I see you running around making all your phone calls thinking you're such a fucking mover. If you could see yourself, you might puke. You're fast-talking and pathetic. It's funny watching you do your routine. Hanging up the phone and laughing about the suit you think you just stiffed when you need him to exist and he needs you like he needs another bill in the mail. You don't see that you're just another in a long line of fuckheads who come up to the plate and take a swing. The big house on the hill looms large in your mind, but you're still under lock and key. You'll always work for the man you say you hate. You will always kiss his ass because it's all you know how to do. People like you get used until there's nothing left, and all the while you think you're in paradise. You're weak and disgusting, but you never get in my way.

All my children are broken bones. I can close my eyes and see myself in a dirty room. I can smell my mother's anger. I can smell all the men who walked through the place. I can hear the screams of the years of fear. I can smell the leather as it slammed into my skin. The scars talk to me. All I can do now is exhale, inhale, vent the rage. I wonder if real life has started yet. Is this it? Is the killing wound the only wound to hatch from? Can I reinvent myself in blood and stone? Burn muscle into forged fury? Once a veteran always a veteran. Shock to shock. There is a dark room always ready to receive. Always a room on the highway that has my name on it. Always a fucked-up memory to cause more brain cancer. Some people will never stop. They have no control over the rolling tragedy that is their lives. A walking accident that loves to happen. Revenge is not the operative. It's caged animal sickness, that's all.

Choking hands. He had one of those typical piece-of-shit days. The grind always. At least this time he had the guts to stay away from the bar and not drive home to the wife and kid drunk. He got home and immediately everything pissed him off. Sometimes the way his wife looked at him made him want to kill himself. The way she all of a sudden appeared like a total stranger. The vacancy in her eyes, it was bad. He took his son's favorite plastic mug, the one with the picture of Magic Johnson, and threw it into the trash. He felt better but not much.

You and your glycerin tears. You're a TV actor, and all of a sudden the still life of your fucked-up world of desperate AA meetings and panicked last-chance lunges at Christ's punk-ass salvation are shook loose when reality comes crashing in. Your son is dead. Shot in the face. I wish it were you instead. You couldn't even make it to the funeral. You're a living piece of shit. Why couldn't it have been you? I wouldn't have lost a minute of sleep. It was great to see you in your moments of pain. You looked so good for the camera, so well rehearsed. I swear I saw you do that on Channel 7 once. Am I being too mean, shithead? I'm not sorry. Your weakness is so disgusting and I have a tendency to attack that which I don't respect, so I'm attacking you. It's your only son, and all you can do is try to look good and manage to be late for every meeting while your relatives talk over all the boring, less glamorous details involved in dealing with your son's refrigerated corpse. You seemed more interested in your son's material things than you were in him. What are you going to do? Sell his clothes? You and your designer tennis suits and your arrogant bullshit. I heard you have a history of suicide on your side of the family. I am hoping you're going to do it on New Year's. That would be great to hear about how you shot yourself in the face underneath your fake-ass Christmas tree. Should I just stop right here and put my arms around you and tell you that it's all going to be all right? Should I? Hey fuck you. The more I think about you and your fucked-up little friend who you brought everywhere with you, the more I want to make your life miserable in hopes that you'll kill yourself. Yes, I'd like to help you. I will concentrate all my best blow-my-brains-out thoughts over to you every day, and if the wind is just right, you'll pick up on the signal and check out. Your friends at the wake—fake grief and studio tans. The one ugly, leather-faced bitch who should have kept her sagging breasts covered up was asking me what my sign was. Remember a couple of summers ago, when you kept trying to get me to go on those stupid tabloid TV shows with you? I said no and it really burned you. I saw the footage of you on *Hard Copy* walking to your son's grave with the soft focus and the bullshit music soundtrack. Was it hard to get the cemetery to let you get the film crew inside the lot? Did you have to do a few takes to get the walk right? Who did your makeup? Do you remember you went on the *Joan Rivers Show* and talked all that shit about me? I know someone who was at one of your auditions a few weeks ago. Apparently you were really bad and you finally apologized and told them that you were hungover. I guess you fell off the wagon. I wish you would jump off the top of a forty-story building. You're such a fuckup. Now all you have is your fake friends who will never be there for you when you need them because they're not there for anyone ever, not even themselves. You can't even help yourself. You're the most pathetic person I know.

Sell the tourists human ears. Watch a man get his spine ripped out every day for thirty years. A man alone in his room thinking about killing someone and then wishing he wasn't so lonely. He has no idea that his brain is in hundreds of pieces underneath his scalp. He vomits his bone marrow whenever he speaks. He cuts himself on words. Nothing helps him from destroying himself. This man needs no drugs or alcohol to ruin himself. All he needs is life itself. The fact that he has a mother somewhere is horror enough. The fact that he has touched a woman and still has the skin on his back to prove it is bad enough. Anything that he has to feel is too much to deal with. He lives in the world that does not feel, that does not touch. At night he dreams of not being real. He dreams of getting out of his skin so he can have a breath that's not like breathing in the sorrow of night. The black air of madness. I am falling through the night. I see things out of the corners of my eyes. My spine crawls across the floor and wraps itself around my feet. Nothing gets to me anymore. It's all horrible. I'm free.

Load the guns. Repeat, "They're just ants at the picnic." Walk into the dance with both barrels blazing. When I go to the store and have to walk around all the whores and drug dealers who block the sidewalk, I always wish one of the ones who didn't have a gun would talk some shit so I could mutilate him. I'm not talking about a run-of-the-mill ass kicking. I'm talking about taking eyes out and breaking joints and smashing windpipes. It would be good to do that to a Hollywood neon shitboy and then hang him from a stop sign to let the rest know what happens to them when they open their dogshit mouths to the wrong person. Look. I see it. You can go to all the movies and watch all the television you want. I am the end of all time. I'm not hooked up to the machine. I don't care about being labeled a misogynist, misanthropic hate addict. I don't give a fuck if some human organism calls me politically incorrect. I like the idea of people getting killed in parking lots. I stab every person who passes me. In my mind, I stab them in the face with a fucking knife. If I thought I could get away with it, I would skin you alive. I only fear prison if I get caught killing one of you humans. I hate you all. I don't know anyone. I am the enemy of humans. I am that which spits in the face of humanity.

Boots on, trousers down. Onward to victory. Hello? Yeah man. Look man, your daughter is dead. She got burned on a drug deal and she got wasted. Don't ask me my name, man. Look, it's not me who did it, so don't be getting all harsh on me. I loved her, man. She was my old lady and shit. We left her in a warehouse on Third and Kent downtown. You should get her picked up man, she's been there a few days. If you don't pick her up soon, the dogs will eat her. Yeah, it's pretty fucked. I've seen it before. We didn't know where to find you. I feel bad about it man. Don't come looking, you know what I mean? Cool. Later, man.

If we didn't act our ages and acted our bank accounts instead, I'd be Father Time and you'd be teething. She belted him right in the mouth. It felt good. It had been building up all week. She would come home from work and there he was, sitting with the baby and listening to some shitty punk-rock music. She had no words for him. All she could do was hit. The baby would cry and she would yell and he would scream and cry and the neighbors on all four sides would knock or kick the wall, floor, and ceiling. She didn't care. They would both yell at the neighbors to shut up. It was usually the thing that would get the fight to stop though. He would go see to the baby as she was walking to the box to get a beer. She had planned on being an artist.

You want to be an actress, so you figure you'll work on your technique by dancing naked in front of a bunch of idiots for seven years? I watched her shoot up in the bathroom. We had just finished fucking. I thought she was in the kitchen, so I went to the toilet and she was in there with the door open. I just looked at her. She looked up at me and said hi and went back to shooting the dope into her foot. I didn't know she did that shit. I couldn't tell when we were fucking. I wondered how long she had been doing that shit, but I was afraid to ask. I don't know why I was afraid, I just was. She finished and leaned back against the wall and closed her eyes. I asked her if she was all right. She didn't say anything. She waved me away and I left the fucking place. She had said earlier that she had a boyfriend who was in jail and some of his friends would check up on her from time to time. I don't know what the hell I even went to her place for. I guess I was lonely. She had a hard beauty that I hadn't ever seen in a woman. I thought about her for days afterward. I never saw her again. I heard that she dumped the guy and married some Marine and the two of them moved to North Carolina. People get caught here on earth. We do the time and shit happens. I end up, you end up. Don't try to make any big sense of it. That's the first mistake. The more you try to figure it out, the more it fucks you up. I don't know what the second mistake is.

The room smells like vomit these days. She throws up every morning. She coughs and hacks into the bowl. Her breasts scrape the rim. She wipes her mouth off with a washcloth and gets ready for work. The pigs put the boy in the back of the car. The pigs shoved him in the back without trying to get his head under the roof. I saw them smash his head against the sides of the door like the way old Ma rings the triangle at dinnertime when it's time to "come and git it!" I was standing there with a bunch of other people. The club owner had locked us inside, so watching was all we could do. I felt like an asshole standing in the window watching this guy get worked over, but there's only so much you can do without modern firearms. Which leads me to the conclusion that life would be a lot more bearable if I had access to an RPG or a mortar. Hell, how about missiles, tanks? Thinking about it, I would have to put my money on that good old RPG. A good tool for traffic jams. Fuck it, someone should have shot that pig in the ass while he was fucking with that guy. These shitheads never get what they really need.

All we are is angel dust in the wound. Rats chewed the hands, lips, and nose off a three-month-old girl in the apartment building across the street from me. The mother was on PCP and had her head in the stove trying to kill herself. God angel devil lover. In my house. Make it hot and kill it quick.

A black guy and a Korean guy, arms around each other watching a white guy hang by the neck. United colors of we'll-do-anything-to-sell-these-fucking-clothes-to-you-morons. He shot the guy. Big fucking deal. I saw the whole thing while I was walking back from doing the laundry. The guy just fell over. The gun didn't make much noise. The guy who shot him ran away, and no one went after him—the guy had a gun! I felt absolutely nothing. I think I've been living in this city too long. I work. I hate it but I do it. What the fuck else am I going to do? Rob a bank? I hate my job. I hate my life so what else is new? I've got ten minutes until I have to go to work. Ten whole minutes to myself. What should I do with my big ten minutes? I might as well go into work early. Fuck it.

What about a gaaaaaaaaaaay GI Joe doll? I got your letter today. I should start by saying that I don't hate you. I don't have any problems with you, that is to say that I will not accept you as the blame for my state of being. In the last few years it has been very difficult for me to get by without bad depression. I have been doing a lot of thinking as to the root of all the bullshit that I put myself through. I ask myself why I do all this music and writing bullshit. I know why I do it all. I am trying to get out all the rage that I have. Do you know where that rage comes from? It comes from the way I was raised. I have a rage in me that dries my bone marrow, it goes so deep. All I can do now is make my rent money and eat year after year. It is up to me to get myself better. I know I was a horrible person growing up. I was never good at school, sports. I was a disappointment on all levels. I am only good at one thing. That is the taking and dispensing of pain. I know humiliation, that's why I work so hard. No one will ever walk on me again. I command respect through intimidation and the fact that I will persist after all the rest have given up. My capacity for taking pain is what I am most proud of. It's all I know at this point. I should have died when I was born. I have no happy memories of childhood. I know you did the best you could and I have no regrets and I appreciate all you did for me and I know you gave up a part of your life to raise me. I know there were things you would have done differently if you didn't have me. I also know that I didn't ask to be born. It is hard for me to deal with women past a business level. The thought of intimacy is repulsive and out of the question. I learned about sex by walking down the hall and seeing you and some guy. One of them once told me how good you are in bed. Do you have any idea what kind of shit that does to a freaked-out little boy? To me, every woman is a bitch. I make sure I hurt every one of them mentally when I have sex with them. I like the mental pain I cause them more than I like the sex. I do my best to feel legitimate and that I deserve a life. It is an ongoing struggle. So in the last two years I have had difficulty in dealing with you. This is no fault of yours. I hope that someday I can be your friend. I don't mean to make this a problem. It is a full-time thing for me to maintain. I have bad problems with depression. It's like a plague. It makes me want to either kill someone or kill myself. It sometimes ends with me beating some guy up. I never would take my fists to a female. I think you are a good person, and I know that you want to do good things. The problem with you and me not connecting is a problem that comes from my end. I can't help how I feel though. I wish I didn't feel like this.

I would rather have had a normal life. Not the strange one that I have now. I feel more in common with a guy who murders a lot of people than I do with anyone in my world. So that's it. My life is fucked. You wanted to know what was going on with me, and I told you the best I could.

I guess you all were too young for est. Lucky. I am chained to a steel bedpost. Every few hours my mother comes in and beats me and then she sends in one of her boyfriends to kiss me and hit me with his belt. They always tell me that they love me. I do this alone in my room. I can do it anytime I want. Then I want to go to her house and beat her sleeping body until the brains start coming out. I can smell it all now because that's how it's going to be. It's going to be a smell thing. Blood, shit, and brains. Nothing smells like human brains. It's a thick sweet smell. It will drive you insane.

You should have killed me when you had the chance. You fucking missed me twice. Fuck you. I was walking up Holly-wood Boulevard. I saw a girl sitting on the ground outside of the Chi-nese Theatre. She motioned for me to come over. She wanted to know if I would buy some sunglasses off her for a dollar so she could get money to go to Las Vegas. I asked her why she was asking for a dollar if she was planning such a long trip. She said, "I'm a Hollywood fuckup," and that she was trying to get her shit together. I could tell by her eyes that she was a junkie. She was looking pretty bad. I asked her if she wanted to get high. She said that she was trying to get off the shit but it was hard and she would really dig getting high right now because she had been puking all day. I told her to come with me and she could suck my dick and I'd give her twenty bucks. She got up and we went to a parking garage near my place. I took her around the back to the fire exit that's never watched and never locked and we went in and up the stairs to the second level. I was amazed at how trusting she was. She asked me if I wanted to score with her. She said that she would come over and we could party at my place after we got the shit.

I told her that was cool. I told her, "I love to party," to see if I could make her laugh. She looked at me and said that I looked like it. We got up to the second level, and I walked her to the corner behind the fucked-up van that had been sitting there all summer. She got down on her knees and started trying to undo my belt buckle. I stood her up and hit her in the face as hard as I could. She fell on the ground and put her hands on her head. I kicked her until I was barely able to breathe. I treat humans like what they are, garbage.

It's easy to play God trips on your head. They are talking a bunch of shit late into the early-morning hours. I can hear them from my room. They're sitting in a car outside. I can feel their heat. I can taste the food they ate on their spent breath as it comes out of their mouths. I can sense them totally. I could kill them with my eyes closed, but I had them open the whole time I clubbed the man to death. He was so easy. I went outside and kicked the side the bitch was sitting on, and of course the guy came out and asked me if I had a problem. This made me laugh. There is a big difference between me and that guy. The difference is that I kill people. I hit him in the face as hard as I could with the bat and killed him with one shot. I clubbed his head until I saw his brains and then ran down the alley and through the back door. My block is so fucked up that no one looks out the windows anymore anyway. The cunt just sat in the car and watched. I got away clean. There's a big difference between you and me. I kill humans. I end their lives and ruin the lives of their families. I don't give a fuck about anyone but myself. I know the meaning of life. It has no meaning. I kill you and it doesn't matter. It's the way I can pass time and respect myself you fuckhead.

There's a lady who knows . . . Here's what happened and it's the fucking truth. I was walking from the store. I don't like going out in the day. I can't take the sun. It's not good for me. I don't like all the ugly fucking people looking at me like they do. All I can do is dream of killing them. It would feel so good to just be able to shoot them like the pieces of shit that they are. Their eyes bugging out, their filthy little kids looking and laughing. I go out at night because there are less people out there to fuck with me. I was walking like I said and this pig car pulls up. I stop. Like what the fuck am I going to do, keep walking and mind my own business like I haven't done anything? Fuck no. I stop because I know that the pig will cook up some reason to take me to jail if I don't stop. The pig gets out of the car and asks me where I'm going, and I tell him that I'm walking to the store, and he says that I'm a faggot looking for some dick to suck. He calls me a cocksucking faggot looking for a little meat. He says that he ought to kick the shit out of me right on the spot. I told him I wasn't a faggot. The pig hits me in the stomach and pulls me to the backseat of his car. He puts his gun to my head and tells me to unzip his pants because I'm going to suck his cock right now. I did it. I sucked the pig's cock. What else was I going to do? He had the gun at my head. I was never with a man before, besides some of my mother's boyfriends and my stepbrother, but none of that was my idea. He pushed me out of the car and drove off. I went home. I'm going to kill that fucking pig someday. I'm going to find him and waste his pig ass. It's going to be great. I'll make him suck the gun. Yeah, come on pig. Let's see some feeling. Gimme some soul when you wrap your tongue around that barrel. I hate those big funerals for cops. The ones where the taxpayers shell out too much money so the pigs can shoot guns and make people think that the dead piece of shit was worth the time of day. They should have the funerals at my house. We could party and drink and laugh and play videos of me shooting the pig over and over. Tie up the pig's boyfriend and mother and make them watch it until they pass out and then kill them. If the pig happened to be married to a woman, then I'll have more fun. I'll follow her around for a few days and get her habits down, and then I'll take her out. I'll put a leash on the cunt and take her out for a walk. Fucking pig slut. Come. Heel. Water the flowers with your piss, you fucking bag of shit. You pig fucker. Shoot her in the jaw with a .22 and leave her so she'll be disfigured but not dead. Fuck you pig. I'm going to kill you.

Sorry, but I'm the REAL voice of the village. Ha ha. Ho ho. I never wanted you. At night I prayed that you would die inside me. I used to hit you by running into tables as hard as I could, hoping that you would crack your skull. I drank. Oh god, I drank. I did anything I could to try and kill you while you grew inside me. For nine months I felt like I was full of cancer. I should have killed myself in the ninth month. That would have been master work on my part. I hate you. But still you came out. At first I was happy just to have you out of me. I didn't care what you looked like. The nurse asked me if I wanted to hold you, and I said no. I should have strangled you while you were asleep. I never wanted you. I want you to know that and never forget it. You ruined my figure. You ruined my life. I hate you. Forever. How do I have a normal sex life with a fucking kid in the house? You think a man wants to come and fuck me when he knows there's a kid in the next room? How am I supposed to be with a man when I know that at any minute you're going to come into the fucking room asking me to fix some fucking toy. They never come to the house again. That's why I hit you every time one of them left. You ruined my life. I never had a life after you came along. I hate you. I remember when I got my boyfriends to hit you. I got sick of touching you, even though it gave me great pleasure to hear you scream. I liked it better when the man did it to you. I always stood outside the door and listened to them hit you. I was always hoping that one of them would kill you and you would be gone and I wouldn't have to do time. I hate you. Do you know what makes me the maddest? The fact that I did everything I could to kill you and nothing worked. You are the Antichrist. You didn't die. Now I wait for my life to end. There's nothing for me now. I am old and ugly, and you could come into this room and kill me now if you wanted to. That's why I keep this gun. I hate you. Tonight is the big night. The gun is in my mouth. I am destroying myself tonight. Tonight is the end of my suffering. No more looking in the mirror and seeing this ugly body. The only thing it ever did was give birth to you. I could have been a model. I could have been a stewardess. I could have been anything. But instead, I became a mother. Only one life. Mine is a life wasted because of you. I hate you.

I know, I know, cultivated misanthropic maladjustment. She told me to come into her room. I went in and asked her what she wanted. She said, "I want to give you a nightmare that will last you for the rest of your life." She took out a pistol from under the pillow of her bed and put the barrel in her mouth and pulled the trigger before I could say anything. Her body flew back and landed in the corner. Now she does it three nights a week. It was years ago but the memory is fresh in my mind. The sound of the gunshot roars in my head for hours like a jet engine. Now I have the gun in my hand. I can't sleep. I keep thinking about that shot. I keep thinking about what I need. It's all coming true. Every night I smell the gunpowder and my vomit. I keep telling myself to be strong.

Information. Yesterday the first gunshot came in at 7:36 a.m. No return fire. Pack the gat and spray the suckers that sling the crack. Duck and cover. It's not you yet so don't even think about death. It just gets in the way of the real-life movie you got going on my fucking street. This wild West has no nobility. Live in fear of the ones who have the ability to see that life has no price and for this, you pay endlessly. You pay with fear. Disease wears a cape and dons a shining shield. The stats break it down to sheer numbers. Reality has become a fear trip. Something to choke on. One in every three women in America will be raped. This is science friction. I see it from all sides. I see the direction of the infection. The facts are stacked and packed into your head. You need the two-hour vacation twelve times a day. Spark the joint and park the car. Look up at the stars. Think about it, you're in the hot seat. You're in a huge shark tank. If you want to beat them, you have to join them somehow. The bad guys kill the bad guys. The bad guys kill the good guys. If you want to survive the bad guys, you have to have some bad in you—a lot actually. You have to know what they know. This is high adventure in the great outdoors. I don't know what these people thought was going to happen to them. Too much television, too much bad food, too many magazines. Too much time spent worrying about depressed millionaires getting left by their women. Wondering if the fall-season shows will be what they should be. Anyone who wants to help me doesn't. Anyone who wants to kill me might. Anyone who wants to love me better not. People are poisonous. When was the last time you wanted to kill someone? I mean *really* kill someone? Where you planned all the shit out, like what to do with the body and all that. When was the last time you really wanted to live? Do you ever have to remind yourself that you're alive? I'm not a light bringer, I'm not a gunslinger. I'm a reporter from the port of soul. Front line at the Abyss. If the abyss fits, wear it. Looking into the monster's mouth. The vet turned cop. Man walks a dozen people down the aisle of a convenience store and shoots them. A girl gets raped in the shower a few times and now tries to kill herself often. She's a good American—she'll get it right. Nothing but the facts. I like the ones that make you choke. The truth is my friend. It keeps me warm at night. The truth is your friend even when it's sending you to prison. Even when it kills you and your fuck partner. There will be some bright nights ahead. You'll get used to the smell of napalm. Pigs eating dead bodies and the gun-toting youth who wear your looted watches and rings will not scare you one bit. Feel the fear. And don't forget to get down.

DO I COME HERE OFTEN?

This is a collection of interviews I did with some interesting people I was lucky enough to have the chance to meet over the years, as well as travel journals and magazine articles I wrote, printed here in their unedited form.

Happy Birthday

February 13, 1983. German/
Dutch border: About last
night. The Nigheist got through
one song before skinheads jumped onstage and started attacking
them. One asshole was swinging a mic stand at Mugger's head. The
Minutemen were freaking out before they went on. They thought that
they were going to get killed. It just made me mad. I wanted to kill
those fuckers.

When we played, one skin got onstage and was looking offstage
to show off to his friends and I kicked him off and he fell a long way to
the floor. He didn't dig that too much. Eight hundred fifty people
showed up, but I bet that there will be a lot less people next time. D.
Boon had the best move of the night. During their last song, "Fanatics," D. jumped offstage with his guitar on and ran through the crowd
screaming, "FANATICS!!!" People didn't know what to do. He knocked
those skinheads over like bowling pins.

The countryside is beautiful. I've never seen anything like it.
Thatched roofs on the houses, snow everywhere. The sky is so blue.
I'm twenty-two years old today.

February 13, 1985. Hermosa Beach, CA: Not much went on
today. Got some interesting mail. I walked down Artesia Boulevard to
practice. I use Artesia to monitor the world. Highlights: Walking past
the Lucky Market, saw a man blow up at a phone booth, tried to rip
the receiver away from the booth. The cord wouldn't give. The man

got even madder. He smashed the phone into the booth and stormed off. I was walking past the Gulf station at Artesia and Aviation. I was in the middle of the driveway. This car was pulling in. The woman inside was mad because I wouldn't move fast enough for her liking. She yelled at me. I gave her the old Hitler salute. She bummed. Fine. Saw a kid rip off a *Creem* magazine at the 7-Eleven at Artesia and Phelton. Real slick mover, that kid. He bent down, wrapped it around his leg, rolled his sock over it, and bailed out of the store. Kids in Iron Maiden shirts playing videos and hanging out.

Someday those kids will grow up and they will stand behind the counter. Now it's just a dream. But isn't it everybody's dream? To don that orange and white smock. To have your own little name tag. To stand with your feet planted solidly, facing front proudly. Only turning to fill an order for a Big Gulp or a Slurpee. "Oh, Seven-Eleven, man it's four a.m. Everything's closed. Who can I turn to but you?" (Hey little lady, I'll help you with that microwave!) Have you ever looked into the cold-drink section? Have you ever seen that familiar orange and white smock bobbing around back there? Bet you'd like to know what goes on back there, always hoping that Channel 7 would do a behind-the-scene report. I bet, Hey! Me too! 7-Eleven is the pulse beat of America. I think that Bruce Springsteen should do a little number about a 7-Eleven in Asbury Park but write it in such a way that the entire USA can identify and slurp along with Bruce. Suck for the Boss. Hail the Boss! Hail 7-Eleven!

For the record, sleep is getting bad. The dreams are heavy. The dreams are real. I am a freakout. I have scales. I have feathers. I have fur. I have enlarged incisors. I have claws. I have escaped the crucifixion. Stepped aside, let the parade pass me by, and pass away. I have come to drop fire. I have come to bring them to fire. To unite them with fire. Confessions of the torch: I thought I was in the Salvation Army. The Salvation Army? No! Salvation's Soldiers, saints set on destroy. Purify! Make fire! Let it come down. The joke is killing me. Let's end the joke so I can get some sleep.

February 14, 1986. Tulsa, OK: Last night in Little Rock was a trip. We played this very straight place, you never know where Dukowski will drop you down next. The set was good. The crowd was fairly friendly. So we finish the set and everybody is leaving and they all need to have autographs and stuff and I'm serving them as best I can. In the meantime, I'm looking around for my clothes so I can get dressed. I go to my backpack and I look for my shirts. They are gone. In their place is a shitty punker shirt. I guess the scenario went as such: Thieving fuckup punker goes up to Henry's shit and says, "Fuck, I'll rip off that asshole Rollins." He takes the shirts, then something pops into his vacant brain. "I know, I'll take these two shirts that don't belong to me, being the low prick that I am, and in return, I'll put my shitty punker shirt in their place!" He walks off into the moist Little Rock night.

The next trip was this huge woman who bought me flowers. It being my birthday and all. She came up to me and says, "Do you remember me? I'm the girl who gave you flowers." Of course I remembered her. Fine. "Well," she continued. "That Negro over there"—she points to one of the cleanup guys—"he's been hounding me all night. I hear that they like big women. He just came up to me and said, 'Who do you go with,' and I pointed at you. He says he wants to arm-wrestle you to try and get me away from you." Thanks a lot lady. I walked away from her and sat down on a piece of equipment. Sure enough the man came up to me and asked me to arm-wrestle him. I said to him, "Man, I know why you want to arm-wrestle me. That fat lady told you that she's with me. Well she's not. I've never seen her before tonight. She's full of shit." He said, "I hear you man, check this out." He lifted up his sleeve and flexed his arm. His biceps kept getting bigger and bigger. Finally he twisted his wrist and this golf-ball–size muscle popped out on top, looked kind of sick to me. I said, "That's wonderful, you're more than a match for me." He grinned and walked away.

Minutes later this real tough-looking woman came up to me and pointed to my cock and then to her mouth. I just smiled. She gestured with her hands as to the size of my cock. I took my thumb and index finger and indicated a length of about three-quarters of an inch. She came over and extended her hand and said, "Let's go." I looked at her closely. Man, what a tough-looking broad! She sat down in my lap and said, "Come on, let's go. Just lay back and enjoy it." I asked her name. "Peach Melba." I said, "Peach, my dear, I want to tell you that you have the nicest ass of anyone here tonight, but I can't go with you." Peach asked why. I said, "Peach, you're a man! Now there are certain things that I won't do and I don't want some guy sucking my cock, but shit honey, thanks anyway." *He* asked me if I would have gone for it if I hadn't been able to tell. I skipped the answer and commented on his vivid green panty hose. I said that I had a Madonna record that had a picture of Madonna on it wearing the same shade. We both agreed that Madonna was awesome. He told me how he scammed on C'el and even danced with him. We talked for a while more and he told me that his real name was Tim. I told him that I liked Tim much better. Fuck, that guy had about an inch of makeup on his face. I told him that he shouldn't shave for about three days and then go out in drag with all that stubble. Tim said that he would give it a try. He got up and split.

Thieves. No one is to be completely trusted besides yourself. To trust someone else is an unfair demand on that person. Black Flag "fans" are not to be trusted in the least. Last night they stole from me. I will never trust any of them again. If someone gives me something, I will ask what that person wants in return, and if that person says that he wants nothing in return, I will return the gift. No trust. They always want something in return at some point. I hate having my back turned when they come to collect. None of them are to be trusted. They cheer while you play, and then when you don't play what they wanted to hear, they hurl insults at you. I learned something from that shit. I learned that it's all the same—praise, damnation, love, hate, all the same. No one can tell me different. I expect nothing from everyone. I am rarely let down. I am occasionally pleasantly surprised. No one. I will not trust anyone completely outside of myself except Joe. I hope for the same from others. Complete trust is stupid. Complete trust is for fools. It's right up there with "faith."

February 13, 1987, 12:10 a.m. Amtrak en route to Chicago, IL: Two girls walk by. "Where do you think Henry's going?" I should dress up in a Cyndi Lauper suit. I'm going to Madison, Wisconsin, for a show. The closest Amtrak can get me is Chicago. No sweat. I just turned twenty-six on this train. No more of that "Quarter-Century Man" shit for me anymore, I'm on my way to thirty.

Just spent three days in DC. Finished up all the East Coast shows: New York, Boston, Providence, New Haven, Trenton, New Brunswick, DC. Sure was great to see Ian. It's hard to think of that boy turning twenty-five. I really can't see it happening. Not that I think he's going to die before he gets there or anything, but I thought that maybe he would magically escape aging. There is something about him that transcends age. *Eternal* is such a heavy, clumsy word. I don't want to use it. He's like a season. I know he'll be around. No plane crash will get that guy. Still, it makes me think. What a trip. Ian MacKaye, twenty-five. No way.

The thing I got from this visit is that now it's just like another town. I don't even remember the names of the streets. Most of the people I know have moved away. I don't know most of the people who hang out. I think that the less people I know, the better. I'm not going to visit there anymore, only to play. I don't need any time among friends. When I open my mouth, I waste my time when I do those things. I lie to myself. There's no use in that. When I'm in the room with them, I feel uneasy, they feel uneasy. It's a lie, it doesn't work. It doesn't have to work. People games tangle me up. Get me caught in games with myself.

The whole car of this train is alive with noise. All of the people behind me are drunk. I can't see why they put alcohol on trains. The air is thick with the smell of booze and bad food.

A drunk guy in front of me is telling us all about how all these people he knows think he's a genius, and he says, "Hah! To me, it's nothing!"

The old folks across the aisle talk about boring shit, their kids, the Bill Cosby show, and food, that's it. The man with the cowboy hat should be executed. He's walking up and down the aisle yelling, "Does anyone want a beer?"

Some guy yells, "Yeah, I'll take one! He's got a white hat on, he must be a good guy!"

The man behind me croaks, "Yeah! Bring 'em down!"

Now I hear some people up ahead.

"Did you see that guy with the short hair?"

The citizens are a trip. Thank goodness for Bruce Springsteen to keep all these people in line. Hey! Go to work, be the person you hate, suck your employer's ass, come home and drink, it's all right, Bruce Springsteen wrote a song about you. If you didn't get in line and work all day and hate your own guts, then the Boss wouldn't have anything to write about and he'd go out of business. The citizen and the Boss walk hand in hand into the darkness. I don't mind his music though. In a situation like this, I see where he's coming from.

Four more shows on this trip. Then back to LA for four weeks, then out to Trenton for band practice and tour. Looking forward to getting back out here. California is a kicked-back joke.

February 13, 1988, 1:07 a.m. Chicago, IL: I am twenty-seven years old. Did the show here tonight. Had a real cool time. Went for an hour and a half; it felt like ten minutes.

Stayed up late last night. Tried to get the train at 7 a.m., but it was sold out. Had to fly. The airplane was overbooked so they put me in first class. It was cool. It was strange to look back and see all these sorry-looking folks in coach. I couldn't help it. I kept looking back at them and watching them watching me. Got off the plane, did two interviews on the phone at the airport. Took a cab to this neighborhood where I always go to get books. Found *Proud Beggars* by Albert Cossery. Went from there to the club, did two interviews. Took ten minutes to get ready, went out and hit it. Did an interview after everybody cleared out. It was strange. All these people wanted to talk to me. I'm signing all these books and then they had to leave and they freaked. They started shoving all this stuff in front of me to sign and started grabbing me. A trip.

So tired from the last few days that I can't even think straight enough to write. The interviews are hard to do. I don't know how much more I can keep this up. I have to get some sleep. Every day has been a brain fry.

I can feel the beast crawling into my bones. My friend is back. There's that hard skin I lose when I'm back there. It's coming back. That's when I'm on—when the beast is running through my blood. I can feel it and it's so good. I knew there was something missing and now it's back. The longer I'm out, the better it gets. It's so easy to forget. When I'm back there, it destroys parts of me, makes me dull. It takes a while for the hard shine to come back. What I really need is the music. This spoken thing is good but I need the pain that the music inflicts on my body. That's when I'm at my best. Hard to explain to other people. I have to stay away from women. The longer I go without sex, the better. When I'm with a woman, I get weak. No one is close to me, and when I'm in close contact with a woman, I try to get out of myself. I lie to myself and that's bullshit. For me to do what I need to do, I can be close to no one.

I have been frustrated the last few weeks because I haven't had enough stimuli. I keep wanting to be back in Europe in the fourth month of the tour, meaner than shit. I haven't been tested since December. I need it bad. I don't think I should ever come off the road. If I do, I should go to a place where I don't know anyone. Association weakens me, waters me down. I will not let anyone pull me off the trail. I must reread the iron reminders that I wrote a few months ago. They are the truth. The part about how the work comes before anything and anyone, even me. The mission is the only thing that matters. Sex, relationships come second place, third place, last place. The work is all there is.

I remember a while ago. I was with this girl, I told her that the work comes before anything. She got offended. Hey fuck that shit.

Females play a smaller part in my life than they used to. As soon as they get in the way of the work then it makes me not like them. They don't know me. No one knows me. The work knows me. The road knows me. The beast knows me. Conflict knows me. Women make all that stuff taste cheap. I was with this girl recently. When I hit the road, I missed her for about a day, and now I don't think of her at all. Time to fall out. Tomorrow is Madison, Wisconsin. Another day. Bring them all on. Let them destroy me, let them try. I welcome the hard things.

2:40 p.m. Madison, WI: Got here a couple of hours ago. Been outside a long time. Now I'm inside Victor's coffee store listening to two men discuss why drinking coffee makes them feel guilty. I'm so cold that I can hardly hold the pen. I got a pot of coffee—that will allow me to stay here long enough to thaw out. Have to do an interview soon. It's too cold to go back out there too soon.

Looking at all the brightly dressed college kids walking down the street makes me glad that I chose not to go that route. Hearing the shit they talk about is beyond belief. I can't understand how people of that age can be into such mindless bullshit.

I was thinking about how today is my birthday. I came to this: Who gives a fuck? It's just another day. I was in this town a year ago doing a talking show. Tomorrow is Milwaukee, then on to Boston for the better part of a week. Will be good to move on to another part of the country. I have been out almost two weeks, I can't even tell. I have to look at my interview list to find out what day it is. I like doing the shows night after night without nights off. They get better and better when I do a lot of shows straight. Momentum is important. I find that it helps me to be able to free-associate and work openly while onstage.

While on the street, people pass me, about once a block I hear my name being mentioned. "That's Henry Rollins." "Where?" "There." "Wow." And so on. At this point I thought I would be used to it. I'm not, but it doesn't bug me like it used to. I have learned that there is a space in my head where I can go where no one can get to me. Often when I'm on the street, that's where I am. I have learned to find open fields in the space of the seat on a bus.

Now the coffee place is full of people, and they're knocking into me with their shopping bags. I put the headphones on and I'm out of there. Every once in a while I look up and I see all these people looking at me like they want to sit down. Hey fuck them. All the guys look like Robin Williams. Those Docksiders kill me. Maybe they should have to stand. Maybe they should freeze to death.

Walking around here makes me sick. I don't like college towns. The streets are full of people wearing the same clothes. It's like being stuck in a wine-cooler commercial and not being able to find the exit door.

February 23, 1989, 2:56 a.m. Arlington, VA: Have been unable to write for a long time. Hand has been fucked up. The story is long and boring. Haven't written in weeks. Just thinking about it fucks me up. Fucks me up to the point where I don't feel like writing any more right now.

3:02 p.m.: Like I said, it's a long fucked-up story. I'll make it short. A few weeks ago we were in Geelong, Australia, playing. We're doing the show—all is well. This guy is standing in front of me, spitting mouthfuls of beer in my face. After a few mouthfuls, I got fed up and punched him. My fist hit his mouth. He fell out. His friends dragged him away. Moments later he came back up to the front. His face was bloody. He pulled his upper lip up and his front teeth were gone. I felt bad about it. Not because I hit the guy but because I knew that the police would be there soon to arrest me. I looked at my hand and there was a hole over the knuckle, deep enough to where I could see my tendon working. I showed it to our drummer and he was not at all interested.

A few moments later something hit the stage. Our guitar player picked it up. It was the guy's teeth—bridgework. Not much to me, another drunk asshole in my face who got destroyed, but I held on to them all the same. I figured they would be a good souvenir.

The next day the band had a day off and I had a talking show and interviews. My hand had started to swell, and the pain was getting harder to take by the hour. The next day we left for the airport. My hand had turned purple, and looked like it was going to explode.

The plane ride was hellish. The pain was enough that I was passing out and coming to all the way there. I was running a fever as well.

I got to LA about fourteen hours later and had to exchange the Australian money and handle all this business while in excruciating pain.

I got back to my place, and of course the first thing I did was call up a girl I know and arrange a date for that night. Brainless.

The next day I checked into a hospital after my friend who used to be a nurse saw my hand and threw me in her car and sped me to the hospital. I figured they would give me some penicillin and that would be it. How wrong can a man be? Wrong as I was.

I went into the emergency room and the lady took one look at my hand and all of a sudden there was a doctor in my face. He said that I should fill out the forms immediately so that he could start operating as soon as possible. I told him that there wasn't going to be any operation. He said that I could leave and come back tomorrow when they would amputate my hand, or I could get started today and they would try to save what was left of my finger. This sobered me up and I filled out the form.

Minutes later I was on my back in one of those nightgown things, there was an IV thing attached to my hand, and I was heading toward surgery.

At some point I woke up and the doctor came in to see how I was. He pulled off the bandage and there was this big hole in my hand. He said they were going to leave it open so it could drain. Then he gave me a shot of Demerol and I hallucinated for a while and passed out.

To make a long story short, I was in the hospital for six and a half days. On my birthday, I came to the conclusion that I had had enough. I took the IV out of my hand and got dressed. When the doctor came in, I told him to congratulate me because today was the day that I was going home. He said that I wasn't going home for four more days. I just smiled and told him that I was leaving in a few minutes and he better make a prescription for whatever it was that I needed. He got the point and wrote a sheet for something. I got out of there and hit the road the next day. I had shows to do. I spent my twenty-eighth birthday sweating it out in a hospital bed. How weak.

I learned a good lesson this time. No asshole is worth this much trouble.

February 13, 1990, 11:50 p.m. San Francisco, CA: I'm in Don and Jane's apartment. It's cool to see Don, but the situation with Don and Jane is fucked up. She takes every opportunity to rip on him. He takes it without complaining. She says the meanest things to him in front of other people. Don tries to be cool and deal with it, but you can tell it hurts him a lot. They had some people over for my birthday and it was okay, I guess. I appreciate the thought, but it's not my kind of thing.

It was hard to take with a room full of Jane's friends, listening to her lay into Don and make fun of him in front of all of them and their daughter. I will never get married as long as I live. I am around them and it reminds me of when I was growing up and all the acrimony between my mother and father. I watched them battle it out and had to take it from their new wives and boyfriends. There's nothing I can see that is good about marriage. I might be lonely a lot of the time, but at least I have the option to get up and go when I want to. I'll hold on to that one as long as I'm breathing.

Now I'm in their spare room trying not to make too much noise for fear of unleashing the wrath of the beast known as Jane.

I have a show in town tomorrow. I am twenty-nine years old. I am lonely and poor and don't know how I am going to keep my band together and keep the books coming out. Sometimes it's all I can do to not break into pieces. I am wracked with anxiety so bad sometimes that I am unable to sleep. All I can do is get madder and madder and wait for the morning to come so I can get to work and try to keep it all going.

Luckily I am hard as hell and can take this bullshit month after month. Sometimes I feel so tired. I can't seem to get enough sleep. Never seems to help anyway.

February 13, 1991, 12:34 a.m. Trenton, NJ: I am thirty years old. I am in the basement of Sim's mom's house. Have not checked in for a while. Too burned out to do so. It's not as if there's been a lot happening.

Things that happened: We did a demo yesterday. I don't know how many songs. I did the vocal overdubs today. Went fast, just hearing the basic tracks unmixed; it already sounds good to me.

I did the show in Big Bear, California, the other day. I will write more about that soon when I feel more like writing.

The woman who I have been writing about for months, the woman who filled my thoughts with light, she dumped me for some guy. What a put-down. It's hard to take it. I liked her too much I guess. It occurred to me the last time I was with her that if it was this good to be with her, being without her would be bad. I feel better now, feeling better with every day that passes. A few days ago, like last Sunday, I was in the pits. I don't remember crawling like that.

She went away to Europe for a month. All the time she was gone, I thought of her constantly. Sometimes thinking of her was the only thing holding me together. All this time away, she never called, never wrote, nothing. I faxed her three times. It was the only number that she gave me. She finally got back, a few days late. I had been calling her place every day leaving messages. She was back and I was all excited to talk to her, but she was all cool and detached. I knew that something was up. She told me that she had started going out with this guy she was working with and she didn't know which one she wanted, and that she was very confused. I talked to her a few more times trying to tell her how I felt. I knew that she was going to dump me, and I was desperate and pathetic. All the time this was going down, I had to do the date in Big Bear. I had to be with all these people, shake hands and all that shit. I was dying inside the whole time. She said she would call me on Sunday morning. I finally got in touch with her in the evening and I asked her what her deal was. She still gave me the bullshit. I asked her if she had been with him since she had gotten back. She said yes. I told her that she had obviously made up her mind. It went on like that for a while, all bullshit. Finally we hung up. I called her later, but all I got was the answering machine. She broke me pretty good. It hurts to think of her with that guy. I know that he will fuck her up like he fucked up the last woman he was with. I will never understand. If someone had told me that it was going to end like this, I would have told them that they were crazy. All the time that we were together, I thought we were close, it was great. I thought I meant more to her. I was wrong. I definitely learned a lesson this time. I know that I can be broken. I am not as tough as I thought. I see it now. At this point, it's the only thing good that came out of all of this. I know myself better now and know what I have to do. It always comes back to me. There's really nothing else for me but the road and the work. They are always there for me.

It was a mistake to get that interested in a woman. I learned something and I should not forget it. What happened is what should have happened—what would've happened eventually. The only thing that has not abandoned me is the road and the life. It is the one constant in my life. Movement. Constant movement and hard travel. Living out of my backpacks and sleeping on floors. I was not meant to come out of the storm.

Should go to sleep now. I have to go into the city tomorrow to meet with a guy from a record company. Yet another meeting. Over a year of meetings and the band still has no label.

February 13, 1992, 3:20 p.m. Hamburg, Germany: Tonight will be the second night here. The Ahoy. I don't think I've ever played this venue besides last night. Usually we play at the Markthalle. I am thirty-one years old today. Not really an age to think about. I used to think that my birthday was an interesting date, and now I don't care. I know I'll be remembering 12.19.91 forever though. It will be strange when Joe has been dead for a year.

All I can do is keep playing my guts out every night and try to sleep it off. I feel violent all the time these days. I don't particularly hate anyone, but I feel like I don't care about anything. I play the music every night merely to punish it and punish myself.

February 13, 1993, 11:23 p.m. Leicester, England: Don Bajema arrived here all right and the books got in as well. We did a show here tonight. Don was good but he didn't think so. He started a little cold but other than that it was a good show for him. I'm sure tomorrow night he'll really let it rip. I felt good about my set. People were great as they have been for pretty much the entire trip.

Last night I did a show called "The Word." I had to sit around for a few hours before I could go sit on a couch and have my time wasted by a bunch of TV people. The only good things about it were hanging out with the guys in Living Colour and ripping on Bob Geldof when I saw him walking down the halls. His girlfriend, Paula Yates, was on the show with me. She's a typical groupie made good, a total waste of daily feeding and maintenance. The whole thing was a bore until the band that was playing started giving the host shit and he wasn't ready for it and it blew his mind. The record company made it seem like my appearance on this show was the biggest deal in the world, but you know how they are.

I was just in Holland and Belgium and the shows were good but the press got to me. I had to talk to the hag at *Kerrang!* about why I don't like two of her writers. These guys talk shit and I call them on it and they go whining to her about it and she makes it out like the world is on fire. These people are so full of their own shit that they can't see anything. None of their shit matters to me. I don't care about being in their magazine, and I don't want to know about all the stupid fucking bands that they put in it. The magazine didn't like me before she got there, and because she wants to fuck me, I get in the mag. These people should get a life.

I had to waste my editing time talking to this common slag. When that was over, I went right into five interviews and then to the gig. Kicked it for two hours. Felt good. All the shows have been going well. There's nothing much to write about because I don't give a fuck about writing down the stupid common details of my little life anymore. It's all the same shit all the time anyway, so fuck it. These reporters can all go get fucked. So weak—they make me weak too with their bullshit. I must not let them get to me and drag me down. You should have seen that little swine lady with her tape recorder while we were driving. A disgusting business I'm in. I get everything I deserve and deserve everything I get. I am thirty-two years old.

February 13, 1994, 1:24 a.m. Sapporo, Japan: I'm thirty-three. Show was pretty good tonight. I got a workout at a mediocre gym. Hope to find better gyms down the road. We fly in the morning to Fukuoka, which is very south of here. Hope there's a lot less snow than here. I'm too tired to write anymore.

11:29 p.m. Fukuoka, Japan: Took all day to get here. The flight was delayed about three hours because of all the snow. Pretty boring. Too bad we couldn't get a gig for tonight. It was good to get away from all that snow.

Went to Tower here and found a few things. Went out and ate and then the rest of them tried to get me to go to a karaoke bar and waste time. I was out of there. Now I'm here and it's boring. Looks like I'll get an early night and that's it. I'm ready to leave. I don't think I'm in the right mood for this stuff anymore. Maybe it's just something that will pass. I'm just going to keep to myself for the rest of the trip. I don't relate to the rest of them and I feel better when I'm on my own. I wish things didn't affect me so much. It seems that I get fucked up too much over things. I don't know what to do to get better.

February 13, 1995, 1:18 a.m. Los Angeles, CA: I'm thirty-four. Ian called me tonight. It was good to talk to him. He's the same as always—working hard and making music. He's one of the only people I know who isn't fucked up somehow. He does his thing and doesn't mess with anyone. He is a big influence on me. I wish I was more like him in a lot of ways. He has a good grip on things.

I am usually depressed on my birthday. I don't feel like working tomorrow. I have nothing else to do but that. It's late, but not that late. I guess I should try to get to sleep early so I won't be a wreck in the morning.

I went through the other journals to see where I was this time last year. Last year it was Japan. I was in a hotel room—bored, hungry, and jet-lagging. The year before, I was in England. I think the only way to travel and still be able to have some fun would be to do it solo. If I could bring myself to do speaking dates again, that would be the way to go. I worry that I will never be able to do any of those shows again. I want to, but I am having trouble with people. Too bad. If I could go out and do a few weeks of shows, it would be good for things around here. There's never enough money around here. So many things I want to do, but it's always money that gets in the way.

It's strange being in my apartment all these days in a row. I have not been in one place this long since 1983. It's strange having slept on the same mattress for three months. I don't want to get soft. I don't want to lose my edge. It's all I have.

February 13, 1996, 8:30 a.m. Albuquerque, NM: At the airport on the way to Seattle for tonight's show. Last night was pretty good. It went a little long though—three hours and forty minutes. No one left and people seemed to dig it. I have to talk less at these shows though.

Today I am thirty-five years old. It doesn't matter to me what my age is. Sure does go by quickly. Tonight I am going to record the show and hope it comes out as a good one so I can put it out as a live record. Been a while since I did one of those.

I like this town, but it's going to be good to get on to Seattle. Something about this part of America is depressing. All the space, I think. Last night's promoter boy dropped us off at the airport this morning. He was a bit of a whiner. Rick, the road manager, said it took multiple phone calls to get him to wake up.

Last year on my birthday I was in LA. Usually Ian calls me. The shows have been good, but they make me kind of dull on the writing front. I give them all I have at night, and when it comes time to have some other thoughts, there is no energy to put them across.

I wonder if I act like a thirty-five-year-old. I think I was born when my father was this age. I don't think I will ever be the family type. I think it will be a failure to be in a band on tour when I am forty. I think it is time to start thinking of what the next move will be. When I hear the music that bands are making these days, it tells me it's time to get out. It's over for people like me. A weaker, less interesting music is what people want to hear. I still like playing and everything. I just don't think I want to be around to have to listen to it and somehow be a part of it. Because you do become part of it whether you want to or not.

3:33 p.m. Seattle, WA: At the usual hotel, the Edgewater. I was given free dessert at the hotel restaurant, and people have been sending in gift certificates to local record stores here and in New York as presents. It's all very nice. People are very cool to me.

I am looking forward to doing this show tonight. I feel like I am on a roll. Not many left on this one. I'll be back in New York by the end of the week. The next few days will be a bit of a grind with all the drives. The day off is traveling all day to get to Memphis.

The Iron

I believe that one defines oneself by reinvention. To not be like your parents. To not be like your friends. To be yourself. To cut yourself out of stone.

When I was young, I had no sense of myself. I was a product of all the taunts and threats at school combined with the fear and humiliation I dealt with on a regular basis. At school I was told that I would never amount to anything. One "instructor," as they were called, took to calling me "garbage can" in front of the other students. I could never talk back to an instructor, so I had to sit still and take it. I started to believe them after a while. I was skinny and spastic. When others would tease me, I didn't run home crying and wondering why. I knew very well why they antagonized me. I was that which was there to be antagonized. In sports, I was laughed at and never chosen to be on a team. I was pretty good at boxing but only because the rage that filled my every waking moment made me wild and unpredictable. I fought with a strange fury. The others thought I was crazy. I was not respected, just observed to see what I would do next.

I hated myself. As stupid as it seems now, I wanted to be like my fellow students in every way. I wanted to talk like them, dress like them, carry myself with the ease that one does when he knows he's not going to get pounded in the hallway between classes. When I looked in the mirror and saw my sallow face staring back, I wanted nothing more than to be transformed into one of them, just for a night, to see what it would be like to have some of their seemingly well-adjusted happiness.

Years passed and I learned to keep it all inside. I would only talk to a certain few of the boys in my grade who were losers like me. To this day, some of those guys are some of the coolest people I've ever known. You hang out with a guy who's gotten his head pushed into a toilet a few times and you treat him like you would want to be treated, you'll have a good friend there. Some of these guys were so funny. They saw things that the better-looking, more well-groomed members of our school would never see, knew things they would never know. I believe that they were the better for it. They definitely had the best jokes.

I had an instructor in history. His name was Mr. Pepperman. I am forever in his debt. Mr. Pepperman commanded intense respect and fear all over the school. He was an absolutely no-bullshit, powerfully built Viet vet who barely spoke outside of class. No one talked out of turn in his class except once that I can remember. It was the class president. Mr. Pepperman lifted the boy off the ground by the lapels of his jacket and pinned him to the blackboard. That was it, as far as talking out of turn in class, or being late either.

One day in October, Mr. Pepperman asked me if I had ever worked out with weights. Actually he said something like, "You're a skinny little faggot. This weekend, have your mommy take you to Sears and buy one of those one-hundred-pound sand-filled weight sets and drag it home. I'll show you how to use it."

This was encouraging. He was not the nicest person I have ever met in my life, but at least he cared enough to tell me that much.

Since it was Mr. Pepperman telling me to do this, I did it. I figured he would throw me across the room if I didn't. I got the weights into the basement somehow and left them on the floor. I was looking forward to Monday with a strange anticipation I had never felt before in my short life. He had told me to buy the weights, and I had done it. Something was sure to happen.

Monday came. I was called into his room after school. He asked if I had bought the weights. I told him that I had. What he told me next was something I'll never forget. He said that he was going to show me proper ways to lift weights. He was going to put me on a program, and he was going to start hitting me in the solar plexus in the hallway when I wasn't looking. When I could take the punch, then I would know that I was getting somewhere. At no time was I to look at myself in a mirror to see signs of change, nor was I to tell anyone at school what I was doing. I promised. I was going to make a list of all the reps and the weights I was lifting at so I could monitor my progress, if I managed to make any. I was to turn in the chart at Christmas break. Never had anyone given me that much encouragement. He told me that it was going to be hard but I would like it if I gave it my all.

I went home that night and started right in on the exercises he had taught me. It was hard finding what weight was right for each lift, but I soon fell into step.

I never missed a single workout. Sometimes I would do the workout twice. Immediately I noticed that my appetite grew incredibly. I was eating at least twice what I usually did. It felt like I could not get enough food into me. When I would visit my father on the weekends, he started calling me "the locust."

Weeks passed, and every once in a while Mr. Pepperman would give me a shot and drop me in the hallway, sending my books all over the place. The other students didn't know what to think. All the while I had this great secret that I wasn't telling anyone. I hadn't looked at myself in the mirror. I did everything he told me to do down to the letter. As the weeks went by, I steadily added more weight to the bar. I could feel the power inside my body grow.

Exams came right before Christmas break. I was walking to class, and from out of nowhere Mr. Pepperman appeared and gave me a shot in the chest. I laughed and kept walking. That afternoon Mr. Pepperman told me to bring in the chart the next day. I was still not allowed to look at myself or tell anyone of my secret work. I brought in the chart, and he looked it over and asked if I had really come that far. I told him yes and I was proud of myself and I never felt like this in my life. He said that I could go home and look at myself now.

I got home and ran to the bathroom and pulled my shirt off. I could not recognize myself at first. My body had a shape. It was a body, not just this thing that housed a stomach and a heart. I could see the difference big-time. It was the first thing that I remember ever giving me a sense of accomplishment. I felt and looked strong. I had done something. No one could ever take it away. You couldn't say *shit* to me.

It took me years to fully appreciate the value of the lessons learned from the Iron. It wasn't until my late twenties that I learned that I had given a great gift to myself. I had learned to apply myself and that nothing good came without work and a certain amount of pain. You can kick ass in anything you want to do when you apply yourself completely. To this day, all the lessons I learned when I was fifteen are still with me.

I used to think that the Iron was my enemy and I was trying to lift that which does not want to be lifted. My triumph was making the Iron do what I wanted it to do, the thing that it did not want to do—move. I see now that I was wrong. When the Iron doesn't want to come off the hooks, it's the kindest thing it can do for you. It's trying to help you. If it flew up and went through the ceiling, then it wouldn't be doing you any good. It's not resisting you in the least. That's the way the Iron talks to you. My triumph is to work *with* the Iron. The material you work with is that which you will come to resemble. That which you work against will always work against you, including yourself.

I used to fight the pain through the workout. My triumph was to take it and bear it all the way through. Hating the pain and the way it made me feel. Recently the lesson was made clear to me. The pain that fills my body when I hit it is not my enemy. It is the call to greatness. It's my body trying to pull me higher.

People usually go so far. Pain keeps them back. There is pain on many different levels. To change is painful. To go after something that's out of your reach is painful. Pain doesn't have to be a deterrent.

Pain can inspire you to reach past yourself. When dealing with the Iron, one must be careful to correctly interpret the pain. You must seek proper instruction so you don't injure yourself. Most injuries involved with the Iron come from ego. Try to lift what you're not ready for, and the Iron will teach you a lesson in restraint and self-control. I once spent a few weeks lifting weight that my body wasn't ready for and spent a few months of not picking up anything heavier than a fork. It was my ego that made me try to lift weight that was still several months and workouts away.

Through the years, I have combined meditation, action, and the Iron into a single strength. Only when the body is strong can the mind think strong thoughts. It's up to an individual's character what he does with this strength. The difference between a big bouncer who gets off strong-arming people and putting them in pain and Mr. Pepperman and his gift of strength.

The strength I have attained through the combined efforts of what I described earlier is a One Relationship. The mind and body develop strength and grow as a single thing. Go out and see for yourself. The strongest number is One. Aspire to the One and understand strength and balance.

I cannot believe a weak person who says he has true self-respect. I have never met a truly strong person who didn't have it. I think that a lot of inwardly and outwardly directed contempt passes itself off for self-respect.

I have found that the Iron is a great cure for loneliness. Loneliness is a desire for what is not there with you. You can be lonely for an infinite number of things, people, feelings—whatever creates a void in your life with its absence. Sometimes your loneliness has nothing to attach itself to. You're just lonely, flat out. The Iron can pull you through when all else fails. You'll find that it was *you* that got you through. Loneliness is energy. Powerful as hell. People kill themselves sick on loneliness. They drink themselves into the floorboards. They do all kinds of damaging things to themselves to combat their loneliness. The loneliness is real. The energy is real. I can't see what good it does to damage yourself trying to feel better. If one can apply all this real energy to damaging oneself, then isn't it possible to harness all this energy into something positive to combat loneliness?

Time spent away from the Iron makes my mind and body degenerate. I turn on myself and wallow in thick depression that makes me unable to function. The body shuts my mind down. The Iron is the best antidepressant I have ever found. No better way to fight weakness than with strength. Fight degeneration with generation. Once the mind and body have been awakened to their true potential, there is, in many ways, no way to turn back. You might not remember when you started working out, but you'll remember when you stopped, and you won't look back at it with much joy because you know you're depriving yourself of yourself.

The Iron will always kick you the real deal. You work out correctly and patiently and maintain a good diet, and you will become stronger. You don't work out for a while, and muscle will go away. You get what you put into it. You learn the process of becoming.

Life is capable of driving you out of your mind. The way it all comes down these days it's some kind of miracle if you're not insane. People have become separated from their bodies. I see them move from their offices to their cars and on to their homes. They stress out constantly. They lose sleep. Their egos run wild. They become motivated by that which will eventually give them a massive stroke. You never have to lose it. You really don't. There's no excuse for freaking out at the workplace, school, anywhere. No need for a mid-life crisis. You need the Iron mind.

The Iron is always there for you. Your friends may come and go. In the time it takes to blink your eye someone you thought you knew might turn into someone you can no longer stand to be around. Fads come and go, almost everything comes and goes. However, the Iron is the Iron. Two hundred pounds is always two hundred pounds. The Iron is the great reference point, the all-knowing perspective giver. Always there like a beacon in pitch black. I have found the Iron to be my greatest friend. It never freaks out on me, never runs, never lies.

SOLIPSIST

I started writing this in 1993 while living in New York City. I finished the manuscript in the summer of 1996. I was reading the dictionary one night and came across the word *solipsist*. It defined the mood of this work. So far, this is my favorite batch of writing.

A noose of blood to stop a life of hope. When you hear screams coming from down the hall, don't be afraid. It's only me trying to get the ghosts out of my guts by beating my flesh with my fists. When you're about to go to sleep and you hear the strange growling sounds coming through your wall, don't think that you're in danger. It's just me trying to talk my blood cells into shooting themselves in self-defense. I'm packed full of glass and memories, and it all hurts. I'm breeding scars in here. I'll sell you one cheap. Wrap it around you like a shield. You can wear my pain and it will seal out the pain of others. It will help keep the world from turning your mind into a slaughterhouse. If you find that the bathroom mirror has blood all over it, don't worry. It's only me and I can take a lot of pain. I'm good that way. I'm bad the rest of the ways. I carve my face off every night to make masks. You can have one. You can wear it on the street and no one will know you're you and you can be yourself instead of that other person you pretend to be when other people are around. The mask gives you freedom. Use my pain. Benefit from my cowardice. If you pay my rent for another month, I'll hack off one of my hands and you can use it to kill someone. Leave it at the crime scene, and they'll never catch you. Use me. I have no use for myself.

I don't know why it's now that I think of you. Of course I am with someone else. She is lying beside me cold. She has been dead for a few hours. We broke into this place this

morning and no one knows we're here, so when I leave tonight no one will find her for quite some time. I have pretty much forgotten about her even though her body is lying here. I did not kill her. She killed herself. I met her yesterday on the strip. She doesn't matter to me. You do. She's dead and gone and a stranger as well. You were never a stranger to me. I always felt like I knew you somehow. You didn't want me and I was mad for a long time, but now I see that you could never be with someone like me. I know you don't hate me either. I have not seen you in years, but I always think about you. I hope you're alive. I don't know anyone who knows you. I'm moving pretty fast these days, but I think of you still. I had been visiting some friends in Portland. I was taking a much needed break from my overdriven workload in Los Angeles where I work as an editor at a variety magazine that I am too ashamed to mention here. I was hoping it was going to be a temporary gig, but at times I felt lucky to have a job in that city at all. One of my friends threw a small party, and of course I showed up. It was small, about twenty people. Much smaller than the ego-fests I was still not getting used to down south in my newly adopted smog-ridden home. When I walked into the room and saw her I was in love. I had to withstand the entire evening being the only person in the room who had this knowledge. I tried to speak to her, but she was not interested in talking to me. I quickly lost my courage and left her alone. She left in the middle of the event. I asked the host and she didn't know who she was and neither did anyone else. We all thought someone had brought her and it turned out that none of us had. That night I thought about her as I tried to sleep and figured the best way to deal with her was to forget her and move on. As the days passed it was all I could do not to think of her all the time. Months later I was still thinking of her and her disappearing act.

Imagine my surprise when I walked right by her on the sidewalk near my office. I said hello and asked her why she had left the party so early. She just shrugged. I didn't bother to ask her how she had ended up there, I was too busy looking at her eyes and her mouth. I asked her if she lived in town, and she said, "I'm in the process of moving." I asked her if she would go out with me, and she said yes. She said that she would meet me at the restaurant we were standing in front of at seven that evening and walked quickly away. I didn't get her name, and now that I think about it, she didn't smile once.

The five hours until then crawled. I couldn't believe that I had seen her again. The chances of that happening were next to impossible. It started making me think of all that stupid crap like destiny and karma.

At seven she was standing right where I had encountered her before. I asked her what her name was, and she said it was Louise. We went in and sat down. With the food ordered I tried to get her to talk to me, but she'd only answer in short sentences. She worked in video, but she didn't tell me anything more than that. I asked her where she lived, and she replied that she was thinking of moving to San Francisco or Los Angeles but not where she lived. She never asked me anything, so I started talking about myself and you know how fast you bury yourself when you try to make yourself sound interesting to someone who just stares at you. Basically the whole thing was going nowhere. I wanted to tell her that I had been thinking about her nonstop since the night I met her, but I couldn't find the words. I just couldn't muster the courage to make a fool out of my almost-silent date. She excused herself to the ladies' room. I figured that when she got back I would tell her everything that I had been going through. I would force a reaction out of her with my truth and passion. It sounded lame, but it was all I had. So I waited. After twenty minutes I asked the waiter if he had seen her. He said that he had seen her, he had seen her walk out the door right after she got up from the table twenty minutes ago. I paid and left.

Okay, tell me that you don't want the story to end, that you really feel for me and want to know what I did next. Tell me that you want me to get in the car and take a long meaningful drive around the streets looking for her. Tell me that this meant something to you. Tell me that you're not laughing at me right now. Please don't be laughing.

Keep walking empty-eyed man. The first feeling I ever had that I felt was my own was when I was young and riding my bike at night. The sound of the tires on the street and the wind rushing by my ears made me feel good. I felt strong and that no one could tell me what to do. I noticed that all the kids around me were always with other kids. I never saw a person my age walking alone. I hated males my age. They would tease me and beat me up. The humiliation was hard to take. I would eventually learn to engage these males in episodes of my violent fury that they always regretted. I learned there is a lot of strength in having nothing to lose. I saw early that I was always going to be on the outside. I knew this by the time I was twelve.

I started to think of myself as a person from another planet. My hatred for people grew more intense as I grew older and understood more of the ways of the world and just how weak humans were. I was done with my parents by the time I was sixteen and merely listened to them so I could remember what to say and what not to say so I could get around them with more ease. I never tried to do anything to make them proud of me. I never thought they were anything more than people I was staying with until I could get loose and nothing more. I never did anything to learn about their lives, and to this day I know nothing more about them than when I was a teenager. I do not know when either of them died.

The years passed and I grew farther and farther apart from my parents and people in school. The only thing that brought me back a little closer to them was the pursuit of women. I always felt that women belonged to them and their planet and that they could always tell that I had spent most of my time on my own. I had almost zero social skills besides those which I had learned from watching television shows. I knew that life wasn't like that, but I tried to affect the cool of the people I would watch. It did nothing more than alienate people further from me.

As I got older and started living on my own I remained a loner. The farther along I got, the more natural it felt. When I walk the streets alone I can still hear the wind like I did on my bike over twenty years ago. When I am near people I can't hear the wind. Nights are wasted when spent around others.

The years passed and the jobs and addresses changed. I drifted all over America, never staying in any one place for more than a year. The scar tissue on my eyebrows and knuckles became deep lines on my face and hands.

I learned to forget. I learned to hear the sound of the wind rushing by my ears even while working in a mail room or some dank factory. I always lived alone. Women came seldom and went quickly. After a while I stopped looking for company and just thought about it as I walked the streets at night.

I eat at this one place a few nights a week. Usually there's a man sitting in the corner table reading a book or a newspaper. One night he came over to where I was and sat down across from me.

He leaned over the table and looked directly into my eyes. I could tell that he wanted to tell me something that he knew from experience. Whatever was going to come out of his mouth was something that he had lived, was living through, and was doomed to keep living. I could see the pain in his face as he was trying to find the words. He pulled back and looked away from me and sighed deeply. He spoke quickly and quietly. "I've seen you in here a lot. I'm checking out soon. The Agent Orange is pushing through my chest bad, I don't give a fuck. Marine?" I shook my head no. "Doesn't matter, fuck it. Here." He handed me a piece of paper and a war medal. I looked at the medal, it was a Purple Heart. He looked at it and smiled. He shook his head, said, "Fuck it" again, got up, and exited the diner quickly without looking back. I read the piece of paper. Blue ballpoint ink, barely readable.

This may come as a relief to you . . . You will always be alone. Crowded rooms, busy streets, it doesn't matter. Your solitude will be everywhere with you always. You will wake up mornings of all four seasons alone and go to sleep the same way. The years will pass and you will witness your body slowly show the ravages of time. Of course there will be the intermittent crossing of paths with women. Be assured, all these liaisons will be short-lived. If you are not immediately distracted and alienated, you find yourself filled with contempt either real or imagined soon enough. You have seen too much. You know the wrong things. Experience is a well-dressed curse. The higher power has a price. The price is the silence of truth. The ghosts never leave, the echoes never die down. They know you better than anyone living ever will. Until you stop fighting the reality of your life, you will pass the nights looking for someone else to share your isolation with. You will never meet your equal because you have none. You will only be reminded of your discontent, hence your emptiness and contempt while in the intimate company of another. You are uniquely damaged. It's the scars that keep you from ever getting away from what you know, what you are. The sooner you learn to accept your fate the better. The time passes easier, you stop tormenting yourself. I know how it is sometimes, trust me, there is no one who understands except other people like me, ones who are damned and know it. And in my company there is no solace because all we have in common is the Abyss, which life has cast us to walk forever through. And you know you always walk through it alone. This is life's sickness. This is the joke life plays on us. Look too deeply and regret forever. I know you know all this shit. I'm dragging this motherfucker all the way down the drain. Fuck it!

No signature. I left the note and the medal on the table after I finished eating. Didn't mean a thing to me. Never saw the man again. I have learned to forget. I forget it as soon as I learn it, I never actually know too much at any one time. There's nothing or no one I want to know. I don't ponder the great mysteries of life. I don't think there are any, and if there are, so what. I don't think about when I'm going to die. I don't read books, watch television, or go to movies. I just work, walk, and sit. I don't hate people like I used to. I don't remember when I stopped. I don't remember when I stopped being proud of anything or feeling superior to others either. I have never told anyone I loved them but my parents, and I only said it because they did and it seemed like a good idea to repeat the phrase. I never felt anything when I said it. Love never seemed like anything I ever needed. I just move on, live through it. Watch the seasons, walk the miles, survive the time.

Not disabled, unable. In my dream I die and come back as a brick. Yes, a brick. The brick that I come back as is lodged in a wall that was built in 1951. The exposed side of the brick faces the window of a woman who I love but who turned me away years before. Day after day I stare into her room, into her life. I watch her come and go. I see her with different men. I cannot call out, I cannot move. I am embedded in cement. I can do nothing but silently and motionlessly watch. I see her alone. I watch her cry and hold her head in her hands. I am forced to watch relentlessly. Sometimes she stares out the window and looks right at me. It is excruciating to look directly into her eyes and know she does not see me, she only sees a wall. She leaves for weeks at a time, and I wonder where she is. Who she's with. I wait. All the other bricks are just bricks, they do not speak, they don't do anything at all. It is only my discontent that makes me believe that I am alive at all. I have no arms or legs. I feel neither hot nor cold. I do not sleep. I do not hunger or thirst. My face is a small rectangle of smooth red clay, anonymous. Sometimes I think that I am a man merely dreaming of being a brick, but the days pass and I can see enough to know that I am indeed a brick in a large wall. One day she moves away. Days turn into months, and soon the first year of her absence arrives. In this time I have done nothing but think and make up every possibility of her return, to my view a potential reality. Five years pass. My mind has begun to drift. I watch the squirrels and birds in the tree to my left. I watch a few families move in and out. See a few traffic accidents, a robbery. I watch the leaves explode into colors and fall off the branches. But at night when everything is quiet I think of her. She is somewhere. I am here. Always here. Not waiting, just here. Please do not let me live my life untouched and tormented. Please help me escape the tragedy of myself. I envision my face: contorted and agonized, wild-eyed, my mouth frozen in midscream. Never able to say the truth. Forever trapped, suspended inside solid black eternity. Embedded, silent, identical to the hundreds of others symmetrically stacked around me.

Drums made of human skin stretched over ribs beaten with severed arms. Playing all night, paying homage to love's annihilating, all-consuming hunger. The dancers scream as the flesh melts from their bones. They rush forward, begging for extinction. I can feel the blood leaving my body. There is a pool rapidly forming around my midsection as I lie here on the sidewalk. I hear traffic sounds and I can see people peering down at me. People are talking about me but no one is talking to me. I am cold and alone. A moment ago I was walking. I heard gunshots and then something pushed me to the ground. Am I dying? Yes I am dying. I can feel life leaving me. It's strange that amidst all the noise and confusion around me I am clearheaded and my thoughts are calm and rational. All I can think of is you. All the things that I never told you, how much you meant to me. I don't know why it is now that these things come rushing to me so clearly. It is sad that you will never know these thoughts of mine. The things that I am feeling while I inhale the smell of car exhaust and blood. It just occurred to me that it is my blood that I am smelling. You will surely find out of my death but not of these moments. I must tell you that I was always afraid of the fury with which I loved you. It overwhelmed me. I thought it beyond comprehension, therefore my silence. I felt overshadowed by the power of it, so much that I was afraid of it and afraid of you. So strong and pure was this passion that it came out as pure venom. I know that you will always think I hated you. If only you knew how wrong you were. I remember when just the sight of you would send me into a fit of rage so blind and molten I would claw at my flesh until I drew blood, hit myself in the face, and cry. I remember the last time I saw you a few months ago. You were so kind and I was so hard and sullen. It was all I could do to contain myself. A rose trapped inside a fist. If I had not walked away quickly after my short reply I would have been at your feet begging to be at your side forever. It is the only place I ever wanted to be. To me you are more than a woman. You are a creature of beauty, a creation of a higher order. I will die knowing that no one will ever love you as I have loved you all these years. I will now attempt to say your name with my last breath.

I am the flying-saucer man. From another world, trapped on yours until they come to rescue me. The saucer will land, Jimi Hendrix and John Coltrane will open the hatch and tell me to get in before someone tries to blow up the ship. I'll just ask them what took them so long. Within seconds we'll be out of here. Quietly I sit in the hotel room. The door has three locks on it. No one knows I am here except the lady at the front desk, but she doesn't care. Traffic passes by the window, no one yells my name out. People pass my door in the hallway, but no one knocks. The city glitters and blinks outside my window. It's times like these when life is almost bearable. No phone calls, no one's company to endure. I can think my own thoughts. Dodge their arrows and stones for a while. People make me sad and lonely for solitude. I feel better when I'm walking alone. I like eating alone. Movies are better alone. Alone is safer because you attract less attention, and when you're alone, you are harder for strangers to figure out. Also, you only have to look out for yourself and you don't have to worry if the people you're with can handle themselves in a bad situation. I'd rather be outnumbered and alone than have a weak person with me. Music sounds better when you listen to it alone. Books are better read alone in a room. It's great to look at paintings but only when you don't have to listen to someone breathing next to you. People ruin almost everything. Being around people makes me think I have nothing and that I'm a creep. On my own I don't feel half bad. I got tired of being a vulnerable idiot telling someone what was on my mind. I got tired of humiliating myself over and over. Only a fool trusts a human. All you can do is predict what they will do next and prepare yourself for what might happen. Look at all the divorces happening. You would think that people would figure out that it doesn't work and just give it the slip. I hear about people getting their bank accounts cleaned out because of a divorce. It's hard to believe that these people got together because they wanted to spend the rest of their lives with each other. Imagine the feeling of failure that must be. People spend years after divorces in deep depression, they have to go into therapy. They are mad all the time. Can't feel sorry for them, they bring it on themselves. Waco, Jonestown, they always bring it on themselves. Then they'll tell you that if you don't get out there and at least try, you really haven't lived. Haven't really lived in hell you mean. Right now, in some city, somewhere there's a light on in a window. The curtains are partially drawn, and you can't see in from the street. There's music playing and the door is locked. That's me.

The beautiful scarred ones went all over the land, setting buildings on fire and breaking clocks. All structures became an endangered species. Time was destroyed. Real life rose to power. They became true gods immediately. There's no need to speak. We will communicate by touch and instinctual expression. We don't need words. We're well past all that now. It is our destiny to be born beautiful into an ugly age. We breathe life in the face of Death's high command. It is your animal grace that keeps me alive. It is your feral eyes and taut skin that bring my veins to the surface. You are beautiful like demolition. Just the thought of you draws my knuckles white. I don't need a god. I have you and your beautiful mouth, your hands holding on to me, the nails leaving unfelt wounds, your hot breath on my neck. The taste of your saliva. The darkness is ours. The nights belong to us. Everything we do is secret. Nothing we do will ever be understood, rather feared and kept well away from. It will be the stuff of legend, tall tale and endless inspiration for the brave of heart. It's you and me in this room, on this floor. Beyond life, beyond morality. We are gleaming animals painted the color of moonlit sweat glow. Our eyes turn to jewels, and everything we do is an example of spontaneous perfection. I have been waiting all my life to be with you. My heart slams against my ribs when I think of the slaughtered nights I spent all over the world waiting to feel your touch. The time I annihilated while I waited like a man doing a life sentence. Now you're here and everything we touch explodes, bursts into bloom, or burns to ash. History atomizes and negates itself with our every shared breath. I need you like life needs life. I want you bad, like a natural disaster. You are all that I see. You are the only one I want to know.

We willingly drank the toxic water. We stood all day while the jets passed overhead and shelled the city randomly and locusts crawled all over us. Even when we saw the others who were in the line ahead of us going into convulsions and vomiting blood after they drank. We were so thirsty, and besides that, we wanted to get close enough to you to see you smile. I don't think any one of us minded dying that day. I want you to know that if I had another life to live, I would have done it all over again. I watch your mouth move. I listen to your voice. I do everything you tell me to. Minutes later I find myself sitting on a metal chair with my hands cuffed behind my back. I tell you that this is the second time that I have been cuffed in my life, the other time by cops. You say nothing, but your expression makes me think that you don't care about this. I don't mind being in this position because I trust you, and even as uncomfortable as this is I don't mind because it's time spent with you and any time spent with you is special to me. You ask me why I love you, and I tell you that no one ever talks to me like you do. When you call me and we talk late at night it's the most wonderful time I have ever known. You smile and ask me if I want to kiss you. I tell you that I want to kiss you every day for the rest of my life. You lean in close to me, lock your eyes onto mine. You open your mouth slightly and move in closer. In the instant before your lips touch mine I see the glint of the cobra's head inside your mouth. You pull me forward and clamp your mouth onto mine and the cobra goes down my throat. Followed closely by a few more and then several scorpions. You pull back and I can feel the creatures in my guts biting and stinging. I ask you why you have done this to me. You say, "You're mad at me because I don't want to fuck you." I tell you that I don't care about that and why did you hurt me when I have never done anything to you. You stand up and pull out a knife. You start to stab yourself and I ask you to stop. You tell me to beg you to stop. I beg you and tears are streaming down my face. The snakes and scorpions are forgotten, all I can think of is your safety. You say, "I'm showing you how weak and stupid you are." I black out. When I awake I am on the floor of a hotel in the middle of nowhere. The rug is warm and I am glad to be alone. I look up to see the door, and to my great joy it is triple-locked. It's the first thing I do when I come in, never knowing how the curse will manifest itself. Whatever happens, no one can be here unless it's a dream of you or a cobra you might send to keep me company. Alone is perfect because it's all I can handle. I was never able to deal with company who stays too long unless it's you with your flesh-cauterizer words. Almost everything and everyone outlasts their welcome. Human nature is antihuman. I dream of anonymous room-numbered nights on flat ground near major highways. I always stay below the windows, and I never answer the phone anymore. I know it will never be you.

You forgave me in a dream the other night. The more you told me it was all right the worse I felt. I know that you were only doing it because you knew I couldn't possibly hurt you more than I already had. I could see what forgiving me was doing to you. I know that you think I'm too stupid to figure it all out. When you forgave me you knew that it was finally over. The pain would leave me, I would forget you, and you would never see me again except in a dream. It is sad that the things that we saw in each other are no longer there. It is a shame that we tore each other apart looking for things that we needed desperately but couldn't describe. It is tragic that we only wanted to give to each other but only stole from ourselves and blamed each other for the emptiness in our lives. I see you differently now. I no longer fear you. It took years to see you for what you are. I no longer associate you with the screaming and dry heaves. You know what? I see now that you gave me the courage to addict myself to the sickness that your presence in my life offered. The puking and blackouts were just some of the slight side effects from the heights of the crippling pain you inspired me to climb to. Years later when the scars were all that I had to show for all the time I spent with you I would dig at them to make blood come out. It made me feel closer to you. I would be alone in a room, years and several thousand miles away from you, screaming and bleeding and wanting to die, but now I see that I was just trying to get back to you. Yes I am ashamed but it's the truth so there's nothing I can do. When I saw you recently and you put your arms out to embrace me I cannot describe the joy I felt when my flesh started to tear away. So many years alone gouging myself, and the whole time you were waiting to have me back. Your voice of one thousand black-night ravens. Your soul-erasing eyes. I can't believe that I had survived without you and the pain that you caused me to inflict on myself. Can you believe that for a time I hated you? That I wanted to see you dead? And when I didn't want to see you dead I wanted to die myself. I used to spend days at a time thinking how nice it would be to not exist. I wanted to die because I blamed myself for all the hatred you poured on me without end. Now I see that we need each other. All those years I spent away from you. I hate to think of how you got by without me to burn and scar. I hope you don't think that I abandoned you. I was selfish. Now I only want to be near you and to give you everything. It's okay to come out, bright eyes. Sit here. Now like before, talk to me real nice, and gently drain the blood from my veins. Help me destroy what is left of my life with your neurotic, insane screeching. Infect my thoughts so that everyone I meet will seem strange and threatening, causing me to alienate them. Your lips are thinner now that you're older, but they still pull back over your teeth when you're about to strike. Spend a little more time with me so that my last years will be bitter and wrenched. Pass every confusing, enigmatic facial expression of yours on to me so I will see it on the faces of others and always blame myself. And tell me that it's going to hurt, otherwise I'll never get to sleep tonight. Please bright eyes. Some magic, one more puncture wound.

You are all colors. You are the birth of true jazz. You are ten thousand years of flowers blooming at once. You are the flavor of sunset. You are perfect like winter stars that *watch over me in the night sky* **of winter.** I'm in a room with a mattress on the floor and little else. The rent is paid by washing dishes. I clean what they leave behind. I have enough to get by. I have no radio, no way to listen to music except to hear it through the walls from other rooms in the building. I don't read books because anyone who writes them must be oppressive and insecure. If they really had something to say, they wouldn't feel the need to write it down. I only want to know about you. I have a picture of you that I cut out of a magazine. I look at it all the time. Even though my clothes are worn and dirty and I have almost nothing, there is not the slightest trace of filth on your picture. Nights have passed unnoticed as I stare into your eyes. I imagine your mouth. Sometimes all I can think of is what a miracle it would be to kiss you and for you to want me to. Your unmoving face speaks to me. I close my eyes and can see your face clearly. I wonder what I would say if you told me to tell you everything. I never talk to people unless I want to get information from them or want to keep them at a distance. I use language as a shield. So much of what I do is an act. I act like a human. That's why I walk through the city as much as possible. I want to get as many human traits as possible so I can utilize them when the need arises. At work I try to think of things that I could tell you. I have never spoken to anyone because I wanted to know about them or wanted them to know me. I have always spoken out of survival or fear. With women in the past I just repeated things I heard other people say. I used catchphrases. I have never loved a woman. I have been with some but I never knew why. I just went through the motions. I don't know if it felt good or not. Afterward, I would be silent, staring at the ceiling. They would ask if I was okay. I would reply with something I heard somewhere like, "Can't complain," or "No sweat." They thought I was strange. They would always leave me and I never cared. It's different when I think of you though. I never write anything down because I think it's a waste of time. I know what I know, and what I do know I know for a reason and don't need to be reminded. If I forget something, then I didn't need to know it. So, I systematically go through all my thoughts, sifting through the facts of my existence and the things that I use as deception, to keep humans from knowing me. I want to know you. I want you to make me tell you everything about me. I want you to be the only person in the world who will ever know me. I want to hear you say that you want me. I want to feel your arms around me. I want to feel your heart beating against my chest and your breath on my neck. If you want me, you can have me. I have never kissed your picture. Out of respect I never speak to it. I never take it out of the room. I don't love you. How can you love a piece of paper or what you think it represents? Something that could be burned in a few seconds, thrown out and hauled away with tons of garbage. I just stare, prepare myself for our unlikely meeting, and make sure I get to work on time.

The moon will never lie to anyone. Be like the moon. No one hates the moon or wants to kill it. The moon does not take antidepressants and never gets sent to prison. The moon never shot a guy in the face and ran away. The moon has been around a long time and has never tried to rip anyone off. The moon does not care who you want to touch or what color you are. The moon treats everyone the same. The moon never tries to get in on the guest list or use your name to impress others. Be like the moon. When others insult and belittle in an attempt to elevate themselves, the moon sits passively and watches, never lowering itself to anything that weak. The moon is beautiful and bright. It needs no makeup to look beautiful. The moon never shoves clouds out of its way so it can be seen. The moon needs not fame or money to be powerful. The moon never asks you to go to war to defend it. Be like the moon. I trust you from my room. From here we are tight. It is late and the lights are low. I am away from the world finally. Two flights of stairs, double-locked. From here, neither of us is the frustrated, ready-to-explode animal that others see when they pass us on the street. Our eyes are not wild and full of compressed hate. The streets scream. The buildings howl as their backs support floor after floor of sweating lab experiments. It is no surprise to me that hardly anyone tells the truth about how they feel. The smart ones keep themselves to themselves and for good reason. Why would you want to tell anyone anything that's dear to you, even when you like them and want nothing more than to be closer than close to them? It's so painful to be next to someone you feel strongly about and know that you can't say the things that you want to. I have been in that hell many times, and so have you. On that one, we're united. There's nothing like the small room and some music. If you're lucky enough to have that, you know what I mean. The late-night soundtrack takes me away from the one-way strangers from the street, and all becomes as it should. I used to like reality, until they screwed it up and cheapened it so badly. I used to defend reality until they shot so many people and crushed so many spirits that I could no longer stand to be part of it. They tried to break me. Of course, they failed. Johnny Hartman is tonight's late-night soundtrack. He never got his due. I think of him singing like a sad alien in a lounge some-where until closing time and going back to a hotel to chain-smoke himself to sleep. His voice lets me know that he was well acquainted with pain and late nights. He is dead but I know him well. He is part of my self-created reality. He comes here and fills the air with his words and it's good to be alive. It's not a matter of not being tough enough to take what they give out. I can hack it anytime around these parts, but only a fool would waste the time. What do you have to prove? It's hard to find anyone who's worth a second of your time or even the slight-est bit of your truth. But from here we can do it. In this silent, under-stood relationship, I am glad you are here and hope for your well-being. From this room with the anonymous location, we don't have to dwell on the ordinary, grinding tasks that keep us alive and make us dull. Here, in this moment, we are beautiful, nocturnal crea-tures and our thoughts and words are jewels guarded by the moon.

Louis Jordan came home one night and crawled into bed next to his wife. A moment later she started stabbing him. He sustained a puncture wound an inch away from his heart that nearly killed him, deep slashes on his face and hands. The doctors were afraid that he would not be able to play his horn again. For a little while today, I hated you. I hated you for being so beautiful and real. I hated you for waking up at night to find your arms around me. I hated your honesty and the way you make people relax when you are around them. I hated you for loving me unconditionally. You have called me on years of cheap emotion and cruelty that came from my fears. When you look at me and smile I no longer feel scared or feel the need to run out of the room gasping for air. You don't make me feel like life is a waste of time and that all you get is cold sweating, dark moments in small rooms all over the world, spending time with other desperate characters who are tearing a path across the night skies of desolation. *Promotional item. On loan from Warner Cablevision. Not for resale.* Could you believe that I didn't know what to do with your slow, warm affection? Could you believe I was scared by your endless giving giving giving? It took me a while to be able to feel welcomed by your strength that never shows off, never brags, but just nourishes and makes time stop. The feeling of hatred passed in the time it takes for an eye to twitch, and I realized that I have to take care of myself because I belong to someone. Someone is thinking of me right now. I never doubt it. I know you will always be there. Yeah, I'm in my room somewhere. It's freezing outside and I am exhausted. Too many things to do. Too many people to answer to all the time. From here I think of you. My body is wracked in pain and I am burning with fever. *Promotional item. On loan from Warner Cablevision. Not for resale.* A lot of men want a woman to mother them. They get with a woman and all they do is regress to the point where you might think he might not be capable to take care of himself at all. I don't want another mother. I want a woman. I want to rise to the occasion. I want to learn and bask in your glow. I want to protect you and do whatever I can to give you strength. There is no twist to this. I am not about to blow my brains out. You have not cut me up like others have. It's just this. I want to love you with everything in me. I need your help because I don't know anything about it. I am suspicious and ready to leave and hit the cold road for the frozen dawn. I am just going to trust you with everything in me. I see now that it's the only reason to be here. After kissing you, I cannot remember what it was like to kiss any other woman. *Promotional item. On loan from Warner Cablevision. Not for resale.* At this point I am not sure if I ever have.

I missed it before it was gone so I would be ready for the time when it left for real. I knew it was on its way out

because it was made by human hands. Greed always shows its flaws early on. Most don't see. Too busy trying to make one of their own. If it's possible to mainline shadows, I will find the way. Because I want out. I don't hear the voices on the phone. There's nothing they're saying that I have to know. People are best on records and books because you can turn them off or put them back on the shelf. I prefer the crystallized moments of human artistic pursuit than to hear what horrors the idiots have done to each other on the news. People try to talk to me on the streets. I have my filter up to make very sure I cannot understand them. I hear the attempt at language, which to them is just sounds strung together in a mindless stream. I tell them to go cure themselves. Yes, cure yourself. Shut up and cure yourself. Get over it finally. If you're going to beat yourself to death, fine, but don't make me have to suffer your common stupidity. I tried to talk to one of them several weeks ago. It was like going to a movie. All of a sudden I was doing that warm-blooded-animal-stranded-in-a-city thing. I didn't believe a word that came out of either of our mouths. I felt like I was a great actor working with a neurotic script. A method actor so deep in the part that I actually became it. Pretty insane, right? I like the shadows these days. Luckily the city I live in has lots of broken streets where fallen people live. This is where I walk. There are no bars for the idiots to crowd around and line up to get into. There are no clubs where you can wear stupid clothes and show off your hair to the other idiots. Just poorly lit, ruptured streets and sidewalks. And in this shadow world I breathe in darkness like a vaccine.

Seventies bedside memo from Hughes inside a blackout curtained suite in Mexico. I always planned on an early retirement. I was right about it coming, but I didn't expect it to be this soon. A loner I have always been, but a recluse is the last thing I thought I would become. I sit in my small room with hardly anything in it. I wait for night to come so I can venture out. During the day it is too much. The stares and the continual bothering make it impossible to control my temper. I feel like lashing out at those who treat me like a prop for their amusement. It is, of course, my own fault. If you are good at what you do, don't let anyone know. They will only drain you and take everything they can and leave you dead on the floor. They will not notice that they are leeching your blood. All they know is their own desperation. If you aspire to be more than average, then you will have to deal with the flak that comes when you inevitably mix with the multitudes. To be widely recognizable is a mistake. Anything you do to promote this gets you everything bad and you have no right to complain. It is your vanity, ego, and pride that will get you in trouble every time. The smart man knows not to put trust in anything but numbers and the weakness of man. Better to fully understand and accept human nature and deal with people knowing that they are always thinking of themselves even when they are at their most philanthropic. After all, acts of philanthropy are just expensively cloaked ways to demonstrate power. It is impossible for anyone to do acts of goodwill when they do not in some way benefit themselves. You can rule out the concept of friendship early on and make sure you find ways to keep your associates paid and hungry for more. That way they will more often than not be your "friends." Make sure they never know all the facts and never hold all the pieces to the puzzle. In your absence they are capable of conspiring to take you out with their assembled bits of knowledge. It happens all the time. It happened to me. They don't even know that I know.

I could fall in love with a cruel desert that kills without passion, a canyon full of scorpions, one thousand blinding arctic storms, a century sealed in a cave, a river of molten salt flowing down my throat. But never with you. There was a house I spent time in many summers ago. A woman lived there. Imprisoned by her touch and mocking smile, I was passed by time. I did not want to leave. The longer I stayed, the weaker I became. The days passed, and finally my self-hatred grew inside this beautiful house of paralysis, snapping me out of the coma of self-delusion I was in. All at once she was done with me and I was pushed out the door. Years later the memories of the house and the woman inside haunt me when the weather grows warm. Broken dreams of conquest stabbed with failure. Of hope driven mad by emptiness. Of the long march that ends in muted defeat, tricked by bad maps and dry riverbeds. Blood drying silently on stones under an unrelenting sun. All the time the truth was there trying to tell itself to me, but I did not heed the warning. And through the years she has risen out of heat-driven mists like a cobra. Different faces, same killer. Yes, they are all the same. I learned the lesson after many self-inflicted deaths. I understood the truth after mutinous nights where my thoughts threatened to reduce me to nothing. It was a revelation. And now their masks fall away when they attempt to meet my eyes. Our conversations are automatic. They see that they have no control over the situation, and they have no default setting for this. There is at first the display of anger at the secret revealed and then contempt because they know in order for me to know what I know, I have to have suffered the consequences of desire and desperation. Finally, the eyes narrow and a cold, mirthless reptilian smile creases the face with a million faces. A hiss emits from the mouth, and the truth makes a wall between us.

I put cardboard up on my windows. I left small strips to look out onto the street. It's a paper-thin barrier, but it's like blinders for a horse. The less I see the better. I figure it might cut down on sniper attack. I prefer artificial light to that of the sun. If I had my way, it would be night all the time so I make my room perpetual night. At night I am the only one alive. All the creatures outside are just extras in the movie. My face still hurts from the operation. I had tear-duct implants placed inside my nasal cavity. All I have to do to make it look like I am crying is tilt my head forward and squint slightly and tears come rolling out of my eyes one after the other. I need the fake tears for my work. I'm an actor on the great urban stage. I have to get along with people, and since I can feel nothing for them or myself, I had my tear glands removed years ago. I had to get fake ones implanted. Now I see why many I know had them installed years later, or the real smart ones only had them tied off in the first place. I thought it was one of the extras the body comes with that I could do without. Now I can at least give the impression that I care. I can "cry" at movies, funerals, and other moments where it is advantageous for me to have feelings. I have been taking acting classes as well. It's hard work. I can put on a good show when I have to. I do really good "concern" and my look of "understanding" is excellent, so says my instructor. The hardest was "fear." To look like you're "afraid" of something was beyond my comprehension for a long time. My instructor would stand in front of me and make these faces that I found very funny. I asked him what the feeling of fear was like, and he told me to imagine I was about to be murdered and "go with that emotion." We do that a lot. Well, I remember being murdered, and I didn't act like him. I was expressionless when it happened. Once I died I decided to stay dead. I don't occupy places. I haunt them. When I'm by myself I don't feel anything, I don't fear anything, and I don't want for anyone. I spend time with women but it's only for practice. That's where the tear-gland implants are amazing. I'm at a table in a restaurant and she's telling about her dog running away when she was eight and how it still affects her and her work to this day, and right into my spaghetti, the tears come out. The look on her face is priceless—it saves me another trip to the acting coach. When I tell a story like that I will use her facial expressions to get it across. I look over at a guy at a table across from me and he subtly gestures toward his eyes and gives me the thumbs-up; he knows I have the implants. There's nothing to fear. Stay dead baby.

I'll be all that's bad, and you can be all that's good. Would that make you happy? You could be right all the time, and I would be wrong all the time. The only rule is you are not allowed to try and rehabilitate me in any way. You are not allowed to make me yours. You are not allowed to make me become like you. Can you deal with that? Save your breath.

Parthenope calls me on the phone. She asks me how I am, and I tell her that I am feeling better than she ever will. She doesn't get mad at the insult, she's used to this. She starts in again.

"I think you are a good person but you're misunderstood. *I* understand you and I am drawn to you. I hope this is not embarrassing you, but I cannot help the way I feel."

I tell her that I didn't hear what she said, could she say it again? She does, in measured, slow speak. She wants me to hear every word. She says, "I wish you would open up to me. I wish you would give me a chance. I am not like the others. I see you differently than they do."

I tell her the acting classes are doing her some good but she has to get deeper into the part, she's not convincing me yet. "More feeling you stupid cow," I tell her.

This pisses her off. "No wonder you live alone. With the way you are, you'll live alone for the rest of your life. I am ready to give you everything, and all you can do is make fun of me and put me down. You're just showing me what a coward you are. If you were really as tough as you act, you wouldn't insult me so. You're afraid of real love. I am stronger than you'll ever be, and you know it."

I yawn. "Probably. That sounds good, we'll go with that one," I reply.

"You need me you son of a bitch. You motherfucker. You need me."

She's really mad now. I wait a minute for her breathing to calm down and then ask her, "Is there anything else you wanted to talk about, or was it just that?"

I hear the phone smash against the wall and glass break. I got a call the next day from a friend who lives in her building. He told me that she apparently threw herself out of her window and died on the sidewalk. Her body was found on cinder blocks, head, tail and claws cut off, radio gone, torso covered in graffiti.

The sky turned a beautiful blue, and the sun shone. My bank account filled with money, and I got laid three times in a week by three females who never asked my name.

You can get what you want. Never sell out. Don't break. Don't weaken. Don't let the kindness of strangers be your salvation, for it is no salvation at all. Unless you sleep alone, you sleep with the enemy. Never come out of the storm. On the other hand, *you* should. You don't have what it takes to go the hard way. Come out of the cold and sit by the fire. Let them warm you with smiles and the promise of friendship's fortune. Lose your edge. A soft body and a chained mind suit you. Chances are you don't have what it takes to walk the frozen trail. Stay home and relax.

Another night. The temperature is flesh. The moisture in the air is a poor man's sauna. And on a night like this, you must have music. To my rescue comes Gene Chandler singing "The Duke of Earl." The music hangs in the air so righteously. These moments make life bearable. People don't mind their business enough for my liking. All that talk from nowhere. Zero on substance. Their experience knows the bounds of a postage stamp. Yet they tell you how it is and how it's going to be. Booker T. and the MG's playing "Green Onions" just came on. I remember watching Booker Jones, Donald "Duck" Dunn, and Steve Cropper walk onstage and pick up a Grammy. I was on my feet. Not because they won a Grammy, but because we were under the same roof. Honor the respect. It's an honor to encounter someone who you must salute, someone who makes your respect stand at attention. Someone whose life deserves tribute. When you pay tribute to them you're also acknowledging yourself and the heights that you aspire to. I have erased myself. My past is past. People I knew are dim memories. Few faces, names, or events exist in my mind. Now it is night. Summer. I do not remember the nights of my youth. I look at young people on the streets and wonder if I was ever like that. I wonder what they are thinking and if I have ever thought their thoughts. As I'm walking down this street, now that they have left, the silence has allowed my other senses to explore. Moths make furious attacks at the streetlights. The choir of insects is symphonic and seems to hang suspended in the air's moisture. The smell of plants and trees makes the darkness full of rich and strong life. So strong that you can turn your back on it and take it for granted. You don't have to remember it because it is a constant. Somehow truer than fact. One of the few memories I have is of having a memory that held every moment of my life like a vise grip. It was a memory that held every thought, every feeling, perspective, and perception captive. I vaguely remember that I was always angry, sad, or in some kind of need. I do not remember the moment or the events that led to my systematic erasure of my memory and associations with people. Now the seasons pass through me like a breeze through thin curtains. I remember no names when I am introduced. I don't even know my own name or if I had one. I'm sure I did, but like every other fact on this planet, it just does not matter.

My flag is the color of late-night ceiling. On my flag are stars. They have all blown their brains out. Their shattered brilliance is scattered all over the worn cloth. In my removed-from-the-world room I am glad you are there, veteran. I am glad to know you are in a room somewhere silently bleeding. It is good to know that you know that no one will understand you. No one will know your wordless panic and empty stepping, slow-moving desperation. You are alone but not alone. You are crowded in with people who are alive yet who have not lived. When they reach out to you their well-meaning arms are but amputated stumps. Their concern is mutilated with guilt and is limited to the confines of their tiny lives. You have been cast adrift in a sea of humanity and are shipwrecked invisibly. You are not alone. My fist hit the wall as yours did tonight. My phone did not ring as yours did not. The scars of my knowledge and regret are rising off my flesh as yours are. I know you're out there in my night as I am out there in yours. Doesn't matter if you've seen war or not. There are many ways to see too much. Experience comes back around to trap you in its claustrophobic, vast abyss. Those who want to be close only make you feel threatened. You like them, so you don't want them to have to get a glimpse of the horrific clarity with which you perceive. How you see the end of the story at the beginning and go along with it anyway until the pain becomes so all-consuming that all you can do is sit alone and wait for it to pass. When you live as a warrior you don't think that dying as one would take this long and be dragged out with such agonizing, dishonorable tameness. The minutes alive humiliate. The days mock and the voices fill you with rage. Wear it silently and walk on. Keep moving up the trail. Stay inside the tree line and never give yourself up because the natives are grotesque in their friendliness. They will kill you and you will go out worthless. Alone is the only way to walk the line, and you know it.

She smiled at me and told me everything was going to be all right. Then she tightened down the clamps that held my head still. The first blow of the hammer hit above one of my eyes, and then I passed out or died. When I could open my eyes again I saw that all my internal organs were nailed to the wall. I was still tied down to the floor, but my head had been released from the clamps. That's how I was left. Alive, but emptied and ugly. I got out of the restraints and put myself together again. I am not bitter about it. Maybe I won't get disemboweled next time. I am trying. If I believed in a higher power, I would tell it. I would say something like, "Lord, I am trying to be good and I am trying to like people. I know that everyone is doing the best they can. I will try to do better." Instead, I just tell myself to be a good person. I work at it. I am not strong enough to maintain it. I am, for the most part, failing. There are moments when I triumph. I stood in front of the woman with the bad breath as she told me the same thing three times. I did not run away. I did not say, "Your breath is disgusting." I stood there like a stuffed animal and took it. I did not attack the man who chased me on his bike trying to take my picture today either. I kept my head down and walked to work. I was polite to the drunk soldier who followed me for two blocks shaking my hand every five paces, telling me the same thing over and over. I did not say, "Could you please stop saying the same thing over and over to me while you breathe on my face? Would you stop holding my hand?" But he's doing the best he can, right? Just like me. I should take that into consideration. There are the times when I am not strong enough. Someone smiles at me and my face freezes blank and my eyes go to the ground. Someone calls after me on the street and I hear them plain as day but I pretend that I don't and keep walking to where I set out to go. I get tired of stopping when I want to go. I get tired of talking when I want to be silent. I get tired of answering endless questions and tired of the petty abuse for which I have no recourse. I try to be good hoping that maybe they'll give me a sliver of space to exist in outside of this room. An insect-sized space I can be where they won't invade and take everything away. I want for this because I just don't have what it takes to keep taking it day after day. Liking people is the hardest thing I have ever tried to do. I am not cutting it. I feel myself slipping too often.

THREE SHORT STORIES

These were adapted
from a speaking engagement
I did in Los Angeles in 1992.

Bun Bun the Rabbit

I worked at this pet shop. Sometimes I would work in the fish department scooping out so many dead fish. That place had more dead animals than it did live ones. I would go in there on Saturday and clean the shit and everything, and half the store's population would be dead and dried out. All the rodents, they dry up, they don't have much moisture, they don't really rot. They just kind of dry up, and they always die with the most horrific facial expressions. Like every mummy you see. When they dig up some mummy, "Oh my god, look, it's a man with a bunch of bandages around him, he must be a mummy." Maybe they bury those guys while they're still alive because they look so mad, their lips are all pulled back. I wonder if they were in midscream or something. "I'm the fucking king you bastards! You can't leave me in here! I'll come back in another life and fuck you up!"

Animals were dying left and right because I could only come in a little bit during the week, and on the weekends I would come in and do the best I could. I was the only real staffer there except my friend Ian. So on Saturdays we would go in there, and man, there'd be all these animals dead, and this is after my old boss, Skip, had bailed on the shop and sold it to this man who didn't really care about the place I guess. We had to invent all kinds of lies because we couldn't clean all the cages before all the customers came in. That's how we invented the Australian Sleeping Rat. A woman comes in and there are two dead rats in one of the rat cages. And the other rats are eating off them and stuff. "Hey, it's a big free lunch in the corner there." This woman comes up and says, "Excuse me, gentlemen, um, I think two of the rats are dead."

And I was trying to cook up some excuse like, "Well, I . . ." And Ian smiles and says, "Those are Australian Sleeping Rats. They're very lethargic." And he picks up this dead rat and says, "See, it's alive."

And the woman says, "Oh, well, it looked dead to me."

"I know, a lot of people are fooled. They're not very good pets, but we have them anyway. And all the rats running around the cage, those are just normal rats, but these, these two kind of odiferous ones, they have a strange smell about them. They smell of rotting animal. Yeah, they're good old Australian Sleeping Rats." And the lady went away. Ian was brilliant.

We faked people out all the time. "Excuse me sir, there's, young man, there are four dead angelfish in that tank over there. Maybe you should clean them out?"

"Oh, no, no, no, no, no. Those aren't dead. They're just at the top waiting to get fed. You know, they're floating like that because they want to be close to the food. They do that. They're very healthy and voracious fish."

Around Easter we'll get in thirty-five bunnies, sell thirty-five bunnies, by Monday twenty bunnies come back because they are all dying. And why are they dying? Because the people who buy the rabbits don't listen to the young guy at the pet shop who says please feed them these Purina rabbit-chow pellets, do not feed them carrots, do not feed them lettuce. This is not Bugs Bunny. Domestic rabbits cannot eat carrots because they can't digest them, so the poor bastards eat the carrots, swallow, they don't digest, and they shit big chunks of carrot, which rips them up from inside. It's like passing shrapnel out of your ass. You would look like Nancy Reagan after that.

One of the rabbits came back, and it was all messed up. It had the carrots coming through it, and this crazy mom had bought the rabbit for her kid. This woman was nuts, she named it "Bun Bun." But this woman talked like this: "This is Bun Bun the rabbit. We can no longer keep Bun Bun. Bun Bun is sick." And Bun Bun was actually hanging in pretty well. When rabbits are ailing they will sit in the corner of their cage and pant—they're really bummed. You can see the pain on their faces.

So anyway, they bring in Bun Bun and me and Ian are trying not to laugh in this lady's face. She's got the cage with Bun Bun and the cedar shavings are falling all over the place, and she's got these two kids who are holding on to her legs, and asking, "Do we really have to give away Bun Bun?"

"Honey, we can't keep Bun Bun. Please take Bun Bun back." And I say, "Well, you know, the boss says there's no refunds."

"I don't want any money. I just want you to take good care of Bun Bun. We love Bun Bun."

And the kids say, "We love Bun Bun."

So, I say, "Okay, we'll take Bun Bun. See you later." And then the two kids and the crazy woman leave. And so we're contemplating Bun Bun and I say, "Ian," and he says, "Yes."

I say, "Upstairs, you know what's in the big python tank."

He says, "A big python?"

I say, "Yeah. I think the big python is hungry."

And he says, "Let's feed Bun Bun to the python." Pythons have to eat too. So I took Bun Bun out of the cage, put a ruler behind Bun Bun's neck, put Bun Bun's chin and head on the countertop, and pulled very hard. Bun Bun didn't know what hit him. It's called a cervical snap. I killed Bun Bun's little rodent ass.

Here's the reason why I offed Bun Bun. What would be better if you were Bun Bun: if I just kill your ass that fast, or if I take you up live and kickin' and throw you into a cage with a huge snake that's going to chase your scared ass around the cage for a good five minutes, bite you with teeth that to your size ratio are going to be huge, grab you, squeeze you until your shit comes out and your eyes bulge, until you die? It takes a good five minutes. Would you rather that happen or me just turn your lights out?

So, I killed Bun Bun and I'm about to take Bun Bun upstairs to feed him to Mr. Python. The door of the pet shop opens. It's the crazy lady and her two kids. Bun Bun goes behind my back. "We've changed our minds. We want Bun Bun."

What do you say? "Ah, you know, you're not a rabbit person. Ian, she's a goldfish person. Don't ya think? Madam, we will give you a bowl, three goldfish, free water. Everything you need to have a goldfish. A rabbit person you are not. You are into aquarium fish, and we're going to start you right away on it. Ian, why don't you take her upstairs and show her our wide array of goldfish?"

"I want Bun Bun. Where's Bun Bun?" She was not going to leave. So, this is where a nine-to-five, horribly paying job turns into art. I hold out Bun Bun. Bun Bun is really dead. "Oh my God! Bun Bun. Bun Bun!" And the old "it's an Australian Sleeping Belgium Rabbit" trick would not work because Bun Bun's neck is really broken and there's blood coming out of Bun Bun's nose. Bun Bun's really dead.

I say, "Here's Bun Bun. You can just put him in the cage and take him out of here." This woman was horrified. She hated my guts. And I just explained, "Well, you bailed, and I figured the python could—" And she called me all kinds of names, and left. We never saw her again.

Go Fish

We had these big fish tanks with goldfish that we'd get for a nickel each. They were for feeding other fish. We had a big tank of goldfish, and on Saturday people would come in for up to fifty at a time. We would give them a big water bag full of goldfish. Goldfish were great for kids because they would come in and for twenty-five cents they had a fish. They'd put it in a big mixing bowl, and they'd have a pet fish. Goldfish are amazingly hardy. They will survive an eight-year-old somehow.

This kid comes into the pet shop. "I want a goldfish."

And Ian says, "Take this young man right up to the goldfish department." And there's this huge tank with ninety million goldfish in it, and there's this one white one.

The kid sees it and says, "I want that white one."

And I say, "I don't see it. Ian, do you see it?"

"No, I don't see it. I just see a bunch of orange fish. Kid, we'll just give you an orange fish."

"No. I want that white one."

"You mean the one over there with the gash in its head?"

"No. The white one. See?" We're stringing this kid along.

After five minutes the kid's almost in tears. "I want that one!"

"The white one right there?"

"Yes."

"Okay." Ian fills the cup half-full of water and I take the net and make this big display of trying to catch this fish which I could easily catch. The kid's on the edge of his seat in suspense. And I get the fish and put it in the cup. I ask him if this is the one he wanted. He says, "That's it. That's the goldfish I want."

And I say, "Ian, that is probably the coolest goldfish I've ever seen."

And Ian says, "I heartily agree. That is a goldfish to be reckoned with most certainly." And we went on and on about how bitchin' it was, and then Ian said, "Henry, it's time."

I said, "Okay." And I pick the goldfish out of the little cup, and I'm holding it by the tail. I ask the kid, "Is this really the one you want? Are you sure?" He nods yes. I say, "This is a great fish," and the kid says, "Put it back in the water." I ate it. The kid goes running out of the place screaming like someone lit his ass on fire. It was great.

The mom called later that day. "I don't know what you have going on in that place, but you should tell your two employees to grow up." Even at that young age we knew we were bound for greatness. You could not convince us otherwise.

The Shit Is on Fire Show

I was home just in time to watch the great TV show that engulfed Los Angeles for three days. No matter what channel you turned on, it was the "Shit Is on Fire Show." On every channel another anonymous strip mall is on fire. It's nighttime, and you see men with garden hoses: "I'll get it." No. Huge Niagara Falls hoses dumping into massive, volcanic walls of flame didn't stop it. It was depressing to watch. They cart out that pig Daryl Gates, and he's saying what amounts to "Well, I don't really have . . . I have no control whatsoever of this situation." And when he said that, he made it almost sound cool. "The situation." He made it sound like he was right about something, you know. It was so disgusting to sit at home and get insulted like that.

One of the days during the riots I was over at a friend's house. She turns on the television, the "Shit Is on Fire Show" was on. And there it is, another big flameout. And then they flash the intersection that is burning like hell. It was like three blocks away from where we were. And we look out the window, and there are dark clouds in the sky, and ash is coming in through the screen. It's like we're in Pompeii when Vesuvius erupted. We're going to be covered in volcanic shit, and *National Geographic* will do a documentary. Five hundred years later we'll be totally preserved. The fillings will be intact, everything. We hear the police helicopters. They're coming so close the building is vibrating. It's chaos. So, what happens when shit is burning, police are in the sky, the National Guard is in the 213 area code, there are guys in cars driving around looking for stuff to fuck up? What should you do? Probably lock your door and cool it. What did we do? "Let's go check it out!" We ran down to the corner.

Here's the scenario: We're looking down the road, and sure enough, fire engines, flames, smoke, helicopters, the sun is setting . . . kind of beautiful in a way. And on the other hand it was horrible. So we're standing there and people from the neighborhood are gathered on the corners checking it out. Across the street is a Sam Goody's record store. All glass, big corner store, glass everywhere with big posters of all the bands behind them. There are two rent-a-cop guys in tan uniforms, no guns. Those guys are a little overweight and they always have a look of slight unease on their face. This time it was a little out of hand. They weren't guarding a parking lot this time. "All right you cement, don't move." They do that for eight hours. "Okay, all the cars are still here. Here's the stick back. Bye." This time there are looters coming up the street. There were five guys standing across the street looking at the record store. If you're a looter, imagine a store full of CD's and stereo accessories and all that glass. If you're a looter and you got a rock and there's no law, you want to put the rock through the window. They're looking at the glass, they're salivating. The two rent-a-cops are trying to maintain what the Los Angeles Police Department calls "command presence." CP is when they pull you over for an illegal left turn and act like it's the invasion of Poland. "Pull your car over to the side. Get out. You have thirty seconds to comply."

"Okay." It's broad daylight. It's just a left turn. "Excuse me, officer?"

"Do not speak." They're in control of the entire situation, everything in the world is in their grasp. "You will do nothing. You will say nothing. You will hand over your ID, registration, and insurance, or you will go to the Pokee." That's command presence. And when one of these pigs pigs you, you are in the grip of command presence.

So, these two rent-a-cop guys are standing in front of Sam Goody's really trying to look heavy to a bunch of guys who fuck shit up for a living. They know it's not working too well. The rent-a-cops come over to us bystanders, and they say, "Hey, we will deputize all of you if you come across the street and stand in front of Sam Goody's. This is your neighborhood, you must protect it." It sounded pretty good. Me being a little bit more cynical than the average person, in fact I'm more cynical than the average stadium full of people, I said, "Man, this guy has about as much legal clout as anybody here. He can't deputize shit." So, let's think about that: Come here and protect your community. Come across the street and stand in front of Sam Goody's. Let me get this straight. What you're saying is you want me to take a rock in the face for Paula Abdul? I'm supposed to take a two-by-four across my chest for Bono? I'm supposed to stand in front of a huge piece of plate glass and try to defend it from fire, gnarly youths who want to go right over my head for Morrissey? Fuckyoufuckyou-fuckyou! None of us moved.

So, they go back to their post—hating it. Across the street some young man picks up a wire-rim trash can and starts going in circles with it, like he's picking up speed, and starts moving toward the liquor-store window. He's going to try and put that trash can right through. At that time a few guys behind me with sticks go running after this guy. They were running as fast as they could. Do you think they're going to run over to the guy and say, "Stop that! What's the matter with you? Are you an animal? Go home!" They're going to try and put this guy's brain through his ears. I see the guy about to break the window, and I say to myself, Man, fuck you. The guy who owns that liquor store is cool, he doesn't need his windows broken. If he's lucky his place is *just* going to get looted, if he's lucky he'll be able to replace all the liquor, sure, he'll get a new window, fine. But what if those guys torch the place? You've got to realize that the people who own stores work for a living. They have families. They have kids they're trying to put through college. Some of these store owners, goodness gracious, they might even be good folks who don't deserve this shit.

So, these guys go taking after this guy, and I think to myself, Fuck you guys too 'cause they're running after him as fast as they can. People behind me are yelling, "Get him! Get him! Go! He's getting away! Kill that motherfucker!" All of a sudden I realize that I'm standing next to guys who are just as fucked up as the guy with the trash can and the guys with the sticks. I look up on the roof of my building right above my head. There's a man with a rifle. I was out of there. Back to the apartment. I did not surface for two days. The day I surfaced was the day I got to go to Los Angeles International Airport and go to the Midwest and speak at some universities.

The cab driver asks me how do I want to go to LAX. I tell him to take me down La Cienega Boulevard. We'll take the surface streets all the way. I figure I'll get to see some carnage and I'll see what's happened. It's not as if you can really go walking around, "Excuse me, are you going to loot that? Can I watch?" In Hollywood there's a Silo appliance store. Apparently it got cleaned out to the point where there was only a washing machine left. Can you imagine people pulling up with a pickup truck? One guy gets out, has a bad back, four gang members help him get that washing machine on the truck. "Hey, hold on man, you're going to hurt your back. Let us help. Fellows, let's pick it up for him. No, no you stand back man, just relax. You're going to hurt yourself. You got that truss on. Come on, we'll do it for ya. Here, take these extra speakers we ripped off too. Have a nice drive home. Do you have enough gas in your tank? Look, here's a five. Fill it up. You've got a long drive back to Chino. Have a good trip buddy."

I'm going down La Cienega, and as we go farther, it gets worse and worse. You start seeing broken windows and then burned stores and then burned cars. And you see what these store owners did to keep their places from getting destroyed. The obvious ones: BLACK-OWNED signs, which don't work so hot if the looters hate black guys. But these guys are just doing anything they can to keep their stores. Pictures of Martin Luther King in the front window, whatever. I thought the best was a computer store. Computer stores are run by people who are pretty smart. The computer store has a single piece of plywood over the door. It says ALREADY LOOTED AND BURNED. TENANTS UPSTAIRS. The place was not looted. It was not burned. There was a roof with nothing on top of it. There were no tenants on top. I can see these computer guys in the back on a virtual-reality trip or just being the cynical geniuses they are. "Oh, there's going to be a riot. I got it, I got it! Do we still have that piece of plywood in the back? Okay, just put it on there and tell them the place has already been burned and looted and just put it out there. No, no, no, no, wait a minute, tell them there are tenants upstairs. All right, let's get the fuck out of here." And they leave. Looters come up and there are ample supplies inside and they're thinking they can go in there and get themselves a two-page color monitor, a laser printer, all the goodies, all the software they can stick up their ass and haul home. Man, if you were like a computer guy, that would be the shit, looting a computer store. You would go home with all the gear you need. So, these looters come up with burning bottles of gasoline and sticks. They're ready to loot and pillage and destroy. "Darn, they already looted and burned the place, and besides fellows, there are people who live up there, it says so on this sign."

Luckily there's a McDonald's on the corner. "Yeah, let's go loot that." And they all went down there and incinerated the McDonald's. You know Ray Krock is squirming in his grave. But as much as it's fun to talk about it, I think looting is fucked.

Photo Credits

The photo that appears at the bottom of each part title page was taken by Joe Cole. The credits listed below are for the photos *above* Cole's photo on those pages, as well as the title page photo.

Title page photo by Albert Watson

Page 1: Photo by Joe Cole

Page 21: Photo by Stephen Stickler

Page 39: Photo by Annika Söderholm

Page 63: Photo by Justin Thomas

Page 81: Photo by Chris Culfano

Page 97: Photo by Anton Corbijn

Page 135: Photo from the author's collection

Page 153: Photo by Stephanie Chernikowski

Page 181: Photo by Glen Friedman

Page 203: Photo by Stephanie Chernikowski

Page 233: Photo by Stephanie Chernikowski

Page 259: Photo by Stephanie Chernikowski

Page 289: Photo from the author's collection

HENRY ROLLINS is the author of several books, including *Eye Scream* and *Get in the Van: On the Road with Black Flag.* Rollins is also a renowned spoken word performer and has made countless appearances in theaters and colleges world-wide. In addition to being a writer and spoken word per-former he is the vocalist for the Rollins Band.